Cities & Urban Sociology

Louis Guay
Pierre Hamel

OXFORD
UNIVERSITY PRESS

OXFORD
UNIVERSITY PRESS

Oxford University Press is a department of the University of Oxford.
It furthers the University's objective of excellence in research, scholarship,
and education by publishing worldwide. Oxford is a registered trade mark of
Oxford University Press in the UK and in certain other countries.

Published in Canada by
Oxford University Press
8 Sampson Mews, Suite 204,
Don Mills, Ontario M3C 0H5 Canada

www.oupcanada.com

Library and Archives Canada Cataloguing in Publication

Guay, Louis, author
Cities and urban sociology / Louis Guay and Pierre Hamel.

(Themes in Canadian sociology)
Includes bibliographical references and index.
ISBN 978-0-19-543376-0 (pbk.)

1. Sociology, Urban--Canada. 2. Sociology, Urban. 3. Cities and
towns--Canada. 4. Cities and towns. I. Hamel, Pierre, 1947-, author
II. Title. III. Series: Themes in Canadian sociology

HT127.G82 2013   307.760971   C2013-902927-3

Cover image: Eastnine Inc./Getty Images

Block quote on page 17 copyright © 2009, John Wiley and Sons.

Oxford University Press is committed to our environment.
This book is printed on Forest Stewardship Council® certified paper
and comes from responsible sources.

Printed and bound in Canada

1 2 3 4 — 17 16 15 14

Contents

Preface

For the first time in history, most of the world's population is now living in cities. If this fact is not important in itself, it nevertheless brings to our attention changes in human settlements that are taking place at a global scale in the sense that the concentration of people in cities continues to grow. Thousands of cities, metropolises, and megacity-regions of the twenty-first century and the people who inhabit them are experiencing changes that would have been unthinkable just 50 years ago. Not only is a new hierarchy of global cities emerging with the booming economy of the global South, but cities and especially metropolitan regions are at the forefront of the new service economy. For this reason, improving urbanism has never been so crucial to urban development.

At the end of the nineteenth century and at the beginning of the twentieth, sociologists worried about the transition from "community" to "society." They were concerned with problems of social integration and anomie. They were also anxious about world disenchantment with processes of rationalization as promoted by modern scientific discourse and introduced in models of social organization. How was it possible that modern societies—which manifested themselves in the first place in major cities of the time—were not swept away by chaos and moral degeneracy as traditional religious values were losing their influence? Such concerns are certainly no longer the focus of today's sociologists.

In the current period of late modernity, researchers are less worried by the negative consequences of mass urbanization. Nonetheless, with climate change and other environmental issues, new concerns are emerging that make urban areas seem more vulnerable than ever. For instance, Hurricane Sandy affected millions of people in the New York City region for many days if not weeks in November 2012. In late modernity, sociology as a discipline of social science is necessarily challenged by constructing theoretical and methodological instruments with enhanced heuristic range and explanatory capacity.

Transformations in lifestyles in contemporary cities and metropolises are certainly different from the changes described at the beginning of the twentieth century. However, issues of social inequality, social exclusion, and social integration continue to be at stake even though their forms are more diversified and complex.

Canadian cities have participated in the making of the modern world. We tend to think of modernity chiefly as a European and an American process, but Canada too has been a member of the long march to modernity. Many of its cities had an industrial past, with all of the problems that went with it.

Later on, especially after 1980, the necessity to adapt urban infrastructure to new economic requirements prevailed.

Canadian cities have also played the globalization card. Toronto is well endowed in talents and skills, in people and infrastructure, to be an agent of the globalization process. Other Canadian cities have also internationalized their economy as well as their cultural production and their way of doing things. Montréal is, for instance, an international cultural centre in some activities and performances, such as dance and jazz. Vancouver is referred to as a model of sustainable development, worth following if not copying.

Finally, there is always a tension between conceptions of the urban way of life. Industrialization and the planning models that responded to urban problems of the industrial city tended to emphasize the functional and economic dimensions of the urban way of life. Cities are places of production, of circulation of people and goods, and of the most efficient means to extract economic value from people's work and ideas. But another conception, for which many urban movements fought, has emphasized a more "interactive" and social way of life. People live in settlements, in neighbourhoods, in a particular locality, either city or suburb, and they are attached to where they live. They are ready to defend it and seek, through participation in urban planning and policy, to improve it. The city presents itself, Janus-like, as a creative tension between these two conceptions.

Acknowledgments

Although books are the product of their authors, none is exempt from the important help of many people at different stages of writing. We would, first and foremost, like to thank Lorne Tepperman and Susan McDaniel who invited us to write a book on cities and urban sociology. They preside over a series called Themes in Canadian Sociology that covers many aspects of a changing Canadian society. We have read other books in the collection, which have inspired us in many respects. We hope this book will respond to their expectations.

We want to thank the staff members at Oxford University Press who have contributed to this text, especially Tanuja Weerasooriya, developmental editor in the Higher Education Division, who has been a competent, invaluable, and understanding adviser all along. We are very grateful to Colleen Ste. Marie for her thorough copy editing and for her many suggestions to improve the book's reading. We would also like to thank the reviewers of our manuscript. We have tried to follow their advice closely, but the final responsibility for the book's content remains with us.

Many students contributed directly to the book content. We would like to thank Émerance Bordeleau at the Université de Montréal, and Nancy Émond and Claire Taugeron-Graziani at Université Laval for the precious help at many stages in the book's production. Many others contributed indirectly. All the students to whom we taught urban sociology and planning over many years were instrumental, although they may not know it, in sharpening the arguments we developed in the book. We are very grateful to all of these students; without whom such a book may not have been written in the first place. University teachers learn a great deal through interacting with generations of students, who also lead them to new questions and problems based on their own experiences of city life.

We received a helpful grant from Villes Régions Monde (VRM), a multidisciplinary network of urban and regional researchers in Québec, for data collection and analysis. We are very grateful to the network and its scientific committee.

Introduction

Cities are the natural habitat of modern humankind, to paraphrase Robert Park, the founder of urban sociology in the 1920s at Chicago University. Urbanization (the process of moving from the countryside to inhabit a city) has historically been a very long process. Although there were cities in the distant human past, only very recently has the world become urbanized, meaning that over half of the world population lives in cities. Urbanization is a key concept, the first "pillar" upon which this book lies.

But urbanization entails change: changes in ways of life, changes in ways of doing things, of relating to people, or of seeing oneself, and of behaving individually or collectively. Sociology has been studying this urban way of life, and has described the manifold fashions it expresses. The urban way of life can be called "urbanity," the second "pillar" of this book. Not that there is always a clear break between living in cities and living in the countryside, for there may in fact be more continuity than what meets the eye. Relationships between town and country have always been tight. Today, the urban way of life has penetrated deeply inside the countryside. What used to pertain to the city, such as technology, education, high culture, and division of labour, now also belongs to the countryside. Sociology studies these two ways of life and shows that relations between town and country are mutually constitutive.

The third conceptual pillar of the sociological study of cities is "urbanism," a term only recently used to stress the material, physical, and technological dimensions of cities, although the term first appeared in a famous article by Louis Wirth in 1938, "Urbanism as a Way of Life," which focused on the process of ecological differentiation in a city and its consequences. Urbanism now refers less to this ecological dimension and more to the set of material objects and technical systems, such as buildings, infrastructure, and facilities, that cities produce over time and that become part of, even essential to, the urban way of life. Urbanism is the "holistic consideration of the built environment within physical, historical, and social contexts" (Ellin, 1996: 225). In taking the long historical view, one is struck by the amount of material objects that cities build and how much of this material is destroyed over time by changing technologies, needs, tastes, and collective aspirations as expressed notably by urban movements and the rise of new social classes, such as the working class in the industrial city. The importance of urbanism in urban studies, as defined as the materiality of cities, has been highlighted by geographers and planners (Dear, 2002a), and by sociologists of technology (Hommels, 2005a, 2005b; Latour, 2005). It is tempting to qualify cities as socio-technical systems in as such as they are heavily characterized by material systems that are socially produced. Whether we think of electricity, streets and roads, water and sewage networks, or communications systems, most of them—if not all—originated in an urban environment before spreading to the countryside and diffusing widely in societies and economies.

So, these three concepts—urbanization, urbanity, and urbanism—should be thought of as key ideas to understand sociologically what cities are and what the urban way of life is all about. These concepts will, as a sort of sociological leitmotif, recur throughout the chapters of this book.

Cities have over their long history changed radically. Two change periods will be examined more deeply: the long rise and consolidation of the industrial city (roughly from 1820 to 1950, with huge time variations between countries), and the recent positioning of cities in the globalization process that has followed. Globalization has impacted cities in at least two ways: cities have become more open to external influences and have taken advantage of what globalization can offer, not only economically but also politically and culturally, including changes in trajectory, some positive, some negative.

Cities may be the chief agents of economic, social, and cultural transformations at the global scale. Not all urban researchers, however, would agree with this statement. But if one reflects upon how innovation of many kinds happens in cities and metropolises, one is bound to take this statement very seriously. Take for instance the global financial system: a few world cities (New York, London, Tokyo) are at the pinnacle of the system, and they bear a large part of all transactions (Sassen, 2009). Immigration is another world phenomenon. It is transforming the social landscape of many large cities in Canada, in the United States, and in Europe, and, perhaps to a lesser degree, in other cities of the world. Note that international immigration to cities is not a new phenomenon but one that has increased in scale and scope.

Moreover, cities have a tendency to grow, to form metropolises and large city-regions. Divisions appear between old and new neighbourhoods, between growing suburbs and declining central cities, between high-technology industrial districts and old manufacturing areas that are on the wane. Cohabitation is not always easy between people of different origins, and the immigration that we mentioned inevitably leads to a process of learning to live together and share urban resources.

Finally, the new environmentalism is much more international and global than the old environmentalism that appeared at the end of the nineteenth century. Cities have had environmental problems of their own, and they are now aware that their contribution to global environmental problem solving, such as climate change and sustainability, is required.

These changes have brought in new challenges for individual and collective social actors who are asking in what type of city or in what kind of urban world they want to spend their daily lives. Urban dwellers have learned about the negative consequences—defined in environmental, social, or cultural terms—of some past planning decisions. Open governance on urban planning and policies has been claimed by different urban movements to make them more responsive to spatial and social justice concerns.

How does a particular city cope with environmental concerns? Are urban actors, citizens, builders, and developers agreed on adopting urban policies that are compatible with environmental principles? Is social integration of immigrants and of low-income households a key political concern? If preventing social exclusion is deemed important, what do cities do? Is gentrification in old industrial neighbourhoods a major social and planning issue? Are vulnerable people, such as children and the elderly, taken into account in urban planning? Can cities build friendlier environments for the disabled persons who need to have adapted access to urban resources?

The book takes a multidimensional approach to cities. It draws heavily from sociology (understandably) but also from a wide set of disciplines that make up urban studies. Urban studies have researched many aspects of city life and change: central-city neighbourhoods' decay, social inequalities and social exclusion, social housing accessibility, or environmental protection, to evoke the most frequent problems. Some solutions imagined by urban planners and policy-makers have not always fared well and have been contested. Cities, large ones in particular, show a contentious stage of diverging interests. If co-operation is not impossible, it must be socially manufactured for it is necessary for urban decision taking.

A Sociological Perspective

Canadians—and they are not the only ones—are increasingly living within metropolitan areas or city-regions (Hiller, 2010a). As a result, we need to better understand metropolitanization and its consequences in terms of living conditions, opportunities, and constraints for city dwellers—thus this book's focus on large cities, metropolitan areas, and city-regions.

Cities remain a complex object of study. And any comprehensive endeavour requires selective choices. At the outset, urban sociology was inspired by the modernity project. Modern societies—and especially urban societies—are characterized by their reflexivity, that is, by their capacity to criticize their own ideas, productions, and institutions. Reflexivity is an intellectual and institutional process; and science, the main road to reflexivity as Anthony Giddens (1990) has forcefully stressed. Reflexivity applies to urban sociology and to urban studies themselves. The knowledge produced by urban sociologists is valuable for its own sake, but is also useful in providing information and knowledge that may help social actors to cope with problems related to the ceaseless self-production of cities.

With the growing urbanization of the world, researchers have come to ask whether urban sociology does not melt into general sociology since modern society is an urban society (Saunders, 1981). Cities remain, however, spatial, organizational, social, cultural, and political entities on their own, entities that require special sociological attention. The role of urban sociology, then, is to unravel the many dimensions of the "urban constellation" and to investigate the choices made by urban actors in coping with a way of life that is constantly changing.

Outline of the Book

This book is made up of nine chapters of equal importance. Each deals with specific theoretical and empirical concerns that are central to urban sociology. As a field of specialization, urban sociology is far from being a unified field of study. First of all, the topics and problems studied are almost unlimited. Second, different approaches and methods are used to examine them. Finally, explanations on the causes and effects of particular urban phenomena do not all agree among themselves. The book must, and will, take stock of this theoretical diversity.

The first chapter introduces the book's framework and its general perspective. We consider cities as an object of study defined from a specialized field of inquiry, urban sociology. Using a historical perspective, we recall the nature of urbanization processes involved in the production of cities and underline the importance of contextual factors. We also explain why urban sociology has been defined as a specialized field of study. Finally, we pay attention to the spatial forms borrowed by contemporary cities in comparison to traditional ones, emphasizing the importance of city-regions.

Chapter 2 shifts the focus to the theoretical contributions in urban sociology, beginning with the Chicago School of urban sociology and its ecological approach. In the 1970s, urban researchers challenged this ecological outlook and replaced it with a political analysis of the production of the city, a key expression of political urban studies. Why such an epistemological shift happened needs to be explained and linked to rising urban movements. Other critiques of urban theory were formulated by a new generation of researchers in the 1980s. Relying on a post-structuralist perspective, these researchers formulated a postmodern critique of past urban theory and put forward a cultural approach to the city.

Chapter 3 deals with the industrial city, its roots, its main problems, and its evolution. It looks at how the industrial city faced its urban problems and what solutions were tested. Problems of the industrial city were difficult to cope with because the city was the breeding ground for contested politics. The industrial city was not isolated from the wider society, and problems solved were experiments that tended to disseminate. For instance, the industrial city was the first to confront sanitation problems, and the solutions designed helped to launch the "Health Century" that followed (Shorter, 1987).

Chapter 4 moves on to suburbanization and its consequences in the shaping of urban development. Suburbs are a fundamental component of the organizational and cultural form of metropolises and city-regions. The current trends at play in the metropolitanization process, starting with urban sprawl, are directly supported by suburban expansion and values. This gives us the opportunity to consider the North American context, raising the issue of its distinctive character.

Chapter 5 considers social diversity and inequality, mainly in Canadian cities. One central question raised in this chapter is whether immigrants cluster in urban space, and if de-clustering is at work and for what reasons. But urban diversity through cultural diversity in cities does not result exclusively from the arrival and settling of immigrants. Canadian cities harbour an increasing Aboriginal population with some particular problems of integration. As well, women's studies have contributed to urban studies by taking women's urban conditions seriously. There are particular problems with respect to women's role and place in cities. Diversity and inequality are not necessarily linked, however. Some degree of urban inequality is independent of cultural diversity, but some diversity may lead to or is produced by inequality. To disentangle these two urban phenomena, or to entangle them when necessary, is theoretically and methodologically challenging. Measures are needed to describe inequality accurately. Inequality has to do with theory (why inequality?) and politics (what do cities do?).

Chapter 6 discusses urban governance and local democracy. The notion of governance is a contested one. Various conceptions, some normative, some analytical, are presented and assessed, followed by a presentation of empirical cases. The governance of two Canadian city-regions, Toronto and Montréal, is examined to discover how urban governance has changed and for what reasons.

Chapter 7 presents planning models that were put forth in the twentieth century to improve city life. These models, while interesting and valuable in themselves, did not have the impact that their designers and thinkers had hoped for. They remain, however, reference models for some planning actions, and they tell something about how cities change and might change.

Chapter 8 re-opens a territory on which the industrial city has already trod. The contemporary city is faced with environmental problems of its own. Although not all environmental problems of the industrial city have disappeared, air pollution is still an urban scourge even though sources of such pollution have changed. New urban environmental problems are more global; climate change and biodiversity decline are typical global problems that have come to town, as well as sustainable development. The relationship between cities and nature necessarily raises the unavoidable issue of the ecological footprint of cities. Answers to these problems follow many path-ways. Some solutions are indigenous, as they are urban grown; others come from higher tiers of government. One of the urban responses is through planning, in which urban form, transport systems, and infrastructure are targeted. Are all these actions leading to the sustainable city? If sustain-ability is a long process of change and adaptation, the answer remains open.

Chapter 9 considers the process of globalization and its effects on cities. Most urban research emphasizes the economic aspect of globalization, which the chapter takes into account. It also looks at the process of urbanization in developing countries as a whole, called the "global urban South," and exam-ines social inequality in some developing countries, which is either growing or reducing in the context of globalization.

1 The Development of Urban Sociology

Learning Objectives

◎ To examine how cities evolved and explain how contemporary cities are both similar to and distinct from cities of the past

◎ To understand *urban sociology*, defined as an intellectually coherent research field and an area of specialization concerned before all by socio-spatial phenomena, considering cities and their spatial forms as part of social relations

◎ To consider internal and external factors regarding the development of cities

◎ To understand the key problems that urban sociology is addressing, such as social inequalities, social integration of immigrants, and environmental issues

Introduction

For sociologists, cities have become an unavoidable object of study. If this was already true at the end of the nineteenth century, it is increasingly the case nowadays due to the fact that the majority of the world population currently lives in cities. But even more important is the growing relevance of cities in regard to economic and social development, to concerns for the environment, to improvement of life conditions, to struggles against poverty and social exclusion, and to social integration processes. Indeed, cities have become a central issue as immigrants are choosing to live in cities rather than in the countryside in order to more fully embrace their adopted country. We see this pattern, for example, among Latino immigrants settling in the United States (Davis, 2000) and among immigrants from diverse ethnic origins in Canada (Satzewich and Liodakis, 2007).

Dealing with problems in cities and of cities is inevitable for sociology. Over the past 50 years, cities have had to adapt constantly to global changes. For example, historical city forms have been significantly altered by economic restructuring. Such restructuring started in the 1960s and 1970s with the relocation of production and manufacturing activities to the fringes of major industrial cities. But this trend was counterbalanced by the growth of the service sector in city cores or at their immediate periphery, particularly in industrial cities—especially those located near the North American east coast—where service industries progressively supplanted manufacturing activities (Beauregard, 1993). Consequently, city planning and management faced new challenges in terms of improving the built environment, including demands made by service-sector workers, who were expecting access to improved urban facilities and amenities.

Urban sociology has traditionally dealt with socio-spatial phenomena (Gottdiener and Hutchison, 2011). By this we mean that cities are not considered exclusively in reference to their physical and architectural aspects but also as an essential part of social relations in societies. We will explore this understanding from a perspective emphasizing the tension between, on the one hand, the historical, physical, and institutional factors determining the face of a particular city—i.e., its singularity—and, on the other hand, the adapting capacity of social, economic, and political actors to respond to the continually transforming external context. In other words, throughout modern history cities have frequently revisited their priorities, their spatial models, and their main functions and activities to adapt not only to social demands but also to economic and environmental constraints. But in spite of these adjustments, cities have achieved, more or less successfully, two central functions: (1) attracting resources, activities, and people; and (2) being influential in their hinterland and even abroad by exporting goods and services.

Some cities have succeeded better than others in expressing greater capacity for change, solving social and economic problems, and reinventing the path to prosperity throughout history. Nonetheless, all cities have had to deal with the tensions we have outlined above.

This chapter examines the main concerns of urban sociology and is divided into three parts. First, we ask what a city is about fundamentally and how its universal representation has changed over time. Second, we contextualize our understanding of cities and urban sociology. What is urban sociology's main goal? Finally, we consider the key social problems that urban sociology is trying to understand.

The Rise of Urbanization and Cities

Cities sprang up quite recently in human history if we consider that they were created around 5500 years ago (Davis, 1996) while *Homo sapiens* emerged approximately 200,000 years ago. As recalled by archaeologist V. Gordon Childe (1996) (see Box 1.1), the rise of cities corresponds to a radical change in the history of mankind. According to Childe, the first cities were created in Mesopotamia around 4000 BCE. But other researchers do not necessarily agree with Childe: they claim that prior to these cities, settlements—while smaller and "less culturally advanced" than the cities of Mesopotamia—were established in ancient Turkey (LeGates and Stout, 1996).

**Box
1.1**

The "Urban Revolution" According to V. Gordon Childe

Childe (1892–1957) was an archaeologist who dedicated his work to understanding the evolution of human development going back to pre-history. In his seminal article "The Urban Revolution," published in *Town Planning Review* in 1950 and reproduced in *The City Reader*, edited by Richard T. LeGates and Frederic Stout (2000: 24–30), Childe specified the main components of the so-called urban revolution that should be associated with the rise of civilizations in "Mesopotamia and elsewhere in the ancient Near East" (LeGates and Stout, 2000: 23).

According to Childe, the emergence and creation of cities in a meaningful way occurred during the last stage of "three evolutionary stages, denominated respectively *savagery*, *barbarism* and *civilization*" (2000: 24). The urban revolution corresponds to the increased number of people living together in a "single built-up area" contributing at the same time to the advent of civilization.

Childe recognized that, in the abstract, cities are "hard to define." Nonetheless, he believed that the following 10 criteria—"all deductible from archaeological data" (2000: 27)—can help differentiate cities from villages:

1. An increase in population, size, and density
2. A concentration of agricultural surplus
3. The introduction of a tax system to favour "the concentration of the social surplus"
4. The erection of monumental buildings for symbolizing deity and/or power
5. The existence of a ruling class able to reassure its subjects
6. The invention of systems for recording information ("writing and numeral notation")
7. The "elaboration of exact and predictive sciences" that make the regulation of the "cycle of agricultural operations" possible
8. The availability of a social surplus to facilitate "artistic expression," providing cities with cultural distinctiveness
9. The ability to pay for the "raw materials" needed for several purposes but not "available locally"
10. The development of "interdependence" between the different categories of producers, rulers, and craftsmen forming a community

Keep in mind, however, that these criteria were applied differently in different regions of the world due to cultural as well as environmental factors:

> Concretely Egyptian, Sumerian, Indus and Maya civilizations were as different as the plans of their temples, the signs of their scripts and their artistic conventions. In view of this divergence and because there is so far no evidence for a temporal priority of one Old World centre (for instance, Egypt) over the rest nor yet for contact between Central America and any other urban centre, the four revolutions just considered may be regarded as mutually independent. (Childe, 2000: 30)

Source: Childe, V. Gordon. 2000 (1950). "The Urban Revolution." In R.T. LeGates and F. Stout (Eds.), *The City Reader* (2nd ed.). London: Routledge, (pp. 22–30).

Due to a lack of knowledge about these settlements, it remains difficult to resolve the dispute regarding the birth of the city. In addition, Childe's definition of the city relies on several elements (as listed in Box 1.1). If only some of these elements were present in settlements in ancient Turkey while other characteristics were missing, would it be possible to consider such settlements as cities? In other words, must all the characteristics as defined by Childe be present or only some of them—the more significant ones, for example—in order for a settlement to be recognized as a city?

Scholars do, however, agree with the general rule that the development of agriculture is a prerequisite for the emergence of cities. Social surpluses coming from agricultural exploitation are unavoidable to support a ruling class that has organizational and planning responsibilities and that is in a position to "reassure the masses" about major upcoming natural phenomena.

Childe's definition of a city relies upon a paradigm shift from the previous Neolithic system of agriculture, in preparation for the coming of the "Industrial Revolution." With the advent of what Childe called the "urban revolution," which followed and broke with the "Neolithic revolution," a new and more complex model of organization clearly emerged that was based mainly on the internal features and strengths of cities.

Even if during the first centuries of their existence cities in different parts of the world were "mutually independent," it was not been long before these social, economic, and organizational units could learn from one another. In other words, a process of learning was transmitted from one generation to the next and innovations were shared over time:

> Even today we use the Egyptians' calendar and the Sumerians' divisions of the day and the hour. Our European ancestors did not have to invent for themselves these divisions of time nor repeat the observations on which they are based; they took over—and very slightly improved—systems elaborated 5,000 years ago. (Childe, 2000: 30)

Cities we are living in nowadays are in many ways the heirs of these first cities. A similar sense of belonging is experienced through social stratification—due to households' revenue, education, and occupation, according to their location in urban space—even though social and cultural recognition are defined differently due to contextual features and the affirmation of liberal values. We also continue to connect cities to increased population size and density. Even the notion of centrality that was indirectly involved in the building of these settlements remains a focal point in the functioning of contemporary cities—although in the case of **city-regions** such centrality is taking on new forms of expression.

Throughout history, as shown by Lewis Mumford (1961), cities have fulfilled several purposes: religious, military, commercial, industrial, and political. And according to the purpose, different urban morphologies arose, including those by recent **megalopolises**. Over time, such morphologies might have been met by shortcomings and failures that no one could have anticipated at the outset.

A city's destiny, however, is impossible to predict over the long term. Internal and external factors cannot be completely controlled by a city's leaders. However, according to Max Weber (1958), the chance to build a stable urban community capable—to a certain extent—of taking its destiny in hand remains specific to the Western world. In these Western cities of the past, priority was given to trading and commercial relations, but the capacity for the inhabitants of those cities to define some form of self-government was also required. In addition, the orientation of European cities toward the economy and its expansion increased with the influence they had on an expanding hinterland.

But it was not until the nineteenth century that cities—according to a contemporary understanding of urban reality—could develop significantly. Up until then, the growth of cities had been constrained by the availability of agricultural surplus. In Europe, "as late as the beginning of the nineteenth century, the produce of nine farms was still required to support one urban family" (Palen, 1975: 33). But as soon as agriculture improved into the nineteenth century and new means of transportation became available, cities could grow at an unprecedented pace.

The Influence of Industrialization

Urbanization is usually associated with what has been called the Industrial Revolution—that is, the emergence of technical innovations and technical change in addition to the presence of large-scale capitalist organizations. Even if scholars disagree about the sudden growth of the productive system accompanying the Industrial Revolution—some contending that the changes were much more gradual then is often suggested by term *revolution* (Schwartz Cowan, 1997)—it is clear that in North America industrialization remains a determining factor for city development.

Indeed, with the Industrial Revolution—or with the technical changes that are often subsumed under the term Industrial Revolution—a clear shift occurred between populations living in rural areas by comparison to populations living in cities: "the cities of the late eighteenth century contained relatively few people, numbering less than 600,000. By the middle of the nineteenth century, capitalist industrialization had created cities of a million or more across Western Europe" (Gottdiener and Hutchison, 2011: 43). And in North America, the number and the size of cities increased rapidly as well: "Between 1870 and 1920, U.S. urban areas (places over 2,500 residents) increased their population from fewer than 10 million to more than 54 million, while Canada's urban population grew from 3.9 to 8.8"

(Macionis and Parrillo, 2010: 62). From 1920 onward, the two countries were predominantly urban, with more than 50 per cent of the population living in urban areas.

This shift from rural to urban can be explained by several factors. First, a large number of the population left rural areas for cities, where they could find jobs and improve their living conditions. Second, the influx of immigrants contributed significantly to the dynamism of industrial cities; coming mainly from Europe, they chose to settle mostly in urban areas. Third, the demographic curve started to reverse by the end of the eighteenth century as the number of births surpassed the number of deaths. The low death rates were linked to better sanitary conditions and to improvements in agriculture productivity (Macionis and Parrillo, 2010; Hiller, 2010a).

Another factor that made possible the expansion of cities was the emergence of urban technical systems (Tarr and Dupuy, 1988). Effective in transportation, communication, and building materials, the new technologies—electricity, telephone, steel structures—were able to redefine the social relations to space, introducing new mobility practices, changing the modes of communicating between inhabitants, and, more generally, altering socio-spatial relations. In brief, these technologies transformed the walking or compact city—where mechanical mobility was the norm—into a networked city characterized by connectivity, rapid communication, and sprawl. Urban changes involved different categories of networks that facilitated both material and immaterial exchanges. If new constraints are following the introduction of a technical rationality, these constraints have been counterbalanced by increased opportunities for everyone. It is not that the networked city was more equitable than the previous city form, but increased mobility certainly triggered social differentiation in relation to work division and, consequently, gave rise to processes of **upward social mobility**.

Social, Political, and Economic Factors

In North America, as across the Atlantic, processes of urbanization were complex. They included a series of interconnected components as they converged with other major factors like industrialization, capitalism, and democracy. In explaining the trends that have supported urbanization and city development, as we have underlined previously, several features need to be considered (demographic, technological, and economical). But political factors were also important because cities, as Weber (1982) defined them, are before all relatively autonomous communities. And this is especially essential when it comes to understanding contemporary cities. In this regard, the evolution of urbanization and its current expansion under the form of **metropolitanization** have introduced a new requirement defined in political terms as regulating private choices and priorities (Lacour and Puissant, 1999: 39). In that respect, political issues are even more central today than for the medieval cities that Weber studied. But it does not mean that political actors are fully in control of metropolitanization, especially in regard to their capacity to influence urban development and city forms.

In his book on the development of American cities and towns, Eric H. Monkkonen has shown that it is complicated to make a connection between, on the one hand, the form and functions of cities and, on the other hand, political decisions: "Because the new city's form and function are in flux, no class or interest group can yet attain the high ground in directing urban policy, because no one knows where the high ground is" (1988: 217). Consequently, even though we can underline the importance of policies in defining city forms, such policies rely mainly on political factors. But other factors, including economical, cultural, social, or geographical ones, are just as important to urbanization. Thus, to understand city development and/or restructuring, we must take into account a series of elements. In fact, it is the *interaction* between these several factors that matters most. In other words, city growth, dynamism, and creativity result from the interplay of several determining elements.

Keep in mind that city or urban development is not a homogeneous reality, nor a mechanical process; it is above all a qualitative issue. The descriptive statistics and the current observation of a given situation do not tell us much about the social and economic forces at play and say nothing about the ongoing social and economic restructuring. Are the power elite or those who are in a position to influence the political regime at the city level also capable of attracting capital investment? Are they also able to persuade households and social actors—i.e., those organized in pressure groups, citizen committees, or social movements—that economic goals will not impair other objectives, such as environmental concerns and/or social justice?

These questions are by no means new or original. Nevertheless, they underlie the multiple choices made by social, economic, and political actors involved in the making of cities. We must consider the complex interaction between actors and processes in the production of cities, from micro decisions taken by households and their members on a daily basis to the major choices made by economic investors, to the frames and orientations elaborated by political elites And this reminds us what city life is made of: above all, human action, organizations, and institutions.

All of this is not to say, however, that the materiality of cities—infrastructure, city forms, urban and architectural design—is meaningless. Historical culture and values of a particular locality are always reflected in these physical facets. In addition, the elements arising from these physical aspects also contribute to the definition of social interactions that take place in the city. By themselves they are important resources for social actors. However, the relevance of the city's materiality remains secondary to more intangible dimensions included in human organizations and institutions.

The capacity to co-operate, to overcome conflict, and to build projects always relies on human agency even though an interaction with structures—the series of interlinked factors and institutions that constrain and provide resources to social actors—is always unavoidable.

Today, we are entering a complex reality comprising interactions, preferences, value-laden systems, conflicts, and compromises, where social and political choices are always limited by the availability of resources and technical possibilities. Industrial cities have made the experience and challenges of **urbanity** more unique than ever before in history. As underlined by Georg Simmel (1950 [1903]), in modern **metropolises** of the industrial era, urbanites are experiencing a novel challenge. At the same time as they feel lonely in the anonymity of the crowd, they also have a strong sense of freedom and self-accomplishment due to the individuality involved in professional life with its new standards—i.e., modernity's new requirements for individuals in regard to work activity. But from understanding the individual experience of urbanites to explaining the choices made by citizens defined as collective actors regarding the future of their cities, we must move from micro to macro concerns.

Industrial city boundaries were open and flexible during the Industrial Revolution, and in the current context of globalization, this is even more striking with urban sprawl. Variations between cities can certainly be explained by internal factors, but external factors like the larger political economy that cities have to adapt to are at least as significant. In other words, in this increasingly globalized world, both constraints and opportunities are provoked by elements predominantly defined outside the city limits. As mentioned by Saskia Sassen, cities are connected in a "wide grid of strategic places" (2004: 651). According to her, a new geography of centrality is thus in the making, underlining the crucial role that cities are playing at a subnational level. As a result, cities are a more pertinent object of study than before.

What Is Urban Sociology?

In adapting to contextual changes, cities have to cope with several challenges in terms of economic development, social integration, or cultural diversity. Until now, this was certainly a central feature of the history of cities. Although it is necessary to take these challenges into account for understanding urbanization and urban changes, doing so is not sufficient. One has to highlight more specifically the way human agency copes with nature and built environments. In introducing a profound rupture with past history, modernity provides a social and theoretical perspective elaborated on the two pillars of freedom and reason as defined through the Western experiment of emancipation. This perspective presents a paradigmatic turn—breaking with previous moral or religious narratives—in the understanding of human action, including human achievement as it relates to city building. In the context of modernity, even though social actors might not be in total control of their passions and actions, they remain responsible for errors in achieving their goals.

It seems impossible to understand cities without understanding society and vice versa (Castells, 2009). And both have been confronted by the challenges raised by modernity. Modernity has introduced a profound separation with past history, providing insights about new historical understandings of freedom and reason: "Modernity is the belief in freedom of the human being—natural and inalienable, as many philosophers presumed—and in the human capacity to reason, combined with the intelligibility of the world, that is, its amenability to human reason" (Wagner, 2012: 4). In giving more attention to the freedom social actors are gaining and to the superiority of reason in human affairs, modernity introduces a new contract between individuals based on the recognition of human rights.

It is true, as underlined by Stephen Toulmin (1990), that modernity is historically difficult to situate. Researchers have long argued over its defining moment: Was it Gutenberg's innovation of moveable type? Luther's challenge of Church authority? The American and French revolutions? Although the notion of modernity is ambiguous regarding, on the one hand, the need for "rational calculations" and, on the other, the acceptance of uncertainty in human relations due to "the complexities of real life" (Toulmin, 2001: 214), modernity as a concept remains useful for understanding the ongoing transformations in "city lives and city forms" (Caulfield and Peake, 1996). Cities always represent a fundamental dimension of society (Castells, 2009) as expressed in the modernity project. In other words, if in its Western version the modernity project was often assimilated with a rationalized behaviour or conduct, its reality is much more complex because it is also including subjective dimensions that are as important as the rational ones.

In that respect, modernity can no longer be associated with an exclusive rational logic, defined in relation to technical and scientific discourses. Modernity may be better defined as a space of individual freedom, reflexivity, and autonomy (Giddens, 1990; Beck, 1997; Bauman, 2001).

With such an understanding, exploring one's self in the face of behaviours that have been entrenched in established institutions can incite people to contest dominant discourses and practices in order to bring in changes in social and political organizations. Individual and collective choices, then, are part of an open project in the sense that no result can be guaranteed at the outset, but also in the sense that no organizational arrangement must prevail, besides historic legacy, which is constantly revised and redefined to achieve a given result.

Historically, modernity has been related to the social differentiation produced through the multiplication and division of social groups as social functions and occupations or professions are becoming more diverse and specialized. As a result, sociologists like Émile Durkheim (1997 [1893]) raised this question: How is it possible to produce social cohesion—the one that characterized traditional societies—in the face of this increased differentiation of social activities occurring in a modern context? In other words, how is it possible to establish social bonds of solidarity while interactions between all depend on freedom and the specialization and singularity of everyone? There is no easy answer to such a question, and, indeed, sociology continues to raise it today.

Nonetheless, how to produce social cohesion in the face of increasing differentiation within the modern cities and metropolises of the industrial era was a burning issue. As a result, it was also during this period that urban sociology emerged as a new field of inquiry for solving problems of and in cities.

From an institutional standpoint, urban sociology was defined by Robert Ezra Park, a leading figure at the University of Chicago. Having been elected president of the American Sociological Society (ASS) in December 1924, he proposed to its members during its meeting in December 1925 to create a research committee dedicated to urban sociology: to studying social problems in and of the city. From then on, Park promoted this new sub-discipline. First, he addressed the university milieu and his peers. In the United States at the time, the university world was in full bloom. Indeed, universities were trying to endow social science with "a new scientific regime." Park engaged in a dialogue with social reformers who were quite involved in two areas: social work and urban planning (city planning had established itself in 1909 as a new profession designed to solve the problems of cities). Park attempted to convince reformers in these two areas that urban sociology could help them make sense of the social problems that concerned them (i.e., the improvement of blighted neighbourhoods and various ills associated in general with cities).

Despite Park's research and influence, it would take more than 25 years before the term *urban sociology* would be adopted in North American university discourse—indeed, not until the 1950s was the term accepted, giving rise to networks of researchers and serious institutional recognition. As Christian Topalov has explained, "what caused the temporary failure of the label, is that it was appropriated by the practitioners of an outdated applied sociology, who did not grasp that they had to redefine social problems in another language so that they could be handled scientifically" (Topalov, 2008: 230).

It was researchers oriented toward quantitative methods who were most highly respected starting from the 1930s, eclipsing human ecology for a while. Thanks to the "provisional triumph" of urban planning and to the emergence of **urban studies** in the 1950s, urban sociology was finally brought to the forefront. Only retrospectively has the label "urban sociology" been attached to the Chicago School of Sociology (Topalov, 2008).

Urban research existed before it was formally or institutionally recognized, however. We may speak of its presence in certain works of Georg Simmel, to whom some sociologists usually associated with the Chicago School habitually returned and whose line of reasoning they followed. But we may point to this same finding for other European sociologists, at least indirectly, to the extent that they linked the social change introduced by modernity to current living conditions in metropolises.

Urban Sociology vs. Urban Studies

The creation of urban sociology from the European tradition and the sociological tradition of Chicago allows us to define a field of research that is open both to macro and micro tendencies in the production of urban space and cities. But what are also important are the relations between the "macro trends and micro-level manifestations" (May and Perry, 2005: 362). Seen from this angle, the economic, social, cultural, and environmental transformations of recent years oblige researchers to consider new issues differently. In other words, the changes brought in by these transformations are related in a way to globalizing factors. It is the relations between the local and the global that are being redefined. But while urban studies emphasize interdisciplinarity, what role should urban sociology assume? Doesn't its specialization—based on a series of specific objects studied since the 1970s connected to housing, transportation, the environment, and/or transversal issues such as the local/global relationships, governance, and rescaling—provide new opportunities for overcoming crises cities are facing (Perry and Harding, 2002)? But how do we set urban sociology within the wider area of urban research studies?

The creation of the field of urban studies in the United States dates from the 1950s when American cities were facing a series of problems resulting from the development that followed World War II. Urbanization and the problems it engendered were at the centre of the political agenda of the American federal government. In getting involved in financing—notably infrastructure, urban renewal, and social housing—the federal government helped stimulate research in urban affairs and urban studies. This also encouraged the recognition, indeed institutionalization, of urban sociology.

Nonetheless, there is no unanimity with respect to defining urban studies as a field of study and an area of research. Urban studies is criticized for being insufficiently conceptualized to merit the status of a "formal academic discipline" (Bowen et al., 2010: 199). Nor is there is unanimous agreement on its definition with respect to other academic disciplines (Bowen et al., 2010). How do we define urban affairs and urban studies?

In the research conducted to determine the precise boundaries of urban studies, William Bowen and his colleagues drew upon a series of complementary processes (interviews with pioneers in the field, a survey of members of the Urban Affairs Association, and content analysis of articles published in the *Journal of Urban Affairs*). This research allowed them to more clearly identify the boundaries of the field. They came to the conclusion that urban studies could be defined in relation to "evolving human settlements" and that the field was structured internally around three dimensions: "the distinctions between (1) people and places, (2) abstract and concrete thought, and (3) the locus of control of individuals over the outcomes of action" (Bowen et al., 2010: 216).

Encompassing a series of specialized sectors (including, urban economy, urban geography, environmental studies, urban governance politics and administration, and urban planning), the field of urban studies allows us to raise questions that the boundaries of traditional disciplines prevent us from posing. Urban studies is also able "to address urban problems using various conceptual perspectives, research methods, and analytical frameworks" (Bowen et al., 2010: 203).

Because of its history and the fame of its founders, until the 1970s sociologists were the leading figures of urban studies; they were the ones framing the theoretical issues at the time. The criticisms urban studies received at the start of the 1970s due to its theoretical deficiencies (Castells, 1972) did not, however, diminish its support—quite the contrary. Nonetheless, from the 1960s the rise in influence of urban studies through the creation of a number of related specialized academic journals, as well as the formation of networks of international researchers associated with that field ultimately challenged the supremacy of urban sociology.

We must remember that urban sociology remained an important factor in the adventure of urban studies even though during the past 20 years this sectorial approach has seen its leadership wane (Perry and Harding, 2002). Yet did urban sociology's purported decline in leadership in the field of urban studies indicate a drop in its theoretical, social, and political importance? If it is true that the most important influence in the field of urban studies, as some claim (Savage, 2005), no longer comes from urban sociology, is this a source of concern? We do not believe so. As we will see in the next chapter, despite the arrival of urban studies at the forefront of research on the city, urban sociology continues to provide research tools and knowledge vital to the comprehension of modern cities' transformation. In this regard, urban sociology remains a dynamic stream of sociology.

Urban Sociology's Role in Addressing Urban Problems

Since the 1950s, urban sociology has expanded rapidly as an intellectually coherent research field and area of specialization. This expansion has allowed for the establishment of a number of research centres and networks of researchers, the organization of dozens of conferences and seminars each year in various regions of the world, as well as an increasing number of academic journals publishing the work of researchers in the discipline.

Although urban sociology's borders are not airtight with respect to other areas of sociology or social science, it is, nevertheless, a well-defined domain of research: "it is an intellectually coherent, distinctively structured, and promising field of inquiry steered by complex, ever-changing, and often-large-scale realities and new-world problems of evolving human settlements" (Bowen, Dunn, and Kasdan, 2010: 199). Thus, one may say that urban sociology has contributed in a dynamic fashion to the analysis and transformation of cities and processes of urbanization.

Discussing urban sociology is not merely a pretext to speak of cities in reference to patterns of urbanization and their social consequences. It is true that it is difficult to consider this field of study without devoting considerable attention to its focus (the urban space), its production (social relations in the city), or the city as a place of sociability, exchanges, and conflicts. Urban sociology also provides the opportunity to consider the increasing autonomy of an important research area in sociology.

Nonetheless, our primary focus is on the relationship to the object, the city. Here, we must note that this object no longer presents itself in the same terms as when Robert E. Park, of the Chicago School of Sociology, thought of formalizing the existence of a new field of study and research in the mid-1920s. The contemporary city, which remains in many respects the heir of the classical city, is also removed from the classical city in many ways. Where the classical city was characterized by some distinctive elements— such as a central forum (an Agora) where economic exchanges could take place along with religious and political life activities; and the existence of surrounding walls to mark city limits and for defence—the contemporary city has an extended form and is fragmented but also stretched, deploying a new "urban morphology." This may be understood through the expansion of large urban regions that assume the form of a sprawling urban settlement, characterized as much by a variety of uses, functions, and social relationships to space as by a redefinition of centrality. Centrality has always been a major feature for defining cities. In the past, centrality entailed relations of proximity from a given place. In other words, the image of a particular city has relied mainly on the dynamism and attractiveness of its centre. Nowadays, the centre no longer corresponds exclusively to functional interactions and/or material connections. Instead, it crosses boundaries more easily. In addition, there has been a proliferation of centres within a single urban area. We are definitely witnessing the emergence of a new metropolitan form with which we may readily associate the contemporary city, which some label city-regions (Scott, 2001) and which others prefer to define as metropolitan regions (Judd and Simpson, 2011), if not "postmetropolis" (Soja, 2000).

Due to social, cultural, economic, and technological changes, the city and its urban environment are undergoing several transformations. We may think of the introduction of new information and communication technologies—which are transforming the "spatial patterns of behaviour into a fluid network of exchanges" (Castells, 1996: 398), facilitating communication for obtaining public services or planning work organization—and their impact on the urban ebb and flow and ways of organizing work or the location of economic activities in the available space. There are also new concerns about the place of nature in the city. It is no longer enough to relegate nature to functional spaces like urban parks or cemeteries. In that respect, urban planners and city managers have no choice but to internalize the costs related to environmental protection (preservation of biodiversity, reduction of greenhouse gas emissions, and the fight against urban hot spots). Consequently, it is becoming increasingly difficult to take the city for granted.

The relationship of households to space is evolving, too—in particular, if we think about people's greater expectations in terms of quality of life—as are ways of envisaging the management and provision of public infrastructure and services in the community. These can no longer simply respond to the needs expressed by everyone. Above all, such infrastructure must contribute to an integrated urban development, where social, economic, and environmental problems must all be taken into consideration.

Does this mean that the city has a new face? In what terms can we understand this? Compared with the city of the past, what characterizes the city of today? Is it only management or planning styles that have changed—leaving the city's personality intact to some degree—or are we witnessing a fundamental modification of representations and values?

While urban reality is ubiquitous—urbanization having spread across all the continents and to every corner of the planet—we may wonder whether it is still appropriate to employ this notion to describe a cultural model that affects the lifestyle of every person and the daily behaviour of each household and individual. Even those who live far from cities or large agglomerations are no less affected by urban culture.

With its standards, codes, and representations, urban life is predominant everywhere, even if its modes of expression are diverse and vary enormously according to historical context and cultural traditions. In the current depiction of things, "[t]he urban dimension is at the centre of perceptions of the world" (Genestier, 1998: 289). Consequently, as others have asked, doesn't the urban reality tend to simply become equivalent to social reality itself?

This is not our position. Although starting with the urban phenomenon to broach the study of cities is neither original nor necessary, doing so does provide a guide for its comprehension and production. In approaching the study of cities by means of the "urban," we are choosing a multidimensional perspective. In that respect, as we will see in the next chapter, urban space is above all an ongoing and open process of social production (Lefebvre, 2003). In this sense, city development relies on the values involved in the choices made by social actors even if those are certainly constrained by a series of structural factors, such as market trends and the availability of resources for households. The capacity everyone has to address city challenges relies on the individual's belonging to the world of urban culture as experienced in daily life.

At the same time, we understand intuitively that all cities are not the same. Living in a city of 10,000 inhabitants is not similar to being part of a megalopolis of 18 million. Social, economic, and political problems experienced in mid-sized or small cities are quite different from those in large agglomerations (Notteridge, 2007). Even if urban culture is pervasive, social transformations involved with urban development and metropolitanization, as we will see in Chapter 4, are bringing in new concerns.

What Are These Urban Problems?

From a historical perspective, regarding economic and social changes largely speaking, we may say that significant transformations have occurred. Certainly, images and representations of the good life have changed. References to diversity in living environments reflect the hybridity of cultures encouraged by trends toward the globalization of economic and social life.

It is the same for urban problems. The poverty that was experienced by a majority of households in several neighbourhoods of industrial cities at the end of the nineteenth century and at the beginning of the twentieth century bears little resemblance to our circumstances today, except with respect to the feeling of social exclusion that continues to haunt the most deprived social groups. Changes and physical mobility that have become characteristic of large agglomerations (the fact that life was organized differently due to the presence of technical networks, like the telephone and the presence of rapid transit facilitating commuting) were already features of the nineteenth- or early-twentieth-century metropolises. However, in our day these features are an intrinsic part of the urban system of city-regions. While the contemporary city is fragmented socially, it is also divided by its functions, which are extended over an increasingly expanding territory. Daily life has necessarily changed. Sometimes, for example, people have to travel dozens of kilometres to get to work, as well as to obtain speciality services or to purchase particular goods, or, failing that, they opt for commerce online, which is happening more and more frequently.

While a number of economic activities are still locally based, whether at the level of the block, the neighbourhood, or the borough, networks and global changes are increasingly visible throughout the territory of agglomerations. This translates into a greater presence of continental or multinational firms, in particular in the area of mass consumption. These interfere insidiously in the development of local spaces, gradually transforming the traditional landscape. This is exactly what Sharon Zukin (2009) explains when she is opposing two distinct visions of urbanism and social relations to space, that of the "urban village" and that of the "corporate city." While the "urban village" is principally oriented toward the use values and lived space,[1] the "corporate city" responds first and foremost to expectations for accumulation:

> Originating in mid-twentieth century American discourse, the corporate city and the urban village are, in one way or another, the pre-eminent socio-spatial constructs of global urbanism today. As material landscapes, they embody the concentration of wealth in industry; in the service sector that coordinates the investment strategies, professional careers and personal lives of those who manage industrial wealth; and in the workers who migrate from villages in distant regions to create the physical products on which modern life depends. As symbolic landscapes, however, they represent contrasting social worlds. The corporate city represents the high end of growth, the cultural hegemony of finance and the standardization of individual desire. It is what we understand to be the ultimate landscape of globalization. The urban village, on the other hand, represents the low-key and often low-income neighbourhood, the culture of ethnic and social class solidarity, and the dream of restoring a ruptured community. It is in many ways the local response to globalization. (Zukin, 2009: 545–6)

The tendencies observed on a macro social scale in link with globalizing tendencies or following the emergence of the new information and communication technologies, as well as their repercussions in terms of space, raise new issues. But a series of other processes also deserve our attention and contribute to the ongoing changes. We may mention the increasingly visible socio-cultural diversity in the urban space, transformations in the organization of work, and the individualization of social relationships. As a result, city-regions become a different type of urban space where local and global rationalities are intertwined and where new land-use patterns, through sprawl and expansion, are mixed with traditional forms. Consequently, the city in question is in no way a classic city. It is not a "bounded unit." Specifically, we are increasingly in the presence of a complex reality that is bringing together different socio-spatial processes and redesigning the traditional model of interaction with urban space (Sassen, 2005).

The city and the urban phenomenon as an ideal location to observe social transformations have proven to be relevant to sociology despite the fact that they were relegated to the background for a number of years, compared with other areas of study, such as the state or international relations. However, it was the socio-spatial configuration of cities that changed, as well as their economic and political significance.

The open form characterizing large agglomerations that are expanding across the land as city-regions include multiple territorial models, ranging from the traditional suburb to the small or mid-sized city, from suburban zones to rural zones in the process of conversion, through industrial waste-lands and lots slated for redevelopment. These various territorial units, the networks and infrastructure that allow them to be viable, and the resources that are invested in them constitute the components of a complex landscape in constant transformation that is not easy to grasp in either its systematic functioning or its administrative and political logic.

In terms of dealing with complex urban problems, city-regions have been experimenting with a variety of governance practices. These have been conceived in reference to co-operation between public and private actors, either on a sector basis—around transport for example—or for general purposes encompassing several domains or issues. (We will discuss these elements in more detail in Chapter 6.) This raises a number of questions that were ignored until recently, not only in matters of coordinating public and private interventions, but also with respect to political responsibilities and issues of democratization.

Social concerns about the practical and political dimensions of the governance of city-regions largely stem from the growing interest in environmental issues, as well as social preoccupation with justice and the reduction of inequalities. With respect to the environment, public action to lessen the risks, reduce the ecological footprint, protect threatened species, fight against air and water pollution, and restore waterways and contaminated soil require coordination of economic agents and local administrations with regard to watersheds that may, of course, exceeds the limits of city-regions. Yet it is still at the level of city-regions that decisions must first be made, given the extent of resources and powers concentrated there.

From the start, the establishment of a metropolitan political space for these city-regions has raised the question of sharing public responsibilities in matters of solidarity. How can a more equitable division of social housing and access to local services be ensured at the level of a metropolitan territory? While higher levels of government attempt to decentralize responsibilities, demands on local authorities are increasing, both from governments and the population. The metropolitan level is necessarily caught in the middle.

Nonetheless, although the feeling of belonging to a metropolitan space is generally shared by the population and the principal actors in local economic development, this does not necessarily translate into a corresponding commitment or a capacity to act at this level (Jouve, 2005; Fontan et al., 2008). In the Canadian context, the issue of immigration is seen from the angle of social and cultural integration/differentiation within a pluralist society. Even though this issue was first raised at the national level, metropolitan spaces are increasingly concerned. Thus, in the face of a series of complex challenges—defined simultaneously in economic, environmental, and social terms—metropolitan governance remains uncertain. This leads us to scrutinize more carefully the territorial composition of this space, as well as the conflicts of loyalty that characterize it.

Conclusion

In this chapter, we have raised several questions about how to understand cities as an object of inquiry from the perspective of a specialized field of research, urban sociology. We have started by paying attention to the processes of urbanization that are involved in the production of cities. By referring to a historical perspective, we have underlined the importance of contextual factors in explaining the production of cities even though internal factors remain crucial as well. Throughout history, cities have been at the forefront of civilization, affected by growth and decline. Urbanization has been supported by agricultural, technical, and demographic transformations. But it was not until the industrial era that cities were able to grow at a rapid pace, and they soon gathered the majority of the world population. Second, we have paid attention to the emergence and trajectory of urban sociology. Above all, urban sociology was created to solve social, economic, and political problems that cities were facing in the United States. After a few decades, this field of study, even if its boundaries are difficult to draw, was revealed to be quite dynamic. The emergence of urban studies, within which urban sociology has continued to evolve, raised new challenges that are interdisciplinary. But we do not think that these challenges threaten the capacity of urban sociology to remain creative and to contribute to the understanding of social relations and their transformation in cities. Finally, we have introduced some of the key urban problems that urban sociology is dealing with. In this regard, we have distinguished contemporary urban forms taken by city-regions from traditional cities.

Questions for Critical Thought

1. What are the main characteristics involved in the definition of a city?

2. Should urban sociologists be concerned with the emergence and development of urban studies?

3. To what extent are contemporary cities similar to and different from cities of the past?

Suggested Readings

Flanagan, William G. 1993. *Contemporary Urban Sociology*. Cambridge: Cambridge University Press. This book focuses on theoretical issues of contemporary urban sociology. It presents a comprehensive reading of the main trends of research within the field of urban sociology, dealing with the city defined as a dynamic object of study.

Hughes, Everett. 2009. *French Canada in Transition*. Don Mills: Oxford University Press. The first edition was released in 1943 by the University of Chicago Press and is written in the tradition of the Chicago School of Sociology. This new edition includes an introduction by Lorne Tepperman and a foreword by Nathan Keyfitz. The book is about the study of an industrial city in French Canada, considering relationships between two cultures. But it is above all a nuanced analysis of industrializing processes at the beginning of the twentieth century, taking into account social inequalities and their possible transformation. Even though it was written by an American sociologist of the Chicago School of Sociology, it is often looked at as part of Canadian sociology, Hughes having taught at McGill University between 1927 and 1938.

Simmel, G. 1976. *The Metropolis and Mental Life. The Sociology of Georg Simmel*. New York: Free Press. First published in 1903, this essay of the great German sociologist remains a must-read for anyone trying to understand the ambivalence of the modern metropolis. Simmel places individuals at the heart of his analyses. He pays particular attention to how an individual's assertiveness within modernity contributes to transform modern social relationships. But he was at first fascinated by the fact that the individual personality was challenged by modernity as expressed in city life.

Related Websites

International Sociological Association (ISA), Research Committee on Sociology of Urban and Regional Development RC21
www.isa-sociology.org/rc21.htm
The Research Committee 21 on Sociology of Urban and Regional Development of the International Sociological Association was created in 1970. It brings together researchers from several disciplines to contribute to the promotion of theory and research in that field. This committee is also facilitating the creation of international networks of researchers.

Cities Centre: University of Toronto

www.citiescentre.utoronto.ca/about.htm

This centre was created in 2007 as a "multi-disciplinary research institute." Dedicated to the development of urban research in Canada and abroad, the centre is providing "a gateway for communication between the University and the broader urban community."

Great Cities Institute at the University of Illinois at Chicago

www.uic.edu/cuppa/gci/

Dedicated to the study of "great cities," this institute focuses mainly on three areas: development, health, and governance. Among other things, the site provides a series of working papers covering mostly empirical research.

2 | Theoretical Perspectives in Urban Sociology

Learning Objectives

- ◎ To present the theoretical approaches to city development and city life
- ◎ To show the pioneering contribution of the Chicago School of Sociology to urban studies
- ◎ To raise criticisms about the ecological approach and show which alternative models of explanation have replaced it
- ◎ To discuss the political economy of urbanization, where urban space is viewed as a social production
- ◎ To present the criticisms of postmodernism addressed to the traditional understanding of cities

---

Introduction

Cities are an amazing object of study. The type of interaction that prevails between, on the one hand, cities' physical components—such as land use, infrastructure, or spatial structures—and, on the other, human action and its capacity to orient or redefine urban forms, remains challenging to understand. As well, the city's changing form over time makes it difficult to highlight in a satisfactory manner the meaning of social, cultural, economic, and political choices of planning the transformation of urban space. Theorizing about cities, as a result, is a controversial endeavour.

Nonetheless, there is a long tradition of theorizing about cities, theories that have been developed by researchers and that have put forward a number of daring perspectives. As Dennis R. Judd has mentioned, "the search for an all-encompassing theory of the city is irresistible, but one must suspect that goal is impossible to achieve. No theory plausibly can explain all of the spatial and social dynamics that govern cities and metropolitan regions" (2011: 17–18). If we agree with such a conclusion, it does not mean that theorizing about cities is useless. Rather, it means that theorizing about cities proved to be incomplete. In fact, as in other fields of inquiry, theorizing in this case was profoundly influenced both by the historical context within which cities were designed and by which explicative model—the organic theory, the systems theory, the perspective of structuralism or post structuralism—was considered to be the dominant paradigm of the times. From that respect, one can understand why theorizing about cities was and still is controversial.

Theories are useful in explaining how empirical reality is produced. They also allow researchers to take a step back from empirical reality to see things a little more clearly. We need theories to elucidate what is going on, to sift through the accumulation of events and details characterizing city life and/or the evolution of a particular city's urban landscape. In that sense, urban sociology, in conjunction with comprehensive or general sociology, has given us some distancing elements that are required for illuminating not only the formal or morphological aspects of cities but also the behaviour of the inhabitants of those cities.

As underlined in the previous chapter, each city has its own personality, so to speak. And both a city's history and the complex interactions among its inhabitants are what produce a distinctive social and cultural reality. Urban theory as elaborated by sociologists is dedicated to better understanding these outputs, even though it is difficult to provide a complete sociological definition of the city (Notteridge, 2007).

The current chapter is dedicated to introducing the theoretical elements that have been central to urban sociology. Even if it is impossible to present a complete synthesis of the theory, it remains important to go through the main theoretical contributions of the discipline in order to first understand the concerns of researchers, and second, familiarize ourselves with the major notions this specialized field of research is based upon.

We should keep in mind that the role of urban theory is, above all, to help empirical research respond to the questions raised by researchers. But its role is also to contribute to finding the missing links resulting from the knowledge produced by empirical research regarding cities and city life. Empirical understanding is never entirely satisfactory, which can be explained by two reasons. First, the social reality that is targeted by the research process is constantly in the making; it is, therefore, difficult to understand its essence. Second, as social transformations occur, new concerns emerge. For this reason, analyses carried out in the past must be reviewed against new information that emerges in the present (such as feminist literature in the 1980s that introduced new concerns about cities).

The chapter is subdivided into four sections. First of all, we will recall the main notions elaborated by the Chicago School of Sociology. Relying on the work done by the pioneers of sociology, urban sociologists of the Chicago School were interested in explaining urban morphology and the pattern of urban development. They also wanted to better understand the relationships among inhabitants living in central urban neighbourhoods. The second section focuses on symbolic interactionism, which is usually linked to the

Chicago School. With the development of industrialization, urban reality became more complex and difficult to apprehend, which led to another attempt to clarify urban issues by elaborating this time on a political economy analysis of the city, as discussed in the third section of this chapter. The last section examines the **postmodern critique**. In the 1980s, urban sociology could not ignore the criticisms that had been made against functionalist and Marxist analyses of the city from a poststructuralist perspective. This postmodern critique is what led many researchers to revise the analytical models that had been developed earlier.

The Chicago School of Sociology

As a discipline, sociology evolved differently on either side of the Atlantic. In Continental Europe, in order to engage in sociological inquiry and to explain the configuration and trends in the social world, the discipline was cast through the notions of social classes and social movements. Sociology there dealt with class conflicts and mass movements that were entrenched in history and that reflected social dissatisfaction with dominant institutions; sociologists there were looking for perspectives able to challenge historicity (that is, the historical accuracy of events). In North America, at the outset, the concerns were quite different. For researchers there, sociology was for focusing on social problems, which seemed to them more appropriate for meeting the issues of social transformations. This duality came from two different traditions or "points of departure": on the one hand, in Europe, having to cope with what was upsetting Europeans—class conflicts and mass movements entrenched in history, reflecting social dissatisfaction with dominant institutions; on the other hand, in North America, finding suitable answers to the troubles coming from a "rapidly industrializing society" (Bash, 1995: 195).

These two traditions define two different theoretical orientations: one that leans toward social constructivism and the other, toward empiricism. In addition, these traditions involve very different ways of understanding and conducting sociology: "In the American social problem literature, acknowledgment of social change tended to be more tacit (than in the European perspective), often arising only by implication and primarily as a backdrop to the problem-specific analysis under consideration" (Bash, 1995: 213). This is precisely the approach that the Chicago School of Sociology was promoting.

The University of Chicago department of sociology was created soon after the university was founded in 1892. Even though that department was not the first to be created in the United States, it was the most influential one for many years (Chapoulie, 2001). The department devoted its attention to "the observation and analysis of the contemporary world" (Chapoulie,

2001: 25). Its "social laboratory" of research was at its doorstep: the city with its working-class and ethnic neighbourhoods, its ghetto, and its slums. At the end of the nineteenth and at the beginning of the twentieth century, Chicago was experiencing an unprecedented urban growth:

> In 1870 the city had a population of perhaps 300,000 living on only 35 square miles of territory. By 1893, the city's population would exceed 1.3 million living in an expanse of 185 square miles . . ., making Chicago during this period the fastest-growing city in the history of the country, if not the world. (Abu-Lughod, 1999: 101)

The Chicago School was not as homogeneous as the term would suggest. A number of differences necessarily prevailed among the professors associated with the department. Although all of them believed in the need for empirical research and the use of social investigation to analyze the transformations at play, as opposed to speculations based on social philosophy, their research varied in its focus due to diverse theoretical perspectives in relation to various influences. Therefore, it would be fitting, as Chapoulie (2001) suggests, to speaking in terms of a sociological *tradition* rather than using the designation "school." This better reflects the reality of the dynamism of the social science research at the University of Chicago.

Initially, two major social and scientific concerns stimulated the research program of Robert E. Park—one of the leading figures of the sociology department at the University of Chicago where he explored mainly three fields (collective behaviour, human ecology, and race relations)—and his colleagues: (1) they wanted to better understand the laws supporting urban development in large cities, and (2) they were concerned with the consequences of urbanization on inhabitants' living conditions and the threatening of the solidity of their relations with the group to which they belonged before moving to the city. For them, the breakdown of traditional sources of control was reflected in the "perceived prevalence of urban crime and vice" (McGahan, 1986: 17). But this statement does not imply a condemnation of urban life. A new form of solidarity based on a "community of interests" can emerge in urban neighbourhoods, which would help people cope with problems produced through urban social relationships.

According to Park, Burgess, and McKenzie (1925), the city can be compared to an ecological system with its specific rules of competition and distribution in space. In developing his conception of "natural zones" and "moral regions," Park starts from the principle that human activities occurring in a given space transform the built environment while the space, in turn, has repercussions for the forms of organization of social life. The materiality of space—that is, the components of the urban fabric and their specific form due to the history of urban development—also comes to affect human groupings and social segregation. As a result, urban zones and areas differ as a function of cultural particularities of group belonging.

Populations share an area based on a spatial model that distributes activities according to an order obeying forces, both social and natural. As a natural entity, the city is not governed by its administrative and legal constraints. The spatial distribution of activities and people is constrained and habilitated at the same time by physical and social factors: "population, technology, customs and beliefs and the natural resource of the locale" (McGahan, 1986: 27). While individuals can sometimes escape from these influences, they participate actively in social differentiation through their social and professional belonging, starting from the division of labour that applies to them and the technical specialization they choose. The city, then, becomes a place of diversification and of opportunities. Trades and professional categories multiply, allowing all individuals to express themselves according to their aptitudes. The relationships between geographic space and society are certainly dynamic.

The Chicago Concentric Zones Model

The Chicago spatial, or concentric zones, model is developed on a few variables only (Burgess, 1925). The model, an ideal-type model never to be found in the real world, is composed of concentric zones that move from the centre outward. The city centre, called the Loop, is the business and commercial zone, broadly described by its main built and functional characteristics. Around this Loop is the second zone, a zone of transition characterized by light industries, which is gradually encroached on by the business activities of the Loop. The third zone contains the working classes, living close to where they work. The fourth and fifth zones are mainly residential zones, and the further one goes away from the Loop, the higher the value of the housing stock. The fifth zone is what we called the suburbs. Social area analysis and factorial ecology constructed complex statistical indices of urban social differentiation built on many more variables than Burgess's model.

Burgess himself refined this basic (too basic) socio-spatial model. Based on the city of Chicago in the 1920s, he observed that inside each zones there were important variations. For instance, the zone of transition was peopled by different immigrant groups and by black households and businesses. Housing was cheaper in this zone, which explains immigrants' preference for it since most of them did not migrate with large financial resources. There also were, in the same transition zone, areas that were downgraded and buildings that were left unoccupied owing to poor conditions. Other types of internal differentiation applied to the other zones. In the fourth zone, Burgess separated areas, subzones so to speak, that were rich and those that were less rich. The type of housing was also an important variable in the socio-spatial model. On the whole, the Burgess model was simple. It was chiefly built on three types of data: social and cultural characteristics, building types, and economic activities.

The Human Ecology Approach

In the ecological vision that Park shares with Burgess and the other members of the tradition of the Chicago School, which was defined and recognized afterward as the human ecology approach, the relations of individuals to space first occur through competition. As we may observe in the world of vegetable and animal biology, in an urban milieu the strongest individuals manage to place themselves in strategic locations, that is, at the centre. The organization of the city in concentric zones—described in the well-known cartographic model that allows representing the spatial distribution of activities and residences as schematized by Burgess (see Park, Burgess, and McKenzie, 1925)—stems from this (see Figure 2.1, Burgess's Model of Concentric Zones). Like any other human establishment, the city takes on the form of an ecological community. Factors such as the size of the population, its concentration, and its distribution influence the possible trajectories of mobility that individuals and groups may follow. Thus, we discover a relationship between property values and the spatial distribution of activities and choices of residential location, property values playing a role both as an indicator of certain behaviour and as a limitation on the choices available to each (Grafmeyer and Joseph, 1979).

Interethnic relations across the city of Chicago were sometimes tense due to successive waves of massive immigration, coming both from abroad and from the southern United States. Ethnic conflicts were most common between recent and earlier immigrants, especially on the subject of employment (Chapoulie, 2001). Thus, it is not surprising that there emerged a series of "urban problems," ranging from the poverty of a large proportion of the recent immigrant population to the unhealthy nature of the built environment to delinquency and racial, interethnic, and class conflicts.

The social transformation of living conditions then corresponded to segregation processes and group membership, as well as to the rejection of the outsider as a member of a distinct social group. All these processes contributed to the creation of a veritable urban culture in Chicago, not simply resulting from the rational choices made by individuals but from a general context linked, for example, to capitalist industrialization, inside of which individuals evolved and which was bound to affect their decisions. Nonetheless, contrary to certain reductionist interpretations (that human ecology had a tendency to explain human behaviour as strongly shaped by ecological characteristics of cities), we should not see in this a simple spatial determinism of social relations. Rather, we should see a desire to consider the role of social relationships

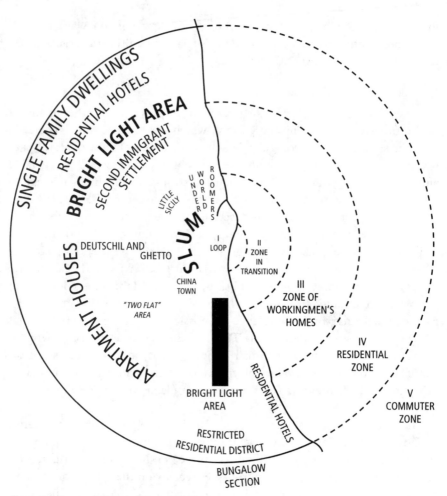

Figure 2.1 Burgess's Model of Concentric Zones
Source: Park, R.E, Burgess, E.W., and R.D. McKenzie (eds.). 1967. *The City*. Chicago: University of Chicago Press, p. 55. Used with permission.

in space, including the forces structuring the social milieu, a dimension rather neglected up until the moment the members of the Chicago School did their studies (i.e., the beginning of the 1920s).

In his seminal article "Urbanism as a Way of Life" (1938), Wirth—one of the principal figures of the Chicago School of Sociology—deals with qualitative aspects of urban development. Even though the "urban mode of life is not confined to cities" (Wirth, 1938: 1), it is in urban settlements that we find the social and cultural characteristics of what is specific to urbanism. Nonetheless, cities remain linked in many ways to the countryside. Urbanization often brings in households previously living in the countryside. Urban and rural settlements should be considered as two opposite spatial forms providing communities with different values and organizing principles:

The city and the country may be regarded as two poles in reference to one or the other of which all human settlements tend to arrange themselves. In viewing urban-industrial and rural-folk society as ideal types of communities, we may obtain a perspective for the analysis of the basic models of human association as they appear in contemporary civilization. (Wirth, 1938: 3)

However, urban culture goes beyond cities. The domination by cities over their hinterland, for example, is something that we are familiar with nowadays. But to explain the characteristics of urban life that are specific to a given city, Wirth suggests taking into account three variables. The first one concerns the number of inhabitants involved in city life, in social and economic activities, and in the system of political representation. The second variable is related to density. Concentration of inhabitants tends to increase "the complexity of the social structure" (Wirth, 1938: 14). The third variable is related to heterogeneity. Increases in the "variety of personality types" evolving in a particular city are favourable to introducing ruptures in traditional behaviour and inducing "a more ramified and differentiated framework of social stratification than is found in more integrated societies" (Wirth, 1938: 14).

If for understanding "**urbanism** as a way of life" it is necessary to start with these variables, researchers also need to connect them to the social structure and institutions as well as take into account their repercussions on the mechanisms of social control. The **human ecology** developed by Park and his collaborators was intended to study "the forces at work within the urban community . . . that tend to produce an ordered grouping, characteristic of its populations and institutions" (Park quoted by Topalov, 2008: 213).

From Ecology to Interaction

The Chicago School's ecological approach to city and urbanism, although dominant in American urban studies for some time, was not without challengers. There were limits to the school's theoretical assertions despite the richness of its empirical studies. Criticisms have focused on the fact that it relied on factors other than social ones to explain social phenomena. Whereas classical sociology, in the Durkheimian tradition in particular, claimed to explain social phenomena by other social phenomena, the ecological perspective to the city opened the door to non-social forces explaining social facts. Classical sociologists broke with the propensity in other fields of study, strong after the Darwinian revolution, to explain social facts by biological causes and by ecological factors. The Chicago School drew heavily on the fledgling American ecological sciences. However, in a complete explanation of complex social facts, many factors are at play. Does this complexity make room for non-social causes? The Chicago School believed so by stressing ecological forces. However, ecological forces leading to space occupation and neighbourhood differentiation have come to be seen as secondary factors that have little influence on people and their social behaviours.

Although it is true that cities are set in space and are subject to physical conditions, these can play as constraining factors to city development as well as enhancing factors. Amos Hawley (1986), one of the last ecological sociologists of the old school, went on to write about the double composition of communities, that is, social as well as ecological. He moreover insisted that the physical has a great bearing on community structure, organization, and evolution. But later urban sociologists turned their back to such an explanation and reverted to the precept that social facts should be accounted for by other social facts. Leading urban sociologists like Gans (1968), Fischer (1984), and Castells (1972) have distanced themselves from a strong ecological approach and its implied model of explanation.

What should replace the ecological explanation? What other models explain more accurately city structure and urbanism as a way of life? To start with, one must recognize that the Chicago School did not put all of its eggs in the sole ecological basket. Although dominant, the ecological explanation was combined with other types of explanations or factors. The problem was that the school entertained a two-tier explanation model. The Chicago School pioneered community studies and investigation of group behaviour in cities, deviant or marginal behaviour in particular (Bulmer, 1984; Chapoulie, 2001). Researchers at the school studied urban communities and neighbourhoods such the *Gold Coast and the Slum* (Zorbaurg, 1929) and the *Ghetto* (Wirth, 1928), although some maintained a strong interest in the ecological basis of community life. Other inquiries focused on the sub-community level: ethnographic studies of the *Hobo* (Anderson, 1923), of a *Street Corner Society* (Whyte, 1942), and of a *Taxi-Dance Hall* (Cressey, 1932) painted a diversified and at times unsettling urban life. Out of this line of research, urban sociologists explored a greater diversity of social actions and interactions in different urban contexts. Thus, the past focus on ecological factors switched to social interactions, group structure, and collective action, as well as to the diversity of reactions in urban space and, in a word, to unlimited forms of sociality in an urban setting.

The understanding of the urban sociological landscape thus changed substantially. Starting from the 1940s, a social interactionist model to city life gradually emerged, consolidated, and replaced the human ecological model (Erickson, 1980; Hannigan, 2010: 51). Interactions among people living under different conditions and sharing different cultures, or world views, grouping together according to stages in family life and to economic means have become a major focus of urban sociology. It is, empirically, a partial break with the past, with the human ecology or ecological model, but the change meant something epistemologically different, for no physical factors are considered in the social interactionist explanation of human behaviours in an urban habitat. Interactions between people founded on a common and shared community have little to do with space as a force but a lot to do with decisions one makes in choosing where to live. People gather in urban space not because of ecological forces but because of social factors, such as sharing a cultural origin, preferring a quiet environment in which to raise children, opting for a thriving cultural life that the central city offers, or doing their best with their family budget in the choice of housing.

Sociality is not lost with a change from a close-knit community to an open community owing to broader social change. In a classic study of an East London community (Bethnal Green), Michael Young and Peter Willmott (1957) showed that when family, friendship, and community relations came under stress, they did not entirely disappear. When a neighbourhood experienced deep physical change, such as a large planning redevelopment, in the course of which members of the old community are spread out to new suburbs, community relations are redefined. Some ties loosen, most undone in the long run by economic prosperity, but people and community are much more resilient, and change in spatial and physical arrangements do not necessarily lead to a breakdown of social relations. Young and Willmott's study can be considered the first example of "social capital" at work when a group of people, a community, is under stress. Social capital—i.e., the set of all social relations—a widely used idea, not only among sociologists but also among international institutions such as the World Bank, can be a helpful concept to a better understanding of social relations as a means to some ends, for instance weathering major stresses and negotiating personal and collective adjustment (Hampton, 2010; Portes and Vickstrom, 2011).

The Emergence of a Political Economy Analysis of the City

Following human ecology, which contributed to a better understanding of the main economic, geographical, and social factors and processes at play in the development of a city, and to a certain extent, taking into account the complexity of social interactions revealed by symbolic interactionists at the beginning of the 1970s, urban sociologists decided to renew the Marxist tradition. Sociologists were not entirely satisfied with the way social and political relations of power had been considered so far in explaining uneven economic development and its impact on cities. The ecological factors involved in shaping the city form did not explain in a satisfactory way capital accumulation in cities and its consequences in terms of increasing class conflicts. What are the main elements involved in the transformation of cities under industrial capitalism? Is it necessary to go back in history to better understand the interplay between economic and political forces in shaping urban forms? For answering these questions and "for stimulating future development in the field" (Flanagan, 1995: 234), sociologists have turned mainly to the heritage of Marxism, paying more attention to class analysis, social inequalities, and capital accumulation.

This has contributed to the emergence of a new school of urban sociology or the **new urban sociology**, which relies on the necessity to better reflect and explain the profound social and economic changes occurring in cities of the Western world at the end of the 1960s (Savage and Warde, 1993). For that matter, among the main significant elements brought to the attention of sociologists, we must recall the relative decline of central cities, the employment decrease in industrial cities at the beginning of the 1970s, the new relationships that were being defined between cities and suburbs and, finally, the different types of riots and/or social mobilizations around urban issues that occurred in cities on both sides of the Atlantic. Urbanites were unsatisfied with their life quality and felt threatened in their location choice by state intervention on infrastructure through diverse urban policies.

The new sociological approach to urban problems tried to consider cities' issues from a new angle. It was no longer enough to describe and explain the mobility patterns of inhabitants during their lifespan. Instead, sociologists had to understand the origin of social inequalities in the city and how economic factors influenced the content and form of urban fabric. For that reason, it was necessary to underscore the cycle followed by capital accumulation and the basic rules of industrial capitalism that are at the basis of many economic decisions involved in the production of the built environment (Harvey, 1973). In that respect, urbanism appeared clearly as the result of class domination relations.

From the outset, the new school of urban sociology challenged the spatial determinism (linking in a simplistic way social behaviour to urban morphology factors) of the first urban sociologists of the Chicago sociological tradition. The new approach was looking for a renewal of the debate on the city in a striking fashion. Manuel Castells (1972) opened the hostilities, so to speak, and provoked a genuine academic debate on the necessity of constructing a theoretical perspective in order to better address the specificity of contemporary cities. According to Castells, the ideological character of urban discourse was concealing that social relations were structured through class conflicts while facilitating the reproduction of the workforce according to dominant interests in capitalist societies. Breaking with this ideological vision of development, Castells suggested considering the urban reality linked with processes of social reproduction, starting with collective consumption.

Aware of the contradictions arising from capitalist accumulation in cities, Castells (1972) defined the urban as an analytical category in reference to issues of collective consumption. He formulated the hypothesis that there was a possible common ground between the interests of the working class and those of the middle classes with respect to problems of housing, transportation, mobility, and access to the urban centre, including the availability of community and proximity services. This hypothesis led him to pay particular attention to social movements in the city. These social actors were aware of the privileges enjoyed by economic and political elites. They challenged the dominant position of these elites in the formulation of urban policies. The new school of urban sociology as defined by Manuel Castells (see Castells and Ince, 2003)—but also to a certain extent by his followers and opponents—tried to redefine urban problems and urban contradictions by revisiting Marxist tradition. Contrary to the sociologists before him, Castells paid special attention to urban social movements, namely the social actors mobilizing around urban issues defined as problems of collective consumption for changing public policies and their underlying relations of domination.

Castells's critique, inspired by both the structural Marxism of Nicos Poulantzas (1968) and the sociology of action developed by Alain Touraine (1965) contributed to the reopening of the theoretical debate on the city and urban sociology. But it also fostered a series of empirical studies on social relationships to space, urban policies, and urban movements.

While Castells was one of the first to contribute to the emergence of the new school of urban sociology, he was not the only one. With his emphasis on political economy processes, Castells's theoretical approach (1972) brought to the fore the fact that the traditional economic model as well as previous sociological templates could no longer account for the ongoing urban restructuring.[1] However, despite the bold and provocative nature of his analysis, divergent views that also contributed to the promotion of the new school of urban sociology were also heard, contributing significantly to the new approach. Among them were the works of David Harvey, Peter Saunders, Jean Lojkine, and Henri Lefebvre. We will focus on the work of Lefebvre.

Lefebvre brought the attention of sociologists and of a broader audience to the emergence of an urban society and the importance of urbanism in shaping social life (see Box 2.1). As Mark Gottdiener and Ray Hutchison point out, "Lefebvre is without question the seminal source of new thinking on the city from a critical and Marxian perspective" (2011: 80).

Lefebvre's first concern was to understand the social production of urban forms. He developed a critical point of view able to articulate economic, social, and cultural dimensions. How do spatial forms and social relations interact in Western societies? What are the advantages of thinking in terms of "urban society"? To what extent is the urban revolution contributing to a radical transformation of social relations in the city for the majority of urbanites?

The role played by Lefebvre's thought and writing in the renewal of urban sociology was important both directly and indirectly. *Directly*, his critical thinking stimulated the urban political economy and the postmodern

Box 2.1

The "Right to the City" According to Henri Lefebvre

Henri Lefebvre (1901–1991) was a French Marxist philosopher who dedicated a large part of his work to understanding the production of cities and, more broadly, the production of urban space while emphasizing the city's social, political, and cultural dimensions by using a multidisciplinary perspective. For Lefebvre, the right to the city meant everyone could take part in choosing and shaping the configuration of what he called the urban society.

There was a fundamental democratic concern underlying "the right to the city" in the sense that such a right opens the door to the participation of all inhabitants, regardless of their social status and difference, in the making of their living conditions. As he wrote in his famous book, *The Right to the City* (*Le droit à la Ville*) (1968), the issue is not only to give everyone the opportunity to have access to traditional urban amenities, but also to allow them to take part in the ongoing management of urban life in a subversive way, and in so doing, overcome relations of domination. Mark Purcell clearly underlines this:

> His right to the city is not a suggestion for reform, nor does it envision a fragmented, tactical, or piecemeal resistance. His idea is instead a call for a radical restructuring of social, political, and economic relations, both in the city and beyond. Key to this radical nature is that the right to the city reframes the arena of decision-making in cities: it reorients decision-making away from the state and toward the production of urban space. (2002: 101)

In this sense, the notion of "urban" underlying the right to the city is, above all, a "mental and social form" that gives inhabitants the opportunity to experience various ways to express their singularity or difference, of gathering and belonging. In this respect, urban space, urban culture, and urban representation—including their materialization in specific cities—provide new meaning to industrial production. At the same time, this gives birth to another world where it is possible to break with the overwhelming rationality of commodification—i.e., transforming everything into commodities—as markets have become the most important mode of social regulation.

Several researchers and activists alike have recognized that the right to the city is accompanied by efforts to challenge the structural and dominant forces that influence the production of cities. A concern for inhabitants' ability to create and design their own spaces is necessarily at stake. Finally, underlying the actuality of Lefebvre's ideas is the growing importance of cities for the future of societies as recognized by the European Charter for the Safeguarding of Human Rights in the City, which was adopted in May 2000 by the network of European Conference Cities for Human Rights.

critique, providing useful insights to researchers and innovative hypotheses about the role of the urban in social transformations. *Indirectly*, he was inviting researchers to put aside traditional ways of thinking and forcing them to clarify their own approaches.

However, Lefebvre's work on the city was not well known in the English-speaking world for at least two decades (Saunders, 1981: 151). His books about the urban reality were not translated into English until the 1990s. In addition, the devastating critique made by Castells in *La Question Urbaine* (1972) regarding his reading of urban history and his analysis of the production of spatial forms did not help the recognition of his work (Saunders, 1981). Nonetheless, Harvey, who contributed to the expansion of the new school of urban sociology in Great Britain, made use of Lefebvre's insights and played a role in the dissemination of his thinking in Britain and the United States (see, for example, Harvey, 1973, 1985a, 1989). In general, the contribution of Lefebvre regarding the revitalization of urban theory and urban studies seems nowadays better recognized due to the dissemination of his thinking, but also due to the originality of his interpretation of urban history (see Savage and Warde, 1993; Goonewardena et al., 2008).

For Lefebvre (1970), the contemporary society is first and foremost an urban society, the third step of the intertwined evolution of three historical eras: (1) agrarian, (2) industrial, and (3) urban. This evolution is the result of the role played in history by the capitalist production of space, but also by human agency. In other words, the changes occurring are not produced exclusively by historical and structural forces but also through initiatives taken by social actors. At the same time, we must keep in mind that Lefebvre's analysis is dialectical, that is, bringing in elements of the past in comparison with recent transformations, and considering these elements in a creative tension. While the industrialization process tends to destroy the mercantile city, the advent of the urban society profoundly transforms the industrial city. The hierarchical model of planning and space pertaining to the industrial city is put aside, at least in theory. Lefebvre is then trying to recreate a new city defined more by its possibilities than by its accomplishments:

> The urban (an abbreviated form of urban society) can therefore be defined not as an accomplished reality, situated behind the actual in time, but, on the contrary, as a horizon, an illuminating virtuality. It is the possible, defined by a direction, that moves toward the urban as the culmination of its journey. To reach it—in other words, to realize it—we must first overcome or break through the obstacles that currently make it impossible. (Lefebvre, 2003: 16)

According to Lefebvre, we should refer to "the urban" as a critical notion because something similar to a political program is involved in the urban.

This notion supersedes the notion of the city itself in the sense that it goes hand in hand with the idea that with the complete urbanization of the world, the city is vanishing as a separate social space, the urban culture being overwhelming. It implies the supremacy of *use values* over *exchange values*.[2] It opens up the field of possibilities for inhabitants. It implies new encounters and relationships among them founded on their needs and aspirations, the recognition of their specificities and differences, and their capacity of empowerment (assertiveness) in front of capitalist domination:

> The urban cannot be defined either as attached to a material morphology (on the ground, in the practico-material), or as being able to detach itself from it. It is not an intemporal essence, nor a system among other systems or above other systems. It is a mental and social form, that of simultaneity, of gathering, of convergence, of encounter (or rather, encounters). It is a quality born from quantities (spaces, objects, products). It is a difference, or rather, an ensemble of differences. The urban contains the meaning of industrial production, as appropriation contains the sense of technical domination over nature, the latter becoming absurd without the former. (Lefebvre, 1996: 131)

The urban revolution that Lefebvre is indirectly referring to in his 1986 book *Le Droit à la Ville*—in the original French version—is more explicitly elaborated upon in his subsequent one, *La Révolution Urbaine*, published two years later. His vision of the urban revolution was somehow premonitory in the sense that he anticipated that the urbanization process was expanding and going to dominate the social reality of our times. The majority of the population was going to live in urban agglomerations, and those who live at their peripheries would nevertheless be influenced by the urban culture in their daily lives. In the context of a service-sector economy—which can be equated with a post-industrial society—life conditions and the control of space are increasingly significant issues that were also included in the idea of the urban revolution. But there is more to it.

A way to achieve the urban revolution, according to Lefebvre, is to secure for all inhabitants an access to centrality, meaning an equal opportunity for everyone to share the exhilarating nature of urban life. For Lefebvre, the claim for a "different urban society" relies on experiences of solidarity and festivity where creativity and self-determination can be expressed (Kipfer, 2008). And this goes with a symbolic and effective access to centrality.

The Postmodern Critique in Urban Sociology

The main directions explored by urban sociology that we have examined in the first three sections of this chapter were unable to grasp satisfactorily the many changes that materialized in urban landscapes after the 1960s, such as the blurring of limits between cities, suburbs, and countryside; the expansion of suburban landscapes through intensive **sprawl** after World War II; and the decentralization of economic and cultural activities that were once concentrated in central cities. The traditional urban form usually associated with the walking city and its social practices has shifted toward "de-territorialization and placelessness" (Ellin, 1996: 1). It is this new urban reality that the postmodern critique in urban sociology wanted to account for. By paying attention to marginalized social actors and minority voices, this critique is also changing the traditional analytical focus. But there is more to it. The problem does not come only from the production of space and cities and the relations of domination underlying this process. It is also the categories of thought—the encompassing concepts associated with the modern era and reflecting its emancipatory perspective—that need to be revised. This is what Jean-François Lyotard (1979) tried to achieve.

According to Lyotard, after World War II Western societies had to face the failure of the Enlightenment project of modernity. Following this failure, society no longer had confidence in the master-narratives elaborated by previous generations of scholars and in their ability to promote the emancipation of the rational subject. Consequently, the past models for understanding and interpreting history, such as Marxism, functionalism, and structuralism, had to be replaced. For that matter, Lyotard suggests making room for minor narrative arguments that are more locally based. And, to a certain extent, we can relate the characteristics of **postmodern urbanism**—i.e., resulting from spatial restructuring due to new trends of development in a post-industrial context—to these types of arguments.

The Rise of the LA School of Urbanism

To better understand the analytical consequences of the postmodern turn in urban sociology and more largely in the field of urban studies and to introduce postmodern urbanism, we must recall the emergence of the Los Angeles School of Urbanism. Before the 1980s, Los Angeles had been neglected by researchers (Dear, 2002a). But during the last two decades, research on this urban region has been thriving. Indeed, numerous studies in urban geography and urban sociology have been devoted to Los Angeles, studies that have contributed to a better understanding of its empirical reality (Dear and Dahmann, 2008). Among the reasons given by the group of scholars who focus on Los Angeles as their main object of research, the one that is most often mentioned is that Los Angeles coincides with "a particular form of contemporary process they labelled as 'postmodern urbanism'" (Dear et al., 2008, p. 101). In Los Angeles, the organization of the production system was already decentralized in comparison with the typical industrial city. During the industrial era, the model of urbanism implemented in Los Angeles broke with the traditional model of the industrial city as defined on the east coast of the United States and Canada. In the industrial cities of the east coast, a clear separation prevailed between industrial activities and other urban functions. At that time, Los Angeles was already characterized by a plurality of industrial sectors but also of minorities dispersed throughout its territory.

In the preface of the book that he edited entitled *From Chicago to LA: Making Sense of Urban Theory*, Michael J. Dear refers to the "potential of a putative LA School" (2002b: vii). He also sees in this potential the promise of the "renaissance of urban theory," mainly because while LA was seen as an exception during the industrial era, nowadays it is becoming the rule: "Every American city that is growing, is growing in the fashion of Los Angeles" (Gareau, quoted by Dear, 2002b: viii).

The questions raised by the reference to LA as the expression of an alternative urban model of development are numerous: To what extent is the LA urban form original and profoundly distinct from the industrial city exemplified by Chicago? What are the economic and social dynamics that are at play in the production of space in LA? Is the evidence regarding the emergence of a postmodern urbanism convincing?

The urban development of the LA region has been linked to the economic expansion resulting from the new opportunities opened up by World War II: "the city was not decisively catapulted into the first ranks of the American urban system until World War II, when the Pacific arena drew the United States into an irreversible involvement with the 'East' (to its west)" (Abu-Lughod, 1999: 404). As LA was included within the new economic configuration of the "entire world system" (Abu-Lughod, 1999: 405), its expansion was more and more related to the transforming possibilities offered by new opportunities.

The Consequences of Post-Fordism

At the end of the 1970s, the traditional industrial system, although still in place, was declining and being gradually replaced by what the LA School called the post-Fordist regime of accumulation (Dear, 2002b). Post-Fordism was corresponding to structural change in capitalism regarding its form of accumulation and its modes of social regulation. Being forced to respond to new economic requirements, business managers and economic leaders bet on decentralization of production activities and increased flexibility of production processes. Workers were given more autonomy. But they also had more responsibility. They were increasingly considered partners instead of subordinates. The rise of *knowledge workers* is a good example. They cannot be supervised the same way workers on an assembly line can be. A different model of management was thus required. Mass production was giving way to flexible and just-in-time production, and to ecological, post-industrial clusters. At the same time, a dual economy was developing. Strong and weak productivity were living side by side. Immigrants were most of the time trapped in activities with weak productivity and low wages, alongside an economy of high productivity. Racial tensions and conflicts necessarily resulted from this situation.

The consequences of post-Fordism on urban space in the case of LA have been documented by many (see Davis, 2006 [1992]; Keil, 1998; Soja, 2000; Dear, 2002a). The authors all agree that the urban landscape of Southern California is a vivid "consequence of this deep-seated structural change in the capitalist political economy" (Dear and Fusty, 2002: 69). Even though it is never easy to link urban forms to economic mechanisms, in the case of post-Fordism the connections are easier to make due to the spatial character of the processes involved in the economic restructuring. Decentralized and flexible production—as experienced in different economic sectors by turning to sub-contractors for obtaining different components of the product, going abroad if necessary to reduce costs, and by adjusting supply to demand—requires a different relation to the territory than mass production. This is reflected in the dispersed location of social and economic activities. And decentralized and flexible production can be implemented with fewer constraints in a region where geography and industrial past are not obstacles to sprawl and dispersion.

The Social and Territorial Reshaping of Postmodernism

The old "practices of community and citizenship" (Dear and Dahmann, 2008: 268) were deeply changed by the waves of immigration coming from Mexico and Latin America, but also from many Asian countries. And the ethnic transformations resulting from this massive immigration led to a great social and cultural diversity whose consequences in economic and political terms have, so far, not been fully recognized (Davis, 2000). For example, researchers have to look at the pressure that the new multiculturalism places on "conventional religions" but also at the redefinition of relations with nature and environment in reference to a "crisis of sustainability" at the heart of the "urban question" (Dear and Dahmann, 2008).

The changes at play in this social and territorial reshaping are diverse and lead, at least up to a certain point, toward what has been associated with postmodern urbanism. Here the break with modernist urbanism is clear:

> [I]n modernist urbanism, the impetus for growth and change proceeds outward from the city's central core to its hinterlands. But in postmodern urbanism, this logic is precisely reversed: The evacuated city core no longer dominates its region; instead, the hinterlands organize what is left of the center. (Dear and Dahmann, 2008: 269–70)

At the outset, postmodern urbanism that has been associated with urban sprawl, spatial diversity, hybridization of cultures, and a revival/integration of historical and contextual features can be easily illustrated by the example of Los Angeles. If these characteristics are valuable for their capacity to initiate a change with universal homogenizing trends and, conversely, for their recognition of differences, they also have a negative side. As Steven Connors underlines, one can find a superficial and transitory character in postmodern urbanism's assertion:

> [W]hen hybridization itself becomes universal, regional specificity becomes simply a style which can be transmitted across the globe as rapidly as a photocopy of the latest glossy manifesto. Paradoxically, the sign of the success of the anti-universalist language and style of architectural postmodernism is that one can find it everywhere, from London, to New York, to Tokyo and Delhi. (quoted by Ellin, 1996: 152)

From a political perspective, postmodern urbanism is facilitated by a "shadow state" or a "shadow government," that is, a form of power influenced by privatization and direct contractual relations for services, with inhabitants defining themselves more easily as consumers than as citizens: "shadow government can tax, legislate for, police their communities, but they are rarely accountable, are responsive primarily to wealth (as opposed to numbers of voters), and subject to few constitutional constraints" (Dear and Flusty, 2002: 64).

The affirmation of an LA School of Urbanism cannot be defined without an explicit reference to the Chicago School of urban sociology, even if the Chicago School did not produced a unified body of knowledge. In the synthesis written by Dear (2002a), the Chicago School mainly relied on the analytical model elaborated by Burgess, Park, and McKenzie in *The City* (1925). This book is then seen as "emblematic of a modernist analytical paradigm" (Dear, 2002a: 14). The assumptions of that paradigm are threefold:

1. The modernist city is presented as a unified whole where the centre is responsible for taking care of its hinterland.
2. The urban condition relies primarily on individuals, whose choices in the professional and housing markets can explain the "overall urban condition."
3. The paradigm is characterized by evolutionism: modernity comes from tradition; society, from community.

The LA School of Urbanism was formed by a group of "loosely associated scholars," professionals, and urban activists who were convinced that what was occurring in Southern California "was somehow symptomatic of a broader socio-geographic transformation taking place within the United States as a whole" (Soja quoted by Dear, 2002a, p. 10). In spite of the divergences among these groups, an agreement was emerging around the fact that the main object of study was "restructuring," whether of the restructuring of "residential neighbourhoods," "global markets," or the "regime of accumulation" (Dear, 2002a: 12). There are four defining characteristics of the LA School:

1. Spatial manifestations are directly connected to the restructuring processes just evoked.
2. The urban form is no longer organized around a central urban core.
3. Private appropriation of space takes priority over the socializing role of public space or of the commons in modern urbanism.
4. Heterogeneity is valued in place of homogeneity for organizing the territoriality.

Consequently, the protagonists of the LA School consider that the Chicago model—which was useful to explain urbanization and urban forms of the modern industrial era in the United States—is long overdue for revision. Cities are no longer built the same way they were during the industrial era. The role of the city centre is completely different nowadays; relations between the core and the periphery are in flux, which is why Dear et al. (2008) consider that the Chicago model is "dead."

It is not possible to make a synthesis of all the arguments that were presented on both sides of the dispute between the LA School and the Chicago School and published in diverse books and journals (see, for example, *City & Community*, 2002, Vol. 1, Issue 1, or *Urban Geography*, 2008, 29). But this confrontation has definitely stimulated theoretical research regarding the production of space and urban forms. It has also encouraged comparative empirical research.

The debate between the LA School and the Chicago School has been played to different tunes. Among those who spoke for the Chicago School, we find some, including Dick Simpson and Tom M. Kelly (2008), who talked of a New Chicago School. For them, the growth model elaborated by Burgess and his colleagues is outdated. The Chicago model no longer corresponded to the dense area of the early twentieth century. That Chicago became an expanded metropolitan region of 12 million inhabitants. For that reason, the previous ecological model has to be actualized.

Perhaps the two approaches need to be nuanced, as suggested by Saskia Sassen (2008), who feels that these two schools cannot capture the varied nature of cities. As she has mentioned, it is not sufficient to describe a reality for understanding the city's dynamic. In order to better understand what is going on empirically, we have to look at the key factors at play in the spatial organization of economic activity: what is the impact of economic processes on spatial concentration or dispersion? For that matter, it is necessary to put aside homogenizing representations of urban forms. Variations due to economic, historical, and geographic constraints seem more realistic in that respect than convergence. Taking into account the scale—the region instead of the city, for example—also changes the nature of the analysis.

Shall we say that the LA model is in continuity with the Chicago model, as Sénécal (2007) contends, rather than in opposition to it? In the conclusion of a co-written paper, Dear brings in nuances in respect to his previous position, mentioning that for the time being we are not able to prove that "we are entering a new era in the production of urban space" (Dear et al., 2008: 109). Nevertheless, he recognizes that "such a radical break is underway: that globalization, the rise of a network society, socioeconomic polarisation, cultural hybridisation, and the sustainability crisis are changing the way we make cities, and the way we understand the urban" (Dear et al., 2008: 109).

Conclusion

The emergence of postmodern urbanism is related to a series of socio-economic and cultural transformations that, up to a certain point, were shaped by the industrial era. By making use of new spatial forms, is the industrial city redefining itself or is it a completely different form, producing a new urban reality? The postmodern turn in urban sociology, however, goes beyond urban forms and connects with discourses and practices that were marginalized in the past but that are being emphasized by the postmodern critique.

In looking for the theoretical perspectives that took part in the development of urban sociology, we have selected the ones that have been the most significant over the past years. These perspectives are far from being homogeneous. Many researchers are involved in their development, contributing to the definition of their main components and to their redefinition over several decades. The emergence of a new perspective does not mean that the previous one is no longer useful but that new factors or new approaches are being taken into account. The relations between the different perspectives contributing to the dynamism of urban sociology are complex and part of a collective effort to better understand cities, their main components, and their future.

We must not lose sight of the fact that these various theoretical perspectives play a proactive role in urban research. In doing so, they enter a debate within a multidisciplinary field that is converging with urban studies, where specialized and sector-oriented objects of study prevail, such as real estate, urban infrastructure, transport, the environment, or local economic development. In this respect, empirical issues should above all serve as a yardstick for assessing the pertinence of the theoretical tools that are available to researchers.

Questions for Critical Thought

1. To what extent can the city as studied by the Chicago School be defined as a modern city?

2. Explain why the social interactionist model has partly been built on the ecological model.

3. What would you consider the most important contribution of political economy to the understanding of city life and form?

4. What does postmodernism bring to the understanding of cities?

5. One major criticism, contained in postmodernism, of previous theoretical approaches is that they are Western-centric and thus have limited ground for generalization. Discuss, using some examples you can draw from your own experience or from other scholarly readings.

Suggested Readings

Dear, M.J. (Ed.). 2002. *From Chicago to LA: Making Sense of Urban Theory*. Thousand Oaks: Sage. Edited by one the main figures of the Los Angeles School of Urbanism, this book offers an excellent introduction to postmodern urbanism and to the main theoretical claims that it is necessary to revise the principles revealed as useful for understanding the industrial city. The book is also an excellent introduction to the principles of postmodern urbanism.

Goonewardena, K., S. Kipfer, R. Milgrom, and C. Schmid (Eds.). 2008. *Space, Difference, Everyday Life: Reading Henri Lefebvre*. New York and London: Routledge. This book is required reading in order to understand the relevance today of Henri Lefebvre's thinking. Based on spatial disciplines and critical theory, the book compares the multiple influences that Lefebvre's work had on the structuring of the urban field and beyond.

Lefebvre, H. 2003. *The Urban Revolution*. Minneapolis: The University of Minnesota Press. The first edition of this book was released in French in 1970. Influenced both by Marxism and by an original thinking about daily life, Lefebvre brought to the fore the tremendous social changes that were occurring through what he called the advent of the "urban" or the "urban revolution." The book was one of the most influential for the new urban sociology.

Smart, B. 1992. *Modern Conditions, Postmodern Controversies*. London and New York: Routledge. This book is a good introduction to the postmodern debate in the field of urban studies. Considering the multidimensional and fundamental changes at play in the contemporary world, this book offers a clear understanding of the social, political, and cultural consequences of socio-economic transformations brought in by the post-industrial society.

Related Websites

Chicago School of Urban Sociology: SAGE Knowledge
http://knowledge.sagepub.com/view/urbanstudies/n46.xml

> The Chicago School of Urban Sociology remains important for urban sociology even though its influence used to be more important than it is the case nowadays. It is the Chicago School of Sociology that defined "the contours of urban sociology for much of the twentieth century." This website provides excellent information about past and recent publications (books, articles, book chapters) related to the Chicago School.

University of Southern California: LA School of Urbanism
http://dornsife.usc.edu/la_school/studies/

> This website is managed by the LA School of Urbanism, University of Southern California. Many papers and articles written by the so-called LA School of Urbanism are accessible through the site. Geographical and historical information about the Los Angeles region are also available there.

Rethinking Theory, Space, and Production: Henri Lefebvre Today
www.henrilefebvre.org/hlt/

> Established by professors in architecture and sociology from Zurich, this website is dedicated to the work and thinking of Henri Lefebvre. But the site is also concerned with recent applications of Lefebvre's theory. One can also find on this site the conferences and seminars that are taking place around the world about Lefebvre's work or regarding his contribution to an understanding of modern and postmodern cities.

3 The Rise of the Industrial City and Its Problems

Learning Objectives

◎ To understand the industrial city in its context

◎ To briefly summarize the origin and evolution of urban Canada

◎ To describe the industrial city's main problems

◎ To examine the solutions worked out

◎ To discuss and criticize utopian models that were developed

◎ To explore the transformation of the industrial city into a new kind of city

Introduction

Urban sociology and sociology more broadly developed following two revolutions: the Industrial Revolution and the political French Revolution. Some, like Nisbet (1993), think sociology to be a response to these events because traditional society was deeply transformed by these two milestones. As we have seen in previous chapters, the city was the locus of much change and one of the breeding grounds of the modern world in as much as sociologists spontaneously match the industrial city with the modern city, although historians believe that modernity started well before the Industrial Revolution.

What was the industrial city? What were its main problems, and how were they confronted and solved, partly or entirely? These questions form the backbone of this chapter and lead to an examination of the main features of the industrial city as revealed by some of its most crucial problems. Urban planning was introduced as a response to the industrial city's problems. But planning, while an old practice, is not an old profession. The industrial city was the breeding ground of the planning profession, that is, a set of regular practices linked to a group of permanent professional actors keen to examine cities' problems and act to provide solutions.

Historically speaking, the industrial city spanned a very long period of time. If we set the beginning of the Industrial Revolution first in England in the last third of the eighteenth century and then in other European countries and North America in the nineteenth century, then we can say that the industrial city lived until the 1950s. However, in planning terms and using other urban categories, such as municipal elections and administrative reform, the industrial city history in fact overlaps the past two centuries! This chapter starts with a brief historical description of the making of urban Canada, followed by a presentation of the industrial city's problems and the solutions found to alleviate these problems. Finally, the chapter ends with a brief examination of the urban models, more or less imaginary, that the period invented.

The Formation of Urban Canada

Canadian urbanization has happened in stages owing to the country's internal colonization. Pre-colonial Canada was not urbanized although more or less permanent settlements did exist—but with population sizes below what is normally defined as a city. Only gradually did an urban society take root in the Canadian territory.

New France (1608–1760)—a colony of settlers in roughly today's Québec and some areas of the Maritimes—was a combination of rural areas and small urban centres. France was highly urbanized when New France was established, and that country transferred some of its own characteristics to the "new world." However, independence could not happen because the French *métropole* had a firm control over its North American colony although it wasn't much interested in the colony's inner development, perhaps for fear of creating an autonomous movement. However, for cities to develop, as historical sociologists such as Max Weber (1982) have shown, some degree of autonomy has to be gained. In order not to be limited by political powers whose base still depended on a rural population and resources, emerging or would-be cities had to acquire some capacity to grow, to specialize, and to deepen the division of labour. Although the French **colonial towns** developed a degree of autonomy and built a small urban economy that fostered some indigenous change, such autonomy was limited for a variety of reasons.

Cities in New France were necessary as hubs for international trade, for shipping goods to the French metropolis, and for trade in goods and services between town and country, including with Aboriginal peoples. But a firm hand on the colony's activities by the king or by his representative was maintained. Moreover, since private or semi-private companies—like the *Compagnie des Cent Associés* (founded in 1645) in New France, much like *The Hudson's Bay Company* (1670) in Northern Canada, whose rights were granted by the king (French or English)—ran the trade in staples (fur and fish) and were instrumental in continental exploration, a tightly knit commercial and governmental elite arose. Thus, for a century and a half (1608 to 1760), urbanization in Canada was commanded by French needs and policies—and English ones for that matter—and no strong and independent urban dynamic and policy developed in the colony. Moreover, the small size of the Canadian population at the end of the French regime hindered city growth and dynamism, since pre-industrial cities drew much of their own numbers from the countryside and from immigration, which remained rather small over such a long period (only 9,000, according to Charbonneau and Harris, 1987). A population of some 60 to 70,000 inhabitants could not support many cities and certainly not any large ones. The urban fabric and hierarchy were, for all practical purposes, composed of Québec (1608), Trois-Rivières (1634), and Montréal (1642), all of them very small in population size (Lafrance and Charbonneau, 1987). In 1743, the population of Québec City, the largest town in New France, had 5,004 inhabitants (about 8,000 in 1759), whereas American cities playing a similar commercial and political role contained two to three times as many people: Boston, 16,382; Philadelphia, 13,000; New York, 11,000 (Hatvany, 2001: 110–11).

Western Urbanization

Urban Canada started in the East, in the Maritimes and in Québec, but expanded westward after the American Revolution and the Loyalists' move to Canada. The Maritimes "cities" were trading and military posts although they also harboured some specialized urban activities (Wynn and McNabb, 1987). Halifax, for example, a commercial and military centre, was a city of 5,000 inhabitants in 1783 (Wynn and McCann, 1987). The Loyalists settled in southern Québec, Ontario, and the Maritimes. The urbanization movement toward the West began with increasing settlements in Ontario. The West remained for some time outside the urbanization movement, but owing to the railway construction in the second half of the nineteenth century Western cities gradually cropped up. Winnipeg, Regina, Saskatoon, Calgary, and eventually Edmonton and Vancouver made up the new urban fabric of Western Canadian society (Hiller, 2010b). Victoria, BC, however, has a different back story. Linked to the British Empire, Victoria acquired a strategic importance in the East Pacific (Hiller, 2010b: 24).

In his long-term view of the urban world, Luc-Normand Tellier (2009) shows that, from ancient times, there is a slow, continuous, and strong western movement in the patterns of human settlement and in city formation. The westward expansion of urban Canada is part and parcel of this movement. There are, however, reasons or factors for such an expansion. Resource availability is a key factor in such a spatial process. Many urban analysts of the political economy persuasion, in the wake of Harold Innis (1995), tend to downplay military factors, focusing on resource exploitation for international markets as a reason for founding cities. But in the case of Québec, Halifax, and Victoria, military factors had to be taken into account in city founding and development. And while both military and resource exploitation factors may reinforce one another, their particular logic may sometimes clash because military needs can quickly be a drain on resource allocation.

Table 3.1   The Evolution of the Canadian Urban Population (% of Total Population, Selected Census Years)

Census Year	Canada	Ontario	Québec	Maritimes	Manitoba/ Saskatchewan	Alberta/ British Columbia
1851	13	14	15	10	NA	NA
1901	37	43	40	25	24	43
1931	54	61	63	38	37	47
1951	62	71	67	46	43	59
1971	76	82	81	56	61	75
1991	77	82	78	51	68	80
2006	80	85	80	54	68	84

Source: Statistics Canada, *Census of Population, 1851 to 2006; Population, Urban and Rural, by Province and Territory.* Accessed February 20, 2012. Reproduced and distributed on an "as is" basis with the permission of Statistics Canada.

Note: The Maritimes includes Newfoundland and Labrador after 1951.

Urban Canada evolved rapidly once Western settlement started (see Table 3.1). And urbanization went hand in hand with industrialization. When the staples economy no longer offered large opportunities for prosperity—although the Canadian economy has remained tightly linked to its natural-resource base—industrialization set in. International capital, at first British and then later American (Naylor, 2006), helped develop a genuine industrial economy. Although for many decades debate has raged about the degree of reliance of the Canadian economy on foreign sources, small and medium-sized countries don't normally have large savings capacity for the industrial takeoff. As a result, they have to rely on foreign capital. They also have to import knowledge and technical know-how because along with the transfer of capital goods, other forms of resources are also imported. Canada has benefited from many forms of transfers, including expert workers and professionals, for its development (Sinclair et al., 1974).

Urban Variations by Region

While in 1851—the first year a Canadian census was held—the urban population was only 13 per cent, between the census years of 1921 and 1931, Canada became an urbanized country as measured by the fact that half its population lived in urban centres. The Canadian definition of *urban centre* is minimal, being set at 1,000 inhabitants with at least 400 people per square kilometre in the urban core. In 1851, 1,000 probably made sense, but with today's cities of over 5 or 10 million people, that traditional cutting figure is less significant. It is, however, still used for historical comparisons.

The urbanization process was very different across the country. Ontario and Québec urbanized more quickly, whereas the Prairies and the Maritimes were slower to urbanize. Ontario was half urban by 1911 and Québec followed suit more or less a decade later. Manitoba became urban much later, between the census years of 1941 and 1951.

A busy weekday on St-Jacques street in Montréal's business centre around 1910.

(© McCord Museum)

Alberta didn't become urban until between 1951 and 1956; Saskatchewan followed suit in the late 1960s. All four Maritimes provinces saw their populations become urban only after 1951 as well. British Columbia is an interesting case because it was the province and region that urbanized first: in 1901, half its population was living in cities as defined by the Canadian Census, twice the urbanization rate of Alberta. This early urbanization can be explained by British Columbia's late settlement, excluding Aboriginals; by an economic structure where agriculture fared less well; and by a pattern of settlement around port cities for exporting goods abroad. Even in 2006, British Columbia was, along with Ontario, the most urbanized province, where 85 per cent of its population lived in cities compared with 80 per cent in Québec and 82 per cent in Alberta. Since the Canadian population was, in 2006, urbanized at 80 per cent (81.1 per cent in 2011), these slight differences are not very meaningful.

Urban and Rural Economies Intertwined

The Canadian urban system, as some like to call it, has been closely linked to its hinterland, which produced staples (resource-based goods) for exportation. Hiller (2010a, 2010b) has stressed linkages of the Canadian urbanization process to the resources economy as well as to the international and global economy even during the early years of the structuring of the Canadian urban system. As he says, "Perhaps the most important theme in Canadian urban history is that towns, villages, and eventually cities were symbols of colonial expansion in new frontiers" (Hiller, 2010b: 20). And indeed, the Canadian industrial city developed with the railways. The railways consolidated the economy of Central Canada but also opened up new territories, notably in the West: "the role of the railway made it possible for new towns and cites to emerge in the interior" (Hiller, 2010b: 26). As the railway industry consolidated and transport developed to bring in food and goods in large quantities from the hinterland, cities grew larger.

The Canadian urbanization example shows that the city economy and the rural economy are closely linked: the development of one is not independent of the development of the other. They reciprocally nourish, properly and figuratively, one another. Moreover, new continents and new frontiers, such as Canada, are linked through a long chain of processes to the international economy. The relationships between town and country are much more complex than the simple thesis that for the city to grow, a food surplus is needed. The production of a food surplus, as exemplified in Canadian history, is not independent of an urban dynamic inserted into a large international dynamic, where innovations like the railways are used to reinforce cities and the countryside at the same time.

The next sections will explore the consequences on the urban way of life of the combined effect of urban concentration and an industrial economy. The period between 1850 and about 1930 may be called the "urban problems challenge." Cities, and large ones in particular, were not necessarily pleasant places to live, at least for the poorest segment of urban dwellers. However, urban conditions improved owing to the combined impact of economic progress and public action. Modern planning, as a response to dire urban conditions, was one factor in city improvement. The story that follows adopts a broad comparative perspective; Canadian cities are and should be viewed within an international perspective. Large Canadian cities faced the same problems as other industrial cities. Conditions were often similar although, to repeat a leitmotif of this book, each city is more or less an island on its own, different from others, each living special local dynamics but sharing large structuring trends, such as industrialization and urbanization (or city growth). Industrialization is much more than just an economic and a technological phenomenon as urbanization is a wider process of change than one limited to demographic and spatial factors.

The Problems of the Industrial City

The Industrial Revolution of the nineteenth century (in Europe it started in the eighteenth century) was a turning point in the history of urban life as cities grew considerably during that period (Hohenberg and Lees, 1985: 218–19). The industrial model took shape and to this day the continuing, almost endless process of first industrial and then world urbanization has not slowed, except for a few periods where its rate of increase slowed but rarely the overall process of urbanization (Bairoch, 1995). But urbanization is more than demographic and spatial change. It is a social change process in full bloom. We may borrow Marcel Mauss's idea in his essay on the gift (1923–1924) that the urbanization process is a **total social phenomenon** (Mauss, 1978: 274) that involves demographic and spatial change but also involves economic, political, and cultural change.

It has been said that people tackle only problems they can solve. This is particularly the case with urban problems. For a large part of the nineteenth century, industrial cities faced mounting problems. Both new and ancient towns and cities where increases in population were large came under pressure because of poor living conditions. As Fernand Braudel (1979) has written, very late in the century many more people died in cities than in the countryside. If cities maintained their growth for the whole nineteenth century, it is because they drew people, the young mostly, from the countryside.

People moved to cities because of different opportunities, real or perceived. Moving to a city involved leaving behind one's family, friends, and relatives. But it also meant moving with no or very little capital. Some people had skills, but many did not. But people believed that larger towns offered better jobs, or at least regular ones; new social contacts; new economic challenges; and a better education for a greater chance of social mobility, which proved to be particularly important in the next century. Were conditions much better in the countryside than in the cities? Critics and contemporary observers at the time were vocal in denouncing urban squalor and the need for progress (Dennis, 2008: chap. 2). When serious, or systematic, investigations were carried out, urban squalor was counter-balanced by rural deprivation as Ebenezer Howard vividly represented in his two "magnets" of town and countryside ways of life. Some people lived off the myth, which great nineteenth-century novels nourished, that cities were no place for men and women to live. Indeed, many moved to cities not by choice, but by necessity.

As the industrial period unfolded, many of these degraded and degrading cities changed course and improved their own living conditions. For almost half a century, an environmental and physical transformation took place in many cities. Such change was not in any way coordinated by a leading authority or government. However, a variety of private and collective decisions; public policies; and charitable interventions, such as those by Jane Addams and the Hull House in Chicago or those by churches, were gradually changing the urban way of life (Gross, 2009). When in 1938 Wirth wrote his essay on urbanism as a way of life, the industrial and modern city had gone through a deep process of physical as well as social change. Chicago, which served Wirth as an "examplar," had come to terms with the urban way of life. Historians have chronicled this deep change in Chicago over a long period, emphasizing the internal dynamics of urban transformations, despite a socially divided city, and its relationship to the hinterland (Cronon, 1991; Miller, 1997). Other American and Canadian cities underwent a similar process of change in social composition as well as in environmental transformation (Abu-Lughod, 1999; Artibise and Stelter, 1979; Stelter and Artibise, 1979; Stelter and Artibise, 1986). Montréal and Québec were both rather small industrial cities compared with the great European and American industrial cities, but they too experienced similar transformations (Germain and Rose, 2000; Morisset, 2001).

Urban problems during this period focused on three urban conditions: (1) public health and sanitary conditions; (2) housing and living conditions, which were for the most part solved by new technologies; and (3) urban mobility, which brought in transport technologies. Each problem had its own evolving context and set of causes; each had it own social actors and movements, who pleaded for solving them; each gave rise to a series of technological, institutional, and administrative innovations. For over 50 years along the nineteenth- and twentieth-century divide (or for a longer or shorter period depending on when one believes that industrialization and urbanization started), gradual change took place, sometimes in a conflicting social and political environment. Three main collective actors, jointly or independently, spurred on the urban transformations: (1) the urban movements, which focused on the industrial question, so to speak—they were concerned with working conditions and wages but were not blind to urban conditions, too, as Castells (1983) has shown; (2) a variegated professional movement composed of new professions, or new specializations within existing professions, in medicine, education, social services, engineering, and the fledgling urban planning; and (3) a political and administrative movement that was instrumental to the long-term urban transformation although it was not always quick to react to pressing problems.

The expression "urban transformation" is deliberately used in this context. What happened in industrial cities was just short of a revolution. We today owe to these three collective actors the groundwork of the contemporary modern city. Their actions were not always coordinated, but in pursuing different objectives—some political, some social, some technological or scientific—they had a huge impact on the city and its way of life.

Public Health and the Sanitary City

Why have sanitary conditions been so important in industrial cities? Why have they become one of the chief political and administrative concerns? Why have they mobilized so many people and resources? The answers seem today obvious. Sanitary conditions, namely urban population health, waste disposal, air and water quality, a clean water supply, and wastewater disposal, could be deadly or healthy. People can die or live depending on sanitary conditions.

The industrial city discovered new diseases and experimented with new public interventions and methods of prevention. All industrial cities were struck by epidemics. Cholera was the most fearful for it came back regularly, but other diseases were as much, if not more, dreadful. Typhoid, a rarer disease; tuberculosis, though not particularly an urban phenomenon; and rickets, owing to lack of light in crowded and dense Northern cities, were not uncommon but tended to be less and less frequent. Some diseases, including cholera, which struck urban populations late in the nineteenth century, were attributed to "miasmas," foul odours emanating from decaying organic matters. Medical officers and chemists, by carefully observing the open water supply in different areas of industrial and large cities, showed that the cholera microbe (a bacteria) was borne in unclean water and that odours had nothing to do with the disease although they might be unpleasant to all (Hamlin, 1990). This bacterial revolution (Melosi, 2000; Porter, 1997) came about gradually and not without opposition from leading authorities. What certainly helped public medicine to overcome resistance was that a **scientific (rationalistic) mentality** was widely adopted, at least by educated people and certainly within the professional groups, to address public health (Perkin, 1969).

The organization of public health raised challenging problems of collective coordination. Churches in Canada, but elsewhere as well, had been prime actors of public health. Private charities, too, played their part. But these organizations had not the means and the resources to act efficiently and to encompass not only targeted neighbourhoods but the whole of urban areas. Progressively, the responsibility passed to central states, but in the preparation of this takeover, municipalities, for obvious reasons, came to play a leading role. Canadian cities started a small administrative revolution on the sanitary and public health issue (Turmel and Guay, 2008). Less used to providing elaborate services, where justice and crime protection were their main responsibilities, municipalities modernized and took over new areas of public action. In order to do so, they had to change their own way of doing things: administrative reform was called for (Dagenais, 2000; Germain, 1984). This administrative and political call for reform was an integral part of a much broader urban social reform movement (Rutherford, 1984; Korneski, 2008; Weaver, 1984). Demands on local authorities grew, the public health issue being the most conspicuous of those requiring management. It would be too strong a statement to say that, from then on, cities and central states that followed suit were starting a vast experiment in public welfare before the welfare state was fully formed. But there is some sense in recognizing that a movement had begun and that it was, as Porter has written, the end of a very long "people-killing" era: "By 1900 civilization had lost its biological population check: infectious disease" (Porter, 1997: 427). Combined with other urban improvements, the urban health revolution was the product of many factors, social actors, and large and small actions:

> Changing public opinion, the labours of medical officers of health, the creation of filtered water supplies and sewage systems, slum clearance, the work of activists promoting the gospel of cleanliness, and myriad other often minor changes—for example the provision of dustbins with lids to repel flies—combined to create an improving urban environment. (Porter, 1997: 426–7)

Urban Housing and Living Conditions

In the industrial city, housing was mainly a private and a market choice (Sutcliffe, 1981). State intervention was considered unwarranted, except in cases where the very poor and the sick had to be housed and cared for (Hall, 1980a). But then, as now, fast-growing cities were prone to speculative behaviours. Landlords and developers looked for opportunities and offered housing "goods," new or converted. High prices can be extracted when demand is increasing, but only up to a point. As noted earlier, all those who moved out of the countryside came to the industrial city for a job or for the opportunities the city offered. Their market power was weak: their revenues were low and capital, nonexistent; and they might not have been able to rely on a large network of relatives and friends to borrow money from to buy a house. Moreover, crowding cast a dark shadow over industrial cities. Pre-scientific surveys helped to evaluate the extent of the problem, and with the passing of time these surveys improved their methodology. For example, when Charles Booth started in London, his more than a decade-long investigation of housing and working-class conditions and his survey methods, based on a questionnaire, were truly innovative. Booth's methods were surely better than the journalistic observations of Herbert Ames in Montréal in *The City Below the Hill*, or of Jacob Riis in New York in *How the Other Half Dies*, which had become a bestseller (Methot, 2003; Scott, 1969: 6–10). Surveys of urban conditions were also part and parcel of the emerging social sciences, notably sociology, and of the administrative modernization (Abrams, 1968; Geddes, 1904).

Was the marketplace adapted to these new urban living conditions? Yes and no, for it could provide housing and lodgings for a growing middle class but could not offer much to the working classes, who lived in crowded accommodations and in environments with no or poor amenities. There were three public responses to these conditions. One was to do nothing or very little and let private actions take the lead. The market could, many believed, respond to housing needs and so there was no need for public action. The second response was regulatory: edict regulations and by-laws to limit crowding in a dwelling or a room and to prohibit some behaviour with dire environmental consequences, such as disposing of waste in backyards or streets (Fischler, 2007, for a case study of Toronto, 1834–1904). Finally, the third response was to build public housing for the poor or the sick. Although this last response received a lukewarm reception, it foretold what local authorities, on their own or with the financial help of higher tiers of government, could do and would gradually learn to do in the twentieth century. Notably, there was a large divide between the response strategies of European cities and those of North American cities. European cities were a little quicker to use the ways and means of public action to resolve housing problems, whereas North American cities relied on the whole on a market solution (Scott, 1969). But, as Peter Hall (1988: chap. 2) has observed, the housing problem of the industrial city was for the first time clearly evident. People knew the problem existed, but mindsets were slow to change, in part because cities had no great means to collect the resources needed for a housing policy. (Although in Germany, with its fledgling welfare state and the pressure of **social democracy**, social housing became a political and municipal issue [Sutcliffe, 1981]).

There was, however, one area that public officials of both industrializing continents agreed to get involved in: it was green spaces and urban parks (Benevolo, 1993: 200–201; Scott, 1969: 10–15). Many, if not almost all, industrial cities designed at least a large park and a few smaller ones in the second half of the nineteenth century. Montréal, Boston, and New York but also London, Paris, and Berlin owed most of their park systems to this crucial period in urban planning. Reasons to design parks were a combination of health and recreation needs. Indeed, many urban parks originated out of the public health movement. Urban residents needed green, open spaces for a healthy life away from urban "miasmas," which were long believed to be the cause of some diseases and epidemics, and to regenerate their good condition. But recreation was another reason for the development of parks; they proved a valuable addition to city life when the bicycle was invented and adopted for sports purposes by men, and for leisure, social, and even economic purposes by women (Bijker, 1997: chap. 2). Sociologists of technology have somewhat downplayed the interaction between urban park planning and the bicycle. Concentrating on "relevant consumers groups" to explain how a technology is created and evolved, these sociologists forgot to look at the broader urban context in which new planning decisions had an effect on the direction and the diffusion of the technology. Without large urban parks, where sports and leisurely activities could be pursued, the diffusion of the bicycle may have been much slower and the bicycle's use, more limited.

Urban Technologies and Modernity

The Industrial Revolution brought to the market cheaper goods and greater diversification. Many of these goods, such as textiles and clothing, were manufactured for private consumers, but the revolution was far from offering only private goods. Public, in particular military, goods were also produced. Capital goods for the machine industry in particular were manufactured in large quantity (Landes, 1969). Moreover, steel and iron were not directly addressed to private consumers but to public and business consumers. Even electricity distribution was first targeted at businesses and public services before reaching private homes (Hughes, 1983). However, some goods proved more useful for private consumers than public ones. The car, for example, fulfilled private needs more than public ones, particularly in rural areas (Kline and Pinch, 1996). If the telegraph was an invention that was closely linked to the business of railways, the telephone was more personal and private (Hugill, 1999). With time, all technologies are beneficial to individuals as well as to organizations. For example, the mobile phone and the Internet are used for business as well as for personal purposes. When a technology has just been invented and hits a market, however, individuals and organizations respond selectively and differently.

Among the great innovations of the late nineteenth century, a fair amount was invented, tested, and adopted in cities (Smil, 2005). Electricity is a good example (Hughes, 1983). Because ideas and information travel faster in concentrated and denser human environments, people are exposed to them more rapidly (Bairoch, 1985: 420–4). And since urban dwellers are on the whole wealthier than rural people, they tend to adopt and buy new technologies earlier. With the proliferation of communications technologies, however, the difference between rural and urban diffusion of new technologies is winding down.

However, the industrial city was the theatre for a diffusion of what may be called the modern conveniences, such as electricity for heat and light, water supply, gas for cooking and heating, and the telephone, which together increased substantially the well-being of the city's inhabitants (Ball, 1988; Fougères, 2004; Gagnon, 2006; Gagnon and Zwarich, 2008). Planning had to accommodate the penetration of these new technologies, making room for them in crowded areas in many cases. Claire Poitras (2000) has shown how the spread of the telephone in Montréal raised problems for the local government because communication lines and poles endangered the urban landscape. Planning had to make do with the new technologies of personal and collective "comfort" and devised means to accommodate them. Creative destruction—the process by which new technologies destruct technologies already in place—is not only true in industrial and commercial businesses but also in the urban space (Gilliland, 2002).

The problem of urban mobility was dealt with through a combination of transport technologies and planning actions. In old towns and cities that experienced rapid growth, traditional means and ways of transport were clearly obsolete; moving people and goods in industrial cities raised enormous problems. Newly urbanized areas and suburbanization helped solve the problem, but the ancient areas were not conceived and built for the new requirements of the industry, nor were they equipped to cope with rapid urbanization. The urban penetration of the train opened avenues for rapid transport, but at the cost of destroying old neighbourhoods. Train stations were architectural and symbolic landmarks in the urban landscape. With their architectural and engineering innovations, they came to represent the whole area of urban industrialization. It is only when they were threatened with destruction in the late twentieth century and heritage groups mobilized to preserve them (some successfully as in Montréal, e.g., the Windsor train station, and others unsuccessfully as in New York) that people realized that a page had been turned in the city's evolution. New public transport, such as the tramway (Linteau, 1988), developed and moved people around relatively cheaply and quickly. However, although the transportation system of the industrial city was adequate, it did not entirely solve the congestion problem. The modern movement in architecture, represented by Le Corbusier, was determined to rethink the modern city in order to help it escape its structural transport problem. In the meantime, roughly between the end of the nineteenth and the middle of the twentieth century, a new personal transport innovation came to the market: the car, which for the last 100 years has been a major agent of change in urban space and planning.

Box 3.1

Constructing Urban Natures

Environmental history is a recent contributor to urban studies and has become a thriving academic study area, examining relationships between societies and particular ecosystems and natural elements, such as forests, water systems, and micro-organisms.

Cities, however, have not been neglected (Cronon, 1991; Boone and Modarres, 2006). A recent collective endeavour, called *Metropolitan Natures* and edited by two historians, Stéphane Castonguay and Michèle Dagenais (2011), has given a picture of the environment of the region of Montréal over a century and a half, and the ways people's needs and power relations are constructed in taming Montréal's capricious nature, especially regarding water.

The book uses the term *socionature* to characterize the end result of many actions taken to master Montréal's natural environment. Technologies are very strong means to change and transform the natural environment. The city has artificialized its environment, but has not totally succeeded in controlling the forces of nature. For instance, water problems, and floods in particular, were difficult to control, despite many attempts. When one set of public works seems to solve floods locally, new floods emerge somewhere else. Moreover, water quantity varies through the year and between years. Planning water infrastructure for variations is a challenging task for engineers.

Other environmental problems have marked Montréal's history. Waste disposal, epidemics of influenza or cholera (environmental hazards), and animals' relationship to humans are dealt with in the book. The term *socionature*, mentioned above, conveys the meaning that the resulting urban environment is the collective product of a permanent negotiation not only with nature, but also between social and political actors about how best to solve environmental problems. The book is keen on showing that an environmental action is basically a political action because social groups compete with one another and also co-operate to decide what needs to be done. An interesting aspect of the book is the link that some authors establish between modern city planning and urban environmental decisions. For instance, the creation of large water reservoirs on and around Mont-Royal is linked to planning green spaces, a major tool of modern planning.

Urban Problems and the Making of the Planning Profession

As problems of the industrial city swelled, persisted, and even amplified, measures of redress had to be coordinated. There was a need for a much broader approach to the city and to the large city in particular. To many contemporaries, **planning** was the way to confront the industrial city problems. To what extent are cities planned, to what extend do they remain unplanned? In a landmark book on the rise of modern urban planning, urban and planning historian Anthony Sutcliffe (1981) describes a slow but continuous movement toward the planned city in industrialized countries (Great Britain, Germany, France, and the United States), starting in the nineteenth century. He stresses large differences between these countries, but also pinpoints similar trends or actions owing in great part to similar conditions. Similar actions were on the whole technological, whereas diverging interventions rested on different political cultures and on the strength of social mobilizations. Without entering into detail, where the state was stronger, such as Germany and France, urban planning was more active. In countries where the state left a great part of the solutions to the private sector, planning was less *dirigiste* (i.e., "interventionist") and more passive. In the latter countries, of which Canada is a member, planning was often dominated by zoning and urban regulation, whereas in more interventionist countries, large state-induced, -designed, and -run projects were socially and politically better accepted. Acceptance was a function of power and class relations, for the transformation of Paris between 1851 and 1870 could not be claimed to satisfy the working classes' aspirations.

Urban planning is not an entirely new profession, or set of practices, although it has, paradoxically, come of age only recently. Cities and human settlements in general have gone through forms of planning; all settlements are established according to some spatial order that reflects some organizing and general, or scientific, principles. In modern urban planning, economic, technological, and social considerations are paramount. In previous centuries, however, cities or villages showed order that was commonly based on the social predominance of some elites, such as the local lord or the religious authority.

Many industrial cities in Europe were built on a medieval layout, which was not a rational plan but a social-order plan. Central to the city was the location of prime institutions: the church, the town hall, and the various trade corporations that dominated city life and city "planning." There was no comprehensive spatial plan but a physical message that these key institutions ruled the grounds. The new industrial cities of the nineteenth century inherited this order, but with time, transformed it radically. New industrial towns, which did not have the constraints of a previous age, were built on other principles. Central to its spatial organization was the factory. Old medium-size industrial towns in Canada and the United States, such as Lowell, Massachusetts, Manchester, New Hampshire, and Shawinigan, Québec, revolved around an industrial powerhouse. Some neighbourhoods were planned: mainly those designated for the owners and managers of the central factory and for the professionals. But working class districts did not always have a discernable plan: they were ruled by regulations and by-laws for fire protection and for the easy, not yet fluid (a very twentieth-century planning idea), transport of goods and people.

Who planned these cities when they were planned? The planning profession did not exist as a specialized field of activities until the beginning of the twentieth century. The ancestors of the planning profession were civil engineers, military engineers, land surveyors, and architects-cum-artists in the Renaissance and Baroque periods and after. In some cases entrepreneurs themselves took part in planning a new industrial town. On both sides of the Atlantic there is a long tradition of philanthropic entrepreneurs who planned, with the help of some professionals, working-class neighbourhoods for their own employees.

Some historical examples are worth noting. Robert Owen (1771–1858), a British industrialist and philanthropist, initiated a movement that continued well into the twentieth century with the example of mono-industrial towns, or company towns, which are towns built around one, usually large, industrial plant. These towns can be found across Canada in resource regions, such as Kitimat in British Columbia, Témiscaming and Arvida in Québec, and Corner Brook, in Newfoundland (Fortier, 1996; White, 2004). Architects and would-be planners lent a hand to these entrepreneurs. Tony Garnier's *Cité industrielle* (1901–1904) was linked to a business development around which he planned a whole city. The Protestant owners of Mulhouse (Alsace) factories contributed to the movement for planning by providing good housing and some public facilities to their employees. Social divisions could be read in spaces, for higher-class districts were differently planned than lower-class areas (Lavedan, 1970; Sutcliffe, 1981). In so doing, planners and entrepreneurs may have invented the reproducible building and district, designed on a model that can be applied to a large number of houses and sites.

Although the industrial city was a hallmark production of the nineteenth century, it lived on and even expanded well into the twentieth century. It is only in the latter century with the Garden City movement and the modern movement in architecture that planning became a recognized profession comprising an institutionalized and professionalized set of activities. The Garden City movement first emerged at the beginning of the twentieth century, whereas the modern movement gained its intellectual coherence and social visibility later in the century with the publication of the Athens Charter in 1941 (see Chapter 7). However, in the industrial-towns era there was a planning movement that could be called a movement *for* planning, comprising a variety of people, some coming from already established professions, such as medicine and engineering, and some from the ranks of political reformists. These people pressed for state or municipal intervention in order to solve urban problems and improve the poor living conditions of many urban residents. According to Leonardo Benevolo (1967), this planning movement was a political and ideological response to social unrest and to the growing fear that urban social movements, centred on the distribution of industrial benefits and ownership of the means of production, might bring about greater and more uncertain changes.

It remains unclear, however, which people were urban planners in the late nineteenth century. New professions always started out as an amalgamation of different people, with different skills, ideas, and interests. Over the course of time, especially when university education formalizes entry into a profession (Freidson, 1986; Starr, 1982), a new professional group develops an identity, a code of practices, and institutional means to communicate with its members and to represent them politically and in the public arena. Entry is limited and competition with others in the marketplace, among themselves, and between other professional groups tends to occupy a great deal of the profession's energy (Abbott, 1988). But at the beginning of the twentieth century, professional planning was not well organized. Coherent and universal training was lacking and even the term *planner* was barely accepted (Sutcliffe, 1981). Also, planning experts were rare and some moved across countries, such as John Adams did at the beginning of the twentieth century in Canada (Hodge, 1985; Ward, 1999). Ideas and experts circulated internationally, or, rather, ideas moved with experts.

On the other hand, the planning movement had produced outcomes, some of them "aestheticizing," such as the 1909 Burnham plan of Chicago or Haussmann's redefinition of Paris's physical and social map (1851–1870), which can both probably be seen as a turning point in planning in as much as they closed a period by showing what planners can do in a grand style. In Paris Haussmann had shown, in a planning style that defined the city for decades to come, that a rational (tainted with some political objectives) approach to city planning was feasible (Benevolo, 1993: 169–88). These planning actions announced a new era: the twentieth-century modern movement in planning and architecture. Planners, mostly architects, had shown their worth in cities and towns that were interested in local improvements and public buildings (Wolfe, 1994). Indeed, in North America the City Beautiful Movement has come to describe the period (Van Nus, 1979; Wilson, 1989). Public buildings but also private developments, such as Maisonneuve City (1883–1918) in the Montréal area (Linteau, 1981), characterized this phase in urban planning history. Private developers and municipal authorities were ready to bet, literally as well as metaphorically, on city building, knowing that urban land and buildings' values would increase with city developments and "beautification." Some of these developers, no doubt, were guided by a sense of civic duty and pride, but economic and financial interests, private and public, could not be ruled out.

This proves that planning as an activity and a profession was and still is closely linked to economic and social interests. Whether planners can arbitrate between these various interests and defend the public interest without jeopardizing the private interests, while maintaining their loyalty to their reformist background, remains to be seen. As Jeanne Wolfe has said:

Planning is about change, and the common belief of all planners, no matter their specialty, expertise, skill or area of endeavour, is that change can be managed for the betterment of the community. Planners argue endlessly about the public good—who is the public and what is good—but all share the sentiment that the human environment can be improved in some way. (1994: 12)

However, this optimistic view of urban planning and planners may no longer be the whole truth and should be subjected to a reality principle. In anticipation of what will be described in the following sections and chapters, while planners appeared to be part of the solution to urban problems in the industrial city, they may have become part of the problem in the second half of the twentieth century.

Urban Models and the Industrial City

The industrial city era produced two contrasting views of the industrial city, leading to two types of urban models: *progressive* and *culturalist*. Models in this sense are ideal representations of what a city should be. Both views belonged, to various degrees, to a strong utopian tradition in Western thought that consisted of imagining better worlds (Manuel and Manuel, 1979). The function of these models may be exploratory, as Karl Mannheim (1936) has thought, but other functions are also possible. The industrial city of the nineteenth century was also a period of deep change and wide conflict.

Françoise Choay (1965), the French historian of planning and urban form, defines this period as pre-planning (*pré-urbanisme* in French). She and other historians of urban planning, including Peter Hall (1988) and Henri Lavedan (1970), insist on its role in setting the stage for the planning ideas and practices of the twentieth century. If some later urban models took their inspiration from the utopian past, there can be no doubt that this tradition has not been a success. Why is that so?

The utopian tradition that set the stage for some of the planning models that followed is marked, as mentioned, by two strands of thought. One is "progressive," to use Choay's term, and is a direct heir to the Enlightenment ideas (Choay, 1965: 7–83). The other is called "culturalist" and got its inspiration in part from a more conservative and traditionalist ideology. Choay finds these two opposing conceptions of planning spanning the last two centuries.

The basic difference between the progressive and the culturalist urban models is that one is grounded on universal principles while the other is based on particularistic principles. For instance, the progressive model is proud to say that it has discovered universal principles on which to plan a city, either entirely or large parts of it, in particular in extension areas that were gradually submitted to a spatial organization. The industrial city presents four basic and universal functions or needs. Some may term them imperatives: to produce, to move goods and people, to house its inhabitants, and to provide spaces and facilities for leisure and recreation. Planning should respond to these needs and provide for them. Consequently, plans and planning styles are likely to be quite similar in all industrial or modern cities.

Culturalist models are not models in the same sense. They do comprise principles but principles that differ according to a city or town's social composition, culture, history, and geography. Needs and urban functions are not universal but, rather, are related to a cultural and physical environment. Instead of planning regular cities, culturalist "planners" design places and spaces according to local values. Their own values must not be grounded in universality but in diversity. Plans are always local arrangements that take into account the human scale of city life.

Finally, whereas the progressive city may be conceived of as an efficient machine for work and circulation of people and goods, the culturalist city is designed and planned for living harmoniously. In a word, the progressive model is *mechanical* whereas the culturalist model is *organic*.

Choay links the progressive "pre-urbanism" tradition to utopian socialism, to thinkers such as Charles Fourier (1768–1830), Étienne Cabet (1788–1856), and others who espoused the nascent socialist ideals. They wanted to build a new society and human community. A socialist community would organize its living space differently: the social divisions of work and place would disappear and, in is place, an egalitarian society would emerge in the way people would occupy space. There were important differences among these thinkers, but the main thrust was for a strong social as well as spatial organization. Regularity in building and in space went hand in hand with regularity of industrial production, which they promoted. Fourier's *phalanstère*,[1] for example, is a social and spatial utopia—*utopia* literally means "a place that does not exist"—in which all is planned and rigorously organized.

The culturalist tradition comprises many social thinkers and urban theorists. According to Choay, different representatives such as William Morris (1834–1896) and Camillo Sitte (1843–1903) gave the tradition its *lettres de noblesse* (that is, its credibility). Morris was a leading figure in the revival of a traditional arts and crafts movement, whereas Sitte was a professional architect who worked in Vienna and was an important leader in the fledgling movement of city and building preservation and restoration. In his 1889 book *City Planning According to Artistic Principles*, he lauded traditional irregular layout and saw in city building the expression of a culture anchored in local space and geography (Sitte, 1996).

Interestingly, the two strands that comprise pre-urbanism (or preplanning) were built on different appreciation of the changing city and society. The industrial society and the industrial city were well under way, and many people were unsatisfied with their evolution and direction. Indeed, one senses that critics were more numerous than defenders of the industrial world (Lees, 1985). Problems seemed to be overwhelming. The progressive thinkers were, on the whole, favourable to the industrial civilization; however, they deplored the nature of its cities and wanted to plan them anew. On the other hand, the culturalists complained about the industrial civilization and economy and wanted to preserve the traditional, medieval city that appeared to them to represent an intimate link between a culture and the art of city building. Industrial work destroyed traditional work and craftsmanship, as well as urban organization.

What's left of this double pre-planning tradition? One is tempted to say "not much" or even "nothing at all." All seems to have vanished with time, and planning practices became more pragmatic, confronting problems as they came along. But solutions to problems do not come about spontaneously. They are structured, as we have seen, by groups of people, by movements, by coalitions of social interests. The industrial city changed with the passing of time. Few well-thought and well-developed models inspired the planning practices. One may even object to the use of the word *planning* in such historical circumstances, for, apart from infrastructure, very few urban actions were actually planned. But others would argue with this, saying that the nineteenth century was the first experimental theatre of urban planning as a deliberate and structured set of actions. All great industrial cities were subjected to change from above: from Baron Haussmann in Paris (1809–1891) to planning large urban parks, such as Mount Royal Park in Montréal by Frederick Olmstead (1822–1903).

Conclusion

This chapter has chronicled the rise of the industrial, or modern, city, which began with the Industrial Revolution. The industrial city encountered difficult new problems that were tackled rather successfully, and responses to those problems were numerous and included a combination of reactions and actions. Reactions are often past- and present-looking, whereas actions are forward-looking. On the whole, responses were pragmatic and problem oriented, but some were more daring, including the development of urban models (although few were actually applied). These models wanted to shape the industrial city's long-term evolution along with solving its more pressing problems. Canadian cities were prompt to adopt these responses. They were inserted in an international movement for city improvement and for the institutionalization of urban planning. At the close of the nineteenth century, the industrial city was in need of perhaps even more innovative actions. Pragmatic solutions were deemed limited or unsatisfactory despite their relative success in improving urban living conditions.

There also was a strong ideological and critical reaction in the creation of the above-mentioned ideal urban models. Progressivism led to utopian communities, which rarely materialized for they were too much against the grain of an industrializing and urbanizing world. Culturalist models were no more adapted to the new situation, but they would eventually give rise to planning practices that tried to preserve some urban landmarks of the past. Preserving the urban heritage would, for many decades to come, remain an issue in urban planning. The roots of the urban preservation movement may have been sowed in the rising industrial city.

In the midst of the industrial city, in large part owing to all these responses—some successful, some less so—a new type of city has gradually emerged. The metropolitan civilization progressively took root as people came to appreciate large urban areas for the benefits they could provide. Large cities of the past were themselves gradually replaced by conurbations and by much larger urban regions of millions of inhabitants. *Conurbation*—coined by Patrick Geddes (1854–1932)—is the spatial organization of the process of growth and urbanization of a set of cities, at first unrelated, which gradually become closely linked to form a very large urban entity. New cities arose and long corridors of joint urbanization grew in size and in importance to form what Gottman (1961) called a megalopolis. The industrial city has lived and thrived, but many changes have prepared for its demise and for its replacement by the post-industrial, or some say postmodern, city.

Questions for Critical Thought

1. What are the special features of Canadian urbanization?

2. What were the main problems of the industrial city?

3. What solutions were found and applied to the problems of the industrial city?

4. Contrast the progressive and the culturalist urban models.

5. How would you describe the planning practices in the nineteenth-century industrial city?

Suggested Readings

Ball, N.R. 1988. *Bâtir un pays: Histoire des travaux publics au Canada*. Montréal: Boréal. Translated from English: *Building Canada*. Toronto: The University of Toronto Press, 1988. This book describes the public works and the infrastructure networks put in place in the industrial city period. All constructions determined the nature and future of the industrial city.

Benevolo, L. 1967. *The Origins of Modern Town Planning*. London: Routledge & Kegan Paul. The author, an urban historian, examines the industrial city and the planning response. The book focuses on Western Europe and Great Britain in particular.

Choay, F. 1965. *L'urbanisme, utopies et réalités: Une anthologie*. Paris: Seuil. Choay's book is an anthology of urban conceptions in the nineteenth and twentieth centuries. The long introduction is worth reading for Choay's typology of progressive and culturalist urban planning models.

Sutcliffe, A. 1981. *Towards the Planned City: Germany, Britain, the United States, and France, 1790–1914*. Oxford: Blackwell. Sutcliffe's is one of the major works on the industrial city and on the movement toward planning. It covers a much wider area than Benevolo's study of the same period and is less interested in ideologies and more interested in practices. The comparative perspective is worth noting and contributes a great deal to anchor urban planning in its social, cultural, and political context.

Related Websites

Federation of Canadian Municipalities (FCM)
www.fcm.ca
> The site of the FCM contains many policy reports on urban problems and challenges. The FCM represents Canadian municipalities in dealing with the federal and provincial governments.

Cities Alliance: Cities Without Slums
www.citiesalliance.org
> Cities Alliance is an international organization of "global partnership for urban poverty reduction and the promotion of the role of cities in sustainable development."

International Planning History Society (IPHS)
www.planninghistory.org
> The IPHS publishes a leading scholarly journal in the history of planning, *Planning Perspectives*.

4 Cities and Suburbs and the Making of a Metropolis

Learning Objectives

◎ To understand the importance and impact of suburbanization on industrial cities

◎ To discuss the causes and consequences of the main factors involved in the suburbanization processes

◎ To critically examine the way in which suburbs play a critical role in metropolitan development

---

Introduction

In the metropolitan era—the current stage of world urbanization—cities and suburbs are jointly created. It is true that cities predate suburban development, but no city in the past and in the present is without some extending fringe areas that the term *suburb* captures well. The word itself is of Latin origin and was already used in medieval times. When suburbs crop up, the central city changes consequently. Once upon a time, suburbs were only residential areas, but this is no longer the case; **suburbia** has, over time, taken on some of the features of central cities. The rapid expansion of suburbia following World War II created a variety of spatial forms, housing types, and social composition. At the same time, other urban functions sprang up: commercial centres, parks and recreation areas, and eventually offices, shops, and even industrial parks. Indeed, the representation of the suburb as a dull, uniform, and socially homogenous living space may have been rather truncated because suburbs have always been rather diversified, open to a variety of people and social and economic activities.

This chapter will examine suburbia in the metropolitan context. Not only does suburbia change, and has changed, but suburbia as a complex socio-spatial phenomenon is part and parcel of the rise of metropolitan era, or **metropolia**, to coin a fitting neologism. The metropolis is jointly invented (only partly deliberately) by suburbia and by a changing central city. The process is a dual one and should be understood as such. The chapter defines what a metropolis is and describes the process through which it emerges, which includes a short sociohistory of suburbs. Next, the chapter returns to the metropolitan context, shedding light on the main forces and counter-forces at play in the production of suburbs in relation to developing metropolises. The chapter ends on a discussion of the fate of suburbs, that is, the likely evolution of suburbs in a metropolitan context.

The Significance of the Metropolitan Order

The term *metropolis* refers to the thing itself (the city), whereas the *metropolitan order* refers to the way the city is organized, distributed over space, and structured in different activities and spaces. The notion of order is borrowed from the Chicago School of Sociology, which found that cities, despite not being planned and designed beforehand, create a socio-spatial order, or what the School called "a double ecological and social order." Impersonal forces rule the ecological order for location—for central location in particular—whereas communication between people and a shared culture govern the social order (Park, Burgess, and McKenzie, 1925). Thus, people with similar cultural backgrounds or similar economic conditions will tend to live in the same neighbourhoods (or close by) and, when their conditions change, will tend to move somewhere else.

The concept of order is a sort of guiding light in the study of variation within large cities and variation between large cities. Questions related to order include the following:

- Is there an urban order to be discovered?
- How does such an order come about?
- What forces are at play?
- How does urban order change?
- Under what conditions does it change?

These research questions remain valid when studying the metropolitan order:

- How does the metropolitan order emerge, and by what forces?
- How does the metropolitan order change?
- What parts do private and public decisions play in changing metropolitan orders, and to what effect?

Let us first define the metropolis. Metropolitan areas are defined differently: size; diversity; internal differentiation; economic, educational, and cultural variety and dynamism; and international linkages can all be criteria for distinguishing metropolitan areas from other types of urban areas

(Antier, 2005: 26). Statistics Canada has chosen a "geostatistical" criterion that defines a **census metropolitan area** (CMA) as "one or more adjacent municipalities centred on a population centre (known as the core). A CMA must have a total population of at least 100,000 of which 50,000 or more must live in the core" (Statistics Canada, 2011). In view of the growing number of very large cities (see Chapter 9), the 100,000 population criterion is not very demanding but is probably significant in the Canadian context because the total Canadian population is of medium size.

Size and number are not everything in understanding city life and change. But they do capture something valuable: the capacity of cities to attract people and to grow further. However, there are metropolitan areas that are stagnating and others that are increasing quickly in size. Table 4.1 focuses on 19 of the 33 CMAs of Canada (all have over 200,000 inhabitants), which are divided into three tiers, forming an urban hierarchy based on population size.

The first tier is composed of the six largest metropolitan areas (the term *city-regions* can also be used), in which close to half (46 per cent) of the Canadian population lives, representing an urban structure where large cities play an important economic, cultural, and social role. These six metropolitan areas are Toronto, Montréal, Vancouver, Ottawa-Gatineau, Calgary, and Edmonton. They may be viewed as centres of a large urban periphery. Centres are, according to Edward Shils (1982: chap. 4), places or institutions that produce a great amount of innovation, which is diffused into the periphery. Although there are obviously innovations in the periphery as well, they tend to be limited. In his book *Cities and Civilization* (1998), Peter Hall gives examples of cities or regions that have created innovations, largely diffused, and have played a leading role in only some particular area of social,

Table 4.1 The Canadian Census Metropolitan Areas (CMAs) in 2011

Urban Hierarchy	Population 2011	% Change 2011–2006 (Weighted)	Population Density per Square Kilometre
Tier 1 (6 CMAs)	15,341,645	8.7	533.91
Tier 2 (5 CMAs)	3,168,723	5.07	329.34
Tier 3 (8 CMAs)	2,475,599	4.57	225.4
Total (19 CMAs)	20,985,967 (62.69% of Canadian population)	-	-

Source: Statistics Canada. 2011. Census, Population and Dwelling Counts: www12.statcan.gc.ca/census-recensement/2011. Retrieved 29 March 2011. Reproduced and distributed on an "as is" basis with the permission of Statistics Canada.

economic, or cultural activities. Detroit, for instance, has been for over a century a centre of car production and innovation, and of diffusion of the car culture. But Detroit has been a centre in only one sphere of activities and innovation, in sharp contrast to New York, where innovation in many guises has been promoted and achieved.

The first-tier cities play a prominent economic role in Canadian society. In their book *Canadian Urban Regions*, examining the changing economic geography of six metropolitan areas, Larry Bourne and his co-writers conclude that "Canada's economy and its major players have become increasingly concentrated in a small number of very large metropolitan areas" (Bourne et al., 2011: 346). The authors have studied five city-regions: Toronto, Montréal, Vancouver, Ottawa-Gatineau, and Calgary. They also pinpoint, following Allen Scott's works (2006), that large metropolitan areas are centres of a "cognitive-cultural economy," which is part of the "immense diversity in the economic structures and trajectories of individual Canadian cities and city-regions" (Bourne et al., 2011: 346).

Tier 1 cities experienced the fastest growth between 2006 and 2011: 8.7 per cent, which is significantly higher than the CMAs in Tier 2 and Tier 3 (5.07 per cent and 4.57 per cent, respectively). It is worth noting that about 63 per cent of the total Canadian population lives in only 19 urban areas, or CMAs. Urban Canada is basically a metropolitan Canada.

What brings people to large urban areas? Reasons and factors, pull and push forces vary, but some do stand out. Job diversity is certainly one of the main reasons people move to large cities and is also insurance when people are made redundant or when firms close. Moreover, there are certain types of work that only large urban areas can offer. High technical and professional jobs, for example, are found only in large cities, where they tend to cluster. Another draw, particularly for young people, is the cultural and social diversity that cities offer. In addition, students born in non-urban regions may move to a large city to profit from the wealth of its education facilities, colleges, and universities, but also from its cultural life. Large cities seem tolerant of behaviours that do not fit well with conventional social norms. Florida (2002) states that social and ideological tolerance is a key factor in the economic dynamism of cities, along, of course, with talent and technology. Large cities offer a variety of services, private and public, which may appeal to many people. Indeed, cultural services have long been a trademark of large and capital cities. The trend is unlikely to abate even though smaller and middle-size cities can now offer a greater variety of cultural goods. These factors may be reinforcing one another in a sort of cumulative advantage that constitutes the metropolitan order.

Recent growth rates of Tier 1 Canadian urban regions give some evidence of this process of cumulative advantage (Table 4.1). There are, of course, downsides to the cumulative advantage of metropolitan areas, such as pollution, noise, travel time to work, perceived or real crime level, and so forth. But these disadvantages have not yet become barriers to metropolitan growth, in part because suburbs offer to many metropolitan residents the triple benefits of a large economic area, the environmental benefit of quieter and green living spaces, and some degree of social homogeneity that some people may prefer.

The Challenges of Metropolitan Areas

Because they are bound to consolidate their leading roles in many respects, metropolitan areas also face challenges, old and new, as the metropolitan order changes over time. There are, of course, many metropolitan challenges, but some are worth pinpointing.

Space and Sprawl

If metropolitan areas are expected to continue to grow at a faster pace than other urban areas, they will face the challenges of containing sprawl or sheer spatial extension accompanied by large costs in infrastructure building and loss of natural and agricultural areas. There is, however, some evidence that metropolitan areas acknowledge the problem (see Chapters 7 and 8) as many regional plans embrace the sustainable development mantra and develop policies for a denser and more compact city. If the Tier 1 CMAs are prepared to curtail spatial expansion, it is by virtue of their overall "spatial footprint" for, as shown in Table 4.1, Tier 2 and Tier 3 cities of the urban ladder are much less dense (5.07 and 4.57 population per square kilometre) than Tier 1 cities (8.70 population per square kilometre). Tier 1 cities could certainly do something to contain urban sprawl in their own backyards. For instance, Edmonton's population density per square kilometre is about an eighth of Toronto's. If Toronto, Montréal, and Vancouver show density figures between 800 and 945.4 (Toronto's being the highest), Ottawa-Gatineau, Edmonton, and Calgary are less dense urban areas, that is, between 123 (Edmonton) and 237.9 (Calgary).

Governing Institutions

Despite many attempts at designing the proper level of governance for metropolitan areas since the end of the 1950s (one or two tiers of government), the Canadian regional governing systems are very different from each other (Sancton, 2005). It is far from clear whether the provinces have chosen the system of governance that fits long-term challenges, both internal as well as external. As Bourne et al. (2011: 346–7) remark, policy and government matter. Large cities are not left to themselves to cope with the internal urban inequalities that resulted, in part, from the 1970s and 1980s restructuring of cities' economic base, from growth problems for some, from international economic competition, from infrastructure building, and from greater demands for environmental protection. While Québec has chosen regional metropolitan governing structures, Ontario has not, and British Columbia has not tampered much with changing structures and has retained its traditional way of governing its urban areas across the province, in what are called regional districts. Boards of directors rather then councils of elected members govern these districts (Sancton, 2005: 324–5). BC's two main urban regional districts, Greater Vancouver and the Capital, have been able to produce regional plans that have taken the sustainable pathway, such as the 2004 Greater Vancouver's Liveable Regional Strategic Plan, "recognized internationally as a model of its kind" (Sancton, 2005: 325).

Urban Infrastructure

Linked to regional governing and planning is the construction of large and regional facilities and infrastructure. Changes in governing structures have acknowledged this particular task for regional governing structures. Canadian municipalities have for some time pressed for investment in large and regional infrastructure that are required to meet new demand or are in need of repair. They have addressed their demand to the federal government and to the provinces. But if all large CMAs want to achieve sustainability, they will have to invest in expensive public transport systems. This is a long-term engagement for them, reminiscent of the 1950s and 1960s when Canadian cities invested heavily in infrastructure and public facilities. However, current needs and aspirations cannot be met with past solutions because problems and ways of life have changed radically. Urban expressways are no longer the sole solution to urban mobility, and urban renewal comprising wide demolition is a policy of the past. Moreover, densification seems to lead urban governments, with the likely effect that traditional zoning has become obsolete. Social and functional mix is the order of the day, although there are obstacles to its implementation.

Public Participation

Not all cities are alike, and public participation is likely to vary a great deal depending on the urban political culture and past local mobilizations. It is not at all surprising that the regional level of urban decision is less prone to large public participation compared with local problems and projects. People seem more likely to participate if a project, coming either from a municipality or a private developer, is planned in their immediate surroundings. If all politics are local, as politicians and political scientists are proud to say, then perhaps public participation is overwhelmingly local. Large infrastructure and facilities planning is more technical, long-term, and complex. Participation is often limited to well-organized groups and special interests. Small municipalities cannot afford to remain outside a consultation process when regional plans affecting all are submitted for consultation. Economic interest groups also show their presence because they may benefit from public investments. The same comment applies well to professional groups. But citizens may feel excluded, although not in principle, from such consultations. They may, as a result, need to organize themselves in public interests or local interest groups. Despite efforts over the years to open the public debate about collective urban decisions, the process is still rather limited to people and groups with special skills, knowledge, and interests (Guay, 2005; Hamel, 2008). Regional governments may face a problem of legitimacy if they are not sensitive to the way consultations are conducted. New ways of engaging people are available, such as design *charettes*, where people are invited to contribute to a project not only by talking about it but also by designing improvements.

Urban Inequalities

Politics are often about redistribution, and urban planning is no stranger to this goal. Large urban areas are marked by visible and invisible inequality. In the past, poor people flocked to the city in order to improve their lot, and this has not changed. Indeed, a great deal of Canadian immigration after 1950 comprised people who wanted a better life for themselves and for their children. There are many kinds of urban inequality (see Chapter 5); if degrading physical and health conditions are no longer on the agenda, poverty, homelessness, and exclusion may be the new order of the day.

Moreover, economic restructuring, or **urban creative destruction**, is at work in large cities, open to international competition and fierce innovation. The work of cities is chiefly the work of innovation (Clarke and Gaile, 1998). But planning for a "liveable city" (Greater Vancouver) or for "sustainable urban spaces" (Montréal Metropolitan Community) cannot be done without a redistributive perspective in mind. *Spatial justice* is a new term describing an old and persistent reality, as well as new realities (Fainstein, 2010; Harvey, 1996; Soja, 2010). Spatial justice is defined by access to urban public services, facilities, and resources for all residents. When people or neighbourhoods do not have access to some public resources, such as public transport and green spaces, owing to their spatial location, there is a spatial justice problem. That keen analysts of urban life and change have written about spatial justice is indicative of a problem that may have recently become more acute.

Global Marketing

Canadian city-regions are engaged in the pursuit of the globalization grail. They cannot avoid this new predicament. Jean Wolfe (2003) has pointed out that too much emphasis has been placed on the global economic context and too little on the local conditions in recent governmental policy statements. A balance should be struck between local challenges and international competition, between a productive and functional city and a sense of place, between belonging and being equally part of a whole community. What is it that cities market internationally? Cities are keen to market themselves as places for investment, as places with great universities, a rich cultural life, and good public services. But as for the rest of what makes up a metropolis, cities are less vocal. Glossy brochures diffused worldwide may show a truncated view of the complexity of a city and of its dark side. Does anyone hear, or read, about a city's vibrant local political culture and the broad public participation in urban policy and planning, not to mention the social tensions and debates over urban resources?

We turn now to a discussion of how suburbs, conceived as integral parts of large cities, have emerged and developed over time. The next sections will focus on *suburbia* (the set of all suburbs as a way of life and as a typical, but changing, urban form) because suburbs are intimately linked to the making of metropolises.

The Suburbanization Process

The history of suburbia is difficult to grasp. Since the classical era, suburbs have contributed to the definition of the city in a dynamic way. At the outset, the destiny of suburbia was linked to the one of the city. Is that still the case today as suburbs are less dependent on the city core and not exclusively defined by their residential function? This question is at the heart of an ongoing debate about suburbs among historians and geographers regarding the status and role of suburbs in post-industrial societies (Nicolaides and Wiese, 2006).

For households who choose suburban life, their decision is not motivated exclusively by practical concerns but also by some utopian conviction. We may even consider their choice an existential one, so to speak. Opting for suburbia is like preferring the countryside and rural areas while continuing to cherish the thrill of city life. In other words, selecting suburbia does not mean renouncing city life, at least completely. Suburban dwellers continue to be in touch with city life. The decision to move to or live in a suburb is a compromise and a paradox: it means leaving the city without breaking completely with urban values. Those who embrace suburban living do not necessarily renounce to their city belonging.

During the twentieth century, when middle-class households moved to the suburbs, their choices were often pragmatic ones. In the suburbs, housing costs were more affordable and the quality of urban services was generally better in comparison to what was available within inner cities. The underlying rationale is one of social upgrading and at the same time one of improvement of living standards. However, if we address collective issues and think in terms of public good, suburban norms and values can be easily criticized for not taking into consideration externalities, especially when it comes to environmental concerns.

The Invention of Suburbia as a Way of Life

Suburbia was not an invention of American culture even though the United States is largely responsible for spreading the myth of conformity that has characterized suburbia over the past 60 years (Nicolaides and Wiese, 2006: 293). In fact, the meaning of the word is linked to the development of the European city. While the word *suburbia* is often traced back to Europe in the twelfth century (Fourcaut, 2000), its initial use can actually be found in the Gallo-Roman era (Vieillard-Baron, 2001). At that time, the designation of human settlements was quite diverse. But the relation between a territory and its periphery was already clearly established. Since the thirteenth century, it is admitted that the root of the French word *banlieue* ("suburb") is *ban*. This word indicates the territory under the jurisdiction of a lord: "Applied to a city, the notion of suburbia began to designate the extent of a country of one league or more—the league varying between regions—submitted to a municipality" (Faure, 2010: 73). In this respect, a suburb is clearly under the control of a particular city. From then on, suburbs were submitted to urban law.

During the nineteenth century in France, and especially around Paris, suburbia played different roles and was linked to contradictory representations. Suburbia was then considered a territory that could be merged with the city in order to contribute to its expansion. Suburbia was associated with recreation and fresh air, a place for escaping from the harmful effects of industrialization. But conversely, the term could also designate the space where rural peasants continued to live next to the city. Suburbia, then, was connected with rustic life and rough manners. Gradually, however, in the late nineteenth and early twentieth century suburbia came to be recognized as a place where workers dwelled while commuting to work in the city. The idea of this pendulum movement became resolutely fixed and with it the representation of "'sprawling cities connected to inhuman rhythms" (Faure, 2010: 75).

If this representation of suburbia could be found in France, the same trends were at play in all industrial countries with cultural specificities that do not alter the model. Everywhere, suburbs contributed to producing a decentralized city that was a response to some of the problems provoked by the industrial city, such as pollution, closeness, poor urban conditions, and traffic congestion. At the same time, suburbia as a response to problems created by industrialization was possible due to innovative technologies that were at the heart of industrialization itself: new tools for communication, a supply of energy that was extracted far away, and enhanced mobility, thanks to the automobile. Mass production and mass consumption, which introduced a novel form of socialization inherent to the industrial society and/or industrial city, contributed paradoxically to the emergence of individualized relationships to spatial forms and urban conditions that suburban life could materialize in an operational way, at least partly.

Detached homes, as in this Calgary neighbourhood, are a hallmark of suburbs.

(© Jason_V/iStockphoto)

Over the years, suburban design and suburban models have been supported by thousands of middle-class households. Detached homes in a rural setting with private access—the dominant image of suburbia in our memory—have remained a collective solution promoted by architects, planners, and builders to what was perceived as a collective problem. While this urban form was adopted in Europe with some success, in Canada and the United States it rapidly and profoundly transformed the industrial city and metropolis. Several factors were involved in this transformation. Modern technologies certainly played an important role. But the rise of **professionalization** was also a factor (Perkin, 1996). Coming directly out of the division of labour within rising capitalism, modern socialization has generated an unavoidable outcome: social specialization. Thus, the notions of profession and professionalization have spread to all sectors of social activities, including urban design and city building. Since the beginning of the twentieth century, the form and role of suburbia has been largely influenced by professionals who were involved in city planning:

> in the case of the US, the mass industrialization that took place in the decade after the Civil War, the mass immigration that began in the last two decades of the 19th century, and the urban condition that gave birth to the progressive movement together brought about the need for the discipline of planning. Suburban plans were responses to the growing urban challenges of the times, whether traffic, urban crime, loss of green space, diminishing

potential for healthy living, declining housing quality, overcrowding, or what was imagined as the loss of "community." (Modarres and Kirby, 2010: 116)

These questions were at the centre of the planning profession's definition from its emergence in the United States at the beginning of the twentieth century. Suburbs were designed to reform urban life: "As the modern city grew in size, density and diversity, many Americans pictured suburbia as its antithesis" (Nicolaides and Wiese, 2006: 164). Thus, progressive reformers saw the suburbs as a way to improve the "living conditions for the urban poor" (Nicolaides and Wise, 2006: 164). For more affluent households, the suburbs were seen as "private havens insulated from the urban masses" (Nicolaides and Wiese, 2006: 164). The same ambivalence mentioned earlier continued to prevail.

If one inspiration of the suburban ideal goes back to the model of "garden cities" as coined by Ebenezer Howard at the end of the nineteenth century in England—i.e., self-contained communities with areas devoted to residence, industry, and agriculture surrounded by a green belt—its realization, which was supposed to combine the advantages of town and countryside, did not necessarily materialize (see Chapter 7). There may be several reasons for this, some of which were underlined in critiques of suburbia that came from diverse perspectives.

Critiques of Suburbanization

For William H. Whyte, in his important work *The Organization Man* (1956), after World War II in US cities the trend in suburban development toward conformity was changing social relations. He described these "mass produced suburbs" as "dormitories" for the organization man. In other words, the professional mobility of managers and other white-collar workers undermined their sociability. Suburbs give them the impression of social refuge, a place to rejuvenate their lost social bonds.

Other critiques of the suburban way of life converge with a Marxist understanding of capitalist contradictions. Indeed, late capitalism goes hand-in-hand with a growing commercialized world, and suburbs play an instrumental role in this process. Suburbs definitely support urban development as a "growth machine" (Logan and Molotch, 1987). The expansion of capitalist markets and capitalist accumulation could not find a better invention than suburbia to support their causes. This was particularly true during the postwar era when suburbs became the "heaven" of mass consumption under capitalist control (Gordon, 1978).

Two other critiques are worth mentioning. One comes from the feminist critique and is directed at the cultural model of patriarchy that hinders the affirmation of women's autonomy and identity. For Betty Friedan, in the 1950s and 1960s, suburbs were reflecting the illusion of a "feminine mystique" (1963). Women felt trapped by the multiple tasks of household work that they were expected to fulfill. But suburbs were also the place where women realized that they were undermined by a "problem that has no name," at least a problem that they could circumscribe easily: "If I am right, the problem that has no name stirring in the mind of so many American women today is not a matter of loss of femininity or too much education, or the demands of domesticity. It is far more important than anyone recognizes . . ." (Friedan, 1963: 32).

During the 1980s and 1990s, the feminist critique about urban and sub-urban development continued to highlight hidden concerns by traditional research. These could be problems of security in the city, preoccupations with the proximity of services, but also new concerns for difference and insurgency in social practices regarding urban planning. As mentioned by Leonie Sandercock (1995), these preoccupations were related to a rethinking of a "public-private divide" and/or to a new reading of planning history that brought to light a hidden dimension of urbanism. This is also what, among others, Caroline Andrew and Beth Milroy (1988) have explored in Canada.

The other critique of suburbs comes from the environmental perspective. The concern about suburban sprawl in North America goes back to the postwar era (Rome, 2001) when people started to notice that there were environmental costs to that model of urban development. Nevertheless, externalities and unpaid costs were not charged to builders or homeowners for several decades.

If some gains were made with respect to environmental protection, thanks to environmental and land use regulation, we have to recall that suburban development is currently consuming more land than previously (Rome, 2001). It is true that the more harmful development practices regarding wetlands or other environmental aspects have been abandoned. However, we still find a lack of awareness about environmental problems, including biodiversity, land erosion, water pollution, protection of wildlife, energy saving, and so on.

Today, the lack of success of efforts to reduce the environmental impact of suburban house building is due to the fact that builders and developers do not entirely take environmental costs into account. In that respect, postwar patterns of urban and suburban development remain to be changed significantly.

Several critiques to suburban development from an environmental perspective have been reiterated by researchers in the field of urban studies since the 1980s, but have not succeeded to transform the mentality of local officials regarding the importance of environmental issues or, needless to say, to change the practices of builders and developers. The difficulty in initiating and carrying out social change remains a central problem of modern, liberal societies.

The Dynamic Nature of Suburbs

Suburbs continue to change, because of, or in spite of, these criticisms. Population shifts in metropolitan areas that are usually connected to the emergence and transformation of suburban development are not recent. According to Benjamin Chinitz (1964), such shifts go back to the beginning of the twentieth century:[1]

> In the larger metropolitan areas, at least, the proportion of population living within the central city has been falling since the beginning of the century. During the same period, or at least as far back as can be measured reliably—generally, since 1929—central city's share of certain employment categories (manufacturing, wholesaling, retailing) has been falling with equal regularity. (Chinitz, 1964: 23)

This global reading of metropolitan trends in the face of suburban development is related to the fact that with the rise of the industrial city, local competition and conflicts were at stake. Suburbs and the central city had been competing to attract wealthy households and economic activities since at least the middle of the nineteenth century (Jackson, 1984). But we must keep in mind the dynamic and contextual nature of suburbs. Like cities, suburbs do not remain unchanged for long. They become caught up in economic, demographic, and social changes that alter their previous status. Here we can recall the example of Brooklyn given by Jackson: "As a result of the continuing exodus and spill over from New York, Brooklyn was gradually transformed from a suburb into a major city of its own right, the fourth largest in the country in the latter part of the nineteenth century" (1984: 30).

This short sociohistory of suburbia we have just recalled insists on the ambivalence of suburbia and its dynamic character in the development of the modern metropolis. In North America, suburbs have been part of the urban fabric for two centuries. But from the standpoint of suburbanization as a global process (Ekers et al., 2012), the reality of suburbia and its evolving status in line with the ongoing development of modern metropolises is much more complex than what we have briefly reviewed.

Like mainstream sociology, urban sociology has taught us to contextualize social practices and social relations, including their historical roots. Emergence, consolidation, and transformation of suburbia under the restructuring of a global economy and culture have to do with the profound social changes characterizing our current modernity (Harris, 2004). During the 1950s and 1960s, Bennet M. Berger explained that in popular culture there was a "veritable myth of suburbia" in the United States (1961). The myth was telling us that suburbanites were "upwardly mobile" and characterized by similar social features and cultural homogeneity. However, at the beginning of the 1960s, Berger was already warning us against simplification and generalization about suburbs and the suburban way of life.

Suburbia in the Metropolitan Context

Suburbia is about form, social composition, economic functions, and culture. Are all these characteristics of suburbia different, very different, slightly different, or not at all different from "**urbia**," to coin a term? We shall try in the following section to review these aspects with some special emphasis on statistical measurement of what suburbia is and on the consequences of a changing suburbia.

The first issue to examine is, of course, understanding what suburbs have become (Bourne, 1996). Although suburbs are an intrinsic feature of large cities, of large metropolitan areas, they are also observed in small and middle-size towns. The postwar trend to own a house, to move outward in lower density areas, to surround one's home with a garden, to live a private life in some functional and at times socially segregated neighbourhood is a phenomenon that is widely observed and valued, at least in North America and some European countries. There are differences between countries, but also between cities as they age. The chief differences are as follows.

The main historical contrast between European and North American cities resides in the fact that in continental Europe, central cities are still the choice of residence for high-income people and families. While in Canada and the United Sates high-income and middle-income people have fled the central city for the benefit of a suburban location, the Western European rich and middle classes have remained centrally located. There are of course important variations on this basic pattern. One can find rich neighbourhoods inside the central city and even close to the economic (or business) centre in many North American cities. For instance, Westmount in Montréal and Beacon Hill in Boston are all high- or middle-income areas fairly close to the city centre. As Firey (1945) has observed, sentiment and attachment may act as ecological variables, that is, people may prefer and be ready to defend a central location because they value "urban centrality." In addition, not all Continental European suburbs are low-income, immigration, and working-class areas. Although Paris, for instance, has its "red"' and working-class suburbs on the eastern side of the metropolitan area, it also has its middle-class and prosperous suburbs on the western side (Pinçon and Pinçon-Charlot, 2004).

Suburbia, at least in North America, has developed on the triple pattern of individual homes, large commercial centres, and the car, with its rapid roads and motorways. But cities are, like musical pieces, prone to infinite variations. For instance, Québec City has shown a diversity of suburbs over time. The first suburbs were designed more or less on the above pattern, with huge variations, but the second and third generations (from 1970 onward) of suburbs were much more diversified (Fortin et al., 2002). Moreover, whereas the first generation of suburbs tended to be ethnically homogeneous, mainly white suburbs including inhabitants of recent immigration are normal features on the socio-spatial map of many large cities in Canada (Charbonneau and Germain, 2002; Ley, 1999). The economic landscape of suburbs has also changed. The commercial centres are supplemented by other business functions and services. Suburbia has, with time, become more like the central city itself, although somewhat younger in demographic composition and economic functions. However, suburbs continue to rely on the city centre for highly specialized jobs and commercial institutional services (Collin et al., 1998).

Suburban planning has often been minimal whereas planning in the central city has always been more *dirigiste* ("interventionist"). Suburbia is the playground of property developers and, according to David Harvey (1985b), of a capitalist class eager to bring their capital to fruition. That suburban planning is more regulatory than conceived and planned is obvious for the first generation of suburbs, but there are exceptions, and the second and third generations of suburbs were much more thought out and, indeed, innovative. Exceptions for the first generation are of course the planned garden cities of the postwar years in numerous cities in Western Europe and North America, including the *Cité-jardin du tricentenaire* in Montréal (Choko, 1988). The highly planned New Towns in Great Britain in the 1950s are examples of what planning can do to improve physical and housing conditions (Newman and Thornley, 1996). France also had its new town planning spree, starting in the 1960s, where planned cities borrow from the garden city tradition but differ from it considerably, making room for denser and higher buildings. A mixture of the functionalist, arising from the Athens Charter, and garden city traditions best capture the kind of planning put in place in the French new towns. However, the *Grands ensembles* model inspired much of the suburban construction in the postwar period in France (Préteceille, 1973). These planning experiments became planning disasters with the eruption of protests and violence in the 1990s and onward (Godard, 2001). If second and third generations of suburbs were more planned, they, however, remain the product of market forces where producers meet consumers' needs and aspirations. Even the widely talked-about new urbanism (see Chapter 7) is at the core of private planning although it has inspired the whole planning profession. The planning profession has long been critical of, if not downright opposed to, suburban development (see Nicolaides and Wiese, 2006, for some telling examples). The rise of new urbanism can be seen as the planning profession's truce with uncontrolled or unplanned suburbs although new urbanism's private direction may not please the planners whose culture has chiefly been oriented to the provision of public goods.

Box
4.1

Metropolitan Planning

Metropolises have learned to plan for their whole areas. The Canadian urban amalgamation process has been instrumental in promoting, even imposing, metropolitan planning. The idea that large urban areas must be planned as a whole is as old as metropolises themselves. But the process of actual planning is much younger.

There are successful historical experiences of large spatial planning for growing urban regions. After World War II, for example, London and Paris embarked on large-scale metropolitan planning. The London plans were focused on "containing urban Britain" (including London, of course, but also other large urban areas, such as Liverpool and Glasgow) and on planning for population and economic decentralization with the help of new towns. And starting in the 1960s, Paris conceived and gradually implemented large plans for the whole urban area, where new towns and connecting transport systems were planned.

In Canada, metropolitan planning took some time to become entrenched practice. In Québec, for instance, it started with the creation of urban communities, in 1969, although there had been exploratory regional or metropolitan plans for Montréal and Québec City before. Most Canadian city-regions are now planning regionally.

There are clear advantages to planning for a metropolis but also some drawbacks or problems. Metropolitan plans are good for building infrastructure and transport systems. Plans are necessary for they are built on long-term investments and political engagement. Public transport demands the coordination of a wide variety of governmental actors—local, provincial, and federal in some cases—as well private actors, such as developers and investors. But there are also problems. Two are worth noting. Metropolitan plans are less responsive to wide public participation, being more expert-driven (engineers, developers, public servants, etc.). As well, they need the strong, long-term engagement of actors whose own agendas may differ substantially. The objectives of central cities may differ from those of suburbs, for instance, and a 20-year period of planning is usually the case in regional planning. Despite these shortcomings, planning urban areas at the metropolitan scale is deemed essential to contemporary city life.

Is there a particular suburban culture that differs from the urban culture? The question has been raised and answered differently. Judgments on the suburban culture have also varied: from enthusiastic approval because of the social and economic mobility suburbs represent to sharp disapproval because of "Creeping Conformity" in Richard Harris's terms (Harris, 2004). Claude Fischer (1984) recognizes, in line with the Chicago School of Sociology's observations, that large cities are a mosaic of cultures.

Not one culture dominates, but many live side by side without necessarily mixing together as Robert Park pinpointed. Herbert Gans (1968) shares this vision and is not convinced that suburbs breed a different culture. However, some research on people's political values and spatial representations shows that suburban dwellers do in fact differ from central-city dwellers. They are often more conservative in political and social terms and they appreciate differently the physical and spatial organization of large cities (Turcotte, 2001; Ramadier and Després, 2004). In a Québec City study on mobility, Ramadier and Després (2004) show that the city centre and the central city are associated with noise, pollution, and congestion, whereas the suburbs offer a quiet and more natural environment, which many suburban people would not be ready to barter for.

A statistical question remains: how can we now define suburbs in a metropolitan context, especially when the neighbourhoods at the periphery of the central city are gradually absorbed into the central city as time passes? Since a city is not an immutable physical and social entity, as neighbourhoods age they are integrated into the fabric of the core area. Older neighbourhoods that in the past were suburbs are later swallowed up by the central city. Political and administrative redrawing of boundaries along with municipal amalgamations (merging of municipalities) have all changed perceptions about what is central and what is peripheral. Statistics Canada has taken notice of this institutional movement. The agency now defines large urban areas—or metropolitan areas—and partitions them differently from the past and from a common understanding of what suburbia is and what "urbia" is (Turcotte, 2007).

The central city has gained ground physically and symbolically. No longer the sole preserve of the city centre and its surrounding older neighbourhoods, today's urban core is much wider and encompasses areas that used to be defined as suburbs. This statistical change, an enlarged urban core, is consistent with changes in urban reality and is mostly relevant to the description of a census metropolitan area (CMA), which we discussed in the beginning of this chapter. The consequence of this statistical redrawing is that suburbia has greatly shrunk, so to speak, at least in the agency's spatial representation of metropolitan areas. CMAs are divided up into an urban core, an urban fringe, and a rural fringe. This statistical and spatial operation may prove the point that we have moved beyond the traditional representation of suburbs. Suburbs are now more and more integrated into the central metropolitan area, and there is thus no need to geographically isolate them.

Suburbia is certainly not dead, however, and has not been wholly absorbed by "metropolia" (the set of all metropolises and their ensuing spatial and social reality; thus, a socio-spatial order of its own kind). Differences still exist in social composition and physical configuration between suburbs and central cities, but, with the new institutions of metropolitan governance, suburbia is more and more integrated into the whole city-region. True, there was for many decades a flight to or, for new urban residents, a choice of suburbia (or is it utopia?), with a corresponding degradation of central-city neighbourhoods. Canadian cities have not entirely avoided the great American divide between suburbia and "urbia." This division between the central city and the suburbs is undoubtedly the result of urban policy and planning which, from the 1980s, have focused on the problems of the central city and have designed interventions and measures attracting people to rehabilitated urban zones (Goldberg and Mercer, 1986; Guay and Hamel, 2010). Urban policies have also built on people's preference for a "new centrality," as is the case in central Montréal with the well-known and sought-after Plateau district (Germain and Rose, 2000). Gentrification and planning decisions have helped to avoid the metropolitan divide, although much remains to be done.

Suburbia and Beyond

Recent research on edge cities, or fringe cities, has shown how traditional suburbs and, for that matter, central cities have changed. For Joel Garreau (1991), who first explored this new urban form and economy in metropolitan contexts, edge cities have a great deal of leasable office space as well as leasable retail space; they also have more jobs than bedrooms. Edge cities have nothing to do with traditional residential suburbs, however, even though the model of pure dormitory space may never have been found anywhere. In other words, an edge city is a proper town, multifunctional in the planning jargon and not unifunctional as the classical suburb is often described and perceived (in Nicolaides and Wiese, 2006: 473).

Urban researchers are increasingly exploring the future of suburbia. They unveil solid trends in the making and offer sound recommendations. For instance, in a long-term study of Québec City suburbia, Andrée Fortin et al. (2002) present the history of suburban construction and planning. They find varying principles of suburban formation and insist that, if some suburbs have become more autonomous in terms of commercial activities and, to some extent, job opportunities—although never completely self-sustaining—new suburbs are mainly produced for residential purposes (but with more planning direction than in the 1950s). Jobs are still not plentiful. The authors also pinpoint that some suburbs, first-generation ones, are aging and may need planning interventions in the near future. Moreover, since the Québec City region is not growing fast, old suburbs may be left to degrade as there will be fewer people to buy them off. Québec City is, of course, a homogeneous urban region and does not show the ethnic, religious, or linguistic cleavages found in other large urban areas in Canada although there are and have been important social and spatial differences (Guay, 1981). Fortin, Després, and Vachon conclude their study, rich in its historical perspective, by suggesting some planning recommendations on making suburbs more ecological, and ready and friendly for an aging population. Along with other Canadian cities, Québec City is preparing a plan for sustainable transport and mobility, and discussions are still open about how best to achieve the double objective of sustainability and adaptability for an aging population because a shift to sustainable transport means investing heavily in public infrastructure and facilities (Québec, 2010).

With this kind of research in mind and of course many more on suburban governance (see Ekers et al., 2012; Modarres and Kirby, 2010), one may wonder about the likely outcomes of suburban development or, perhaps, contraction. There is an urgency to accept suburbia as a spatial order as it is. This order is not likely to vanish despite appeals for compact cities, new urbanism, and the ecological city. Suburbs are spatially obdurate, in Hommels's terms (2005), and it is impossible to change them overnight, even if that were desirable. The dominant planning conception has to make peace with suburbia as it is, and not as what it should have been and should be. However, thanks in part to new urbanism and smart growth (see Chapter 8), suburbia can be better planned. However, it is not always desirable to introduce planning in between land developers and consumers because too much planning may lead to "great planning disasters" as Peter Hall has shown (Hall, 1980b).

There is a need for adapting planning practices to suburbia and not the other way round. If planning regulations have, in the past, been weak, that is no longer the case as there are many examples of planned suburban communities. For instance, the new Sainte-Foy district in Québec City was, in the 1970s and 1980s, more heavily regulated than the old Sainte-Foy: it was denser, had more varied types of housing, and had more public spaces (Divay and Gaudreau, 1984).

In addition, rehabilitation of older suburbs is likely to become an important municipal and planning task. Suburbs built on single-family units and commercial services with few public facilities do not suit today's tastes and aspirations. The detached single-family house as a housing model is no longer the sole model. Restoration, to use an ecological analogy, is not possible. Rehabilitating old suburbs is likely to demand technical, physical, and building innovations.

As many sociological studies have shown and, contrary to people complaining about uniformity and loss of a sense of community (Putman, 2000), suburbs are human and social communities. Sociologists do not understand why spatial order should determine social order, that is, why neighbourhoods in the central city should be more prone to a sense of community than suburban neighbourhoods.

Finally, can suburbs be designed to be more compact in order to reduce their ecological footprint? New urbanism has pledged that it is possible to do so, but not all are convinced that it is the best path to the ecological city.

If, as Edward Glaeser (2011) forcibly and convincingly pleads, compact and ecological cities mean higher and denser cities, there may be some resistance to changing a model that many people think is still desirable.

Conclusion

Metropolitan areas are complex and changing. Canadian metropolitan areas have been studied at great length. The recent publication by Bourne and his co-authors (2011) is one of the latest additions to our understanding of metropolitan trajectories. The authors take the perspective of economic geography, but they are also aware that economic and spatial change does not come about in a political vacuum. Government matters, and in the case of Canadian city-regions, provincial as well as federal government matters a great deal. Not only do provincial governments set up metropolitan governing structures, but they also finance, with the help of federal programs and policies, large infrastructure planning and social housing.

Research on metropolitan areas tend to take a macro perspective, seeing them in governing terms and as economic agents in the international economy, but internal differentiation is no less a feature of metropolises. The most visible differentiation is obviously the separation between suburbs and the central city. We have reviewed, in a brief socio-history, the birth of the modern suburb in the nineteenth century and have moved to the complex development of suburbs, both in the industrial and post-industrial city. Although up to fairly recently suburbia was for the rich and well-off, suburbs have been identified with the middle classes since at least the postwar years. Suburbs represent the realization of a dream of social mobility that the urban growth model of the School of Chicago mapped rather well. Indeed, Burgess's concentric urban model was both spatial *and* social. This model was rarely observed in reality, however, and has been replaced by more complex models. In these new models, suburbia is highly differentiated. There are ethnic suburbs, working-class suburbs, and even suburbs in the process of physical degradation and social downgrading.

Suburbia has also been criticized. One would expect that these not always well-founded criticisms would abate, but, under the cover of urban sprawl, suburbia as a model of social and spatial order still tends to be viewed negatively, especially by some planners. We have pleaded for a more neutral and sociological view of suburbia. Not only is there no specific suburban culture in the strong sense of the word, despite diverging representations and behaviours, but to attach cultural traits to a particular space would be bad sociology. Space is, rather, socially produced rather than socially determining.

There are characteristics and problems to suburbs that differ from central urban problems and features. Both belong, however, to the modern world and should be seen and studied as such. Judgments on suburbs are not very helpful. If suburbs consume more space and resources, and contribute to greenhouse gas emissions, owing to their strong dependency on the car, they can be planned and designed to reduce their ecological footprint, defined as the sum total of natural resources used by suburban dwellers. Suburbs are often targeted as unsustainable, but they are not the sole culprits. City dwellers too consume a great deal of resources, and their ecological footprint may, depending on the suburban model, only be slightly lower than that of suburban dwellers. Both are part and parcel of a civilization, which cities have helped to bring about and develop. Both rely on consuming goods and services, thereby using and abusing natural resources; both have used the environment as a sink and as a dumping ground.

In planning terms, suburbs represent a challenge but so, too, do central cities. The suburban challenge is, however, multifaceted: not only ecological, but also social and physical as some suburbs age and others are created. Urban planning and governance therefore face huge problems in a metropolitan context. Many Canadian metropolises have recently merged component city members, not always smoothly and easily, as was seen in Toronto, Montréal, and Québec City (Sancton, 2000). Tensions still exist between central city dwellers and suburban dwellers; both groups elects their representatives for their own reasons and interests. But municipal amalgamations are a thing done. Learning to live together and to share urban resources, and planning for sustainability are the new challenges that lie ahead.

Questions for Critical Thought

1. What are the main characteristics of suburbanization in North America?
2. According to your understanding, what is the dominant representation of suburbia nowadays?
3. Define the driving forces supporting suburbanization processes.
4. What are the challenges facing suburbia in the future?

Suggested Readings

Fortin, A., C. Després, and G. Vachon (Eds.). 2002. *La banlieue revisitée*. Québec: Nota Bene. Fortin, A., C. Després and G. Vachon (Eds.). 2011. *La banlieue s'étale*. Québec: Nota Bene. The two books are a thorough examination of suburban history and recent developments in the Québec City area. The study combines social with physical analysis and provides planning suggestions.

Harris, R. 2004. *Creeping Conformity: How Canada Became Suburban, 1900–1960*. Toronto: University of Toronto Press. Using a geographical and historical perspective, this book analyzes the rise and transformation of the suburbs in the Canadian context.

Nicolaides, B. M. and A. Wiese. (Eds.). 2006. *The Suburb Reader*. London/New York: Routledge. The publisher has printed some very good readers in urban studies.

This one is a member of the collection. It is different because it is less academically oriented and makes room for contributions by many different people, such as journalists, professional planners, and urban activists in the many roles they take, and from a variety of sources.

Rome, A. 2001. *The Bulldozer in the Countryside: Suburban Sprawl and the Rise of American Environmentalism*. Cambridge: Cambridge University Press. Looking at postwar American suburbia, the author examines how and why buyers, builders, and developers in their social and professional practices are insufficiently taking into account environmental concerns. He also highlights the main reason for the emergence of a new environmental consciousness.

Related Websites

Polis
www.thepolisblog.org/search/label/informal%20settlements
Polis (meaning "city-state" in Antiquity) is a "collaborative blog about cities across the globe," according to its home page, and was founded in 2009. It is a virtual community of people interested in urban affairs, who want to share practices, experiences, and problem resolution toward improving city life and conditions.

The City Institute at York University
www.yorku.ca/city/
Project: *Global Suburbanism: Governance, Land Use and Infrastructure in the 21st Century*. This project on suburbanism is a large international collaborative research project aimed at understanding the multiple changes in suburban living and governing.

5 The City as a Social Mosaic

Learning Objectives

◎ To understand how cities produce and reproduce inequality

◎ To describe the social mosaic of large Canadian cities in many dimensions

◎ To distinguish between positive and negative segregation and attempt to understand how urban clustering is at work and how it is measured

◎ To reflect on urban inequality and spatial justice

Introduction

Large cities are characterized by a great diversity and a large differentiation of social and economic activities. Although Louis Wirth contrasted the urban way of life and the rural way of life, there is now no doubt that we have learned to distinguish between large cities and smaller one. The Canadian urban system is an interesting case, composed of at least a three-tier hierarchy. At the top are the census metropolitan areas (CMA) (urban areas of over 100,000 residents); the middle is occupied by urban areas having between 10,000 and 100,000 inhabitants, which are called census areas by Statistics Canada and by urban researchers; and finally the lowest tier is formed by all settlements of under 10,000 people. We may add a fourth tier at the very top by separating urban areas of over 200,000 (see Chapter 4) from the other census metropolitan areas. Some would argue in favour of creating an even higher tier where urban areas of over a million people are considered because they are far different from the other CMAs. One can see that there is a great deal of arbitrariness in defining tiers in the urban system. But experience has led researchers to use Statistics Canada's divisions, although other divisions, depending on the research purpose, may be possible.

We mention this because while numbers do not tell all, they do matter. Economically, socially, and culturally, large cities are very different from smaller ones. They offer a large variety of goods and services, jobs and other types of revenue, and cultural and educational activities. Large cities are, with some exceptions, much more heterogeneous than small or medium-size cities; indeed, their social mosaic is more diversified and complex. Thus, they need to be dealt with as *sui generis* phenomena.

This chapter presents, in broad strokes, the current social landscape of large Canadian cities and the implications of their ethnic or cultural diversity.[1] Since the 1970s, Canadian immigration has been sustained, even accelerating in the 1990s. Most of those immigrants chose to live in large cities; they chose Toronto, Montréal, and Vancouver as first destinations, but Ottawa, Calgary, Edmonton, and Hamilton also saw a growing number of immigrants. Other cities, all of them over 100,000, such as Québec City, Halifax, and Winnipeg, received far fewer immigrants, but that may be slowly changing.

One relevant research consideration, as well as a political one, is how immigrants integrate into the host society. With multiculturalism as an official policy, we no longer talk about assimilation but about a variable and almost *à la carte* **integration** into Canadian society. Integration is a complex process of becoming fully part of a group or society. Being part of a social entity is partly a subjective judgment, however. While it is clear that second- and third-generation immigrants are, in many respects—such as language, occupation, education, and voting behaviour—very similar to the host society, they can also differ in important ways. For instance, immigrants may, for cultural and religious reasons, live with like people, even past the second generation. This is a simple fact that urban sociology has tried to document and explain for different immigration groups. The follow-up is to determine whether immigrant groups fare well or badly in the receiving urban society: Are they residentially segregated by factors over which they have no control, or are they choosing their own neighbourhoods and clustering in some specific areas?

There may be good and bad reasons for residential segregation (Peach, 1996). Research on ethnic, racial, minority, and immigrant residential patterns is well developed in Canada and the United States (Driedger, 1999; Charles, 2003; Clark, 1986; Clark and Blue, 2004; Fong and Wilkes, 2003; Fong and Chan, 2010; Hou, 1996; Hou and Balakrishnan, 1996; Logan, Stults and Farley, 2004; Massey and Denton, 1988; Mendez, 2009; Spivak et al., 2011; Taeuber and Taeuber, 1965). These studies have painted a complex picture of choices of living areas, and have asked about the impact of economic integration on residential patterns. Some of this research tradition will be explored and assessed in this chapter.

If large cities are diversified, they are also unequal. Here too research has been sustained and has shown that there are many aspects to urban social inequality. The Organisation for Economic Co-operation and Development (OECD, 2011) and the Conference Board of Canada (2011) have shown that inequality of income is on the rise in many developed countries, including Canada, owing in large part to market outcomes, which are tempered by state redistribution. The rise follows decades of decreasing inequality. Inequality tends, in democracies, to be converted into social problems in need of political actions. Social and urban inequality breeds social movements and collective action. The city is a preferred ground for the expression of contention and claims for social justice. There is a renewed—and a new—interest in **spatial justice** and, with the rise of the environmental movement, an interest in environmental justice, in particular in urban areas, though this is far beyond the scope of this chapter.

The chapter is subdivided into five sections. First, we consider the sources and some consequences of urban diversity and inequality. We start with inequality and move to other issues. Second, we highlight how immigration has changed the landscape of Canadian cities. Third, we look at social diversity and how it has changed the socio-spatial structure of cities. Fourth, we consider women and gender issues. Finally, we briefly examine the presence of Aboriginal people in Canadian cities.

Social Inequality as a Social Problem

Social inequality remains a central feature of contemporary urban societies even though in a majority of cases the *principle* of equality—equality of rights and equality of chances—prevails. Sociology and sociologists have always been concerned with social inequality because in the industrial era, when sociology emerged as a specific field of social inquiry, social conflicts and class struggles were strongly intertwined with the social fabric. The structure of inequality was then at the origin of the relationships between individuals and society. For Émile Durkheim (1997 [1893]), to take the most renowned example, the progression of the social division of work, a hallmark of modernity, provoked an increase in social interactions between the constituents of society. Introducing then a rupture in the previous equilibrium that existed in traditional communities, the social division of work raised the question of harmony between what Durkheim calls individual nature and social functions. In other words, Durkheim wondered how to fulfill individual expectations in terms of the autonomy and self-accomplishment that modernity was triggering in the face of the necessity of social integration.

The answer was not easy to formulate. Durkheim was torn between, on the one hand, a radical liberalism and, on the other, a strict state model of control and regulation, guaranteeing that social position be fulfilled by the best candidates, or by those who were the more qualified for the job. Durkheim's solution was a form of social democracy, betting on the absolute equality of chances for everyone (Cuin, 2004). In that respect, if social inequality was threatening solidarity, this was due to the social and economic conditions that were at the basis of this reality and responsible for contributing to their reproduction. The solution was to change those conditions, and the best tool for that was to achieve the equality of chances for everyone.

Durkheim was writing during the industrial era. As Karl Marx has shown, the division between social classes was structured through the relations of production. Two clear distinctive poles were then formed with their respective opposite systems of interests. The clash between the bourgeoisie and the working class was overwhelming. These two antagonistic social categories were profoundly different in many ways—not only in their social position in the production system but also in the distinctiveness of their way of life. Each group had a different approach in envisioning the purpose of human existence and in defining the cultural world within which they operated. In such a context, social conduct could be explained by class belonging. Inequality, then, was necessarily linked to class affiliation.

From a sociological standpoint, it was possible to predict social behaviour or to anticipate the journey of workers of the industrial society through social life—their life course—according to their class affiliation. People would behave according to what was possible for them to achieve given their "class habitus" (*habitus de classe*), to use Pierre Bourdieu's notion (Bourdieu and Passeron, 1970). For Bourdieu, "class habitus" referred to the constant and continuous provisions common to all persons of the same social group that are acquired and internalized through education. If social identities were principally produced in reference to the mode of production, the meaning of social behaviour could easily be revealed by an analysis in terms of social class.

As we know, capitalist industrial societies and modern cities closely evolved during the Industrial Revolution. The capitalist mode of production and the spatial location of economic activities shaped city life through class conflicts. But the expansion of Western modern cities did not follow a steady process. By solving successive crises involving the two antagonist classes, cities, with the help of nation-states, were able to overcome the economic and social divisions at work in spatial organization. In that sense, if there was a stark difference in terms of the quality of facilities that the two social groups had access to—for that matter, the working class neighbourhoods and bourgeoisie districts were easily recognizable—they nevertheless shared common spaces. They often met and shared downtown facilities, and both social groups made use of public utilities. In other words, even if most of the time the members of the two social groups lived apart, they nevertheless shared a common world, one defined by the vocabulary and values brought in by modernity, even though at times they may have interpreted these representations differently.

One can understand, then, why during the industrial era the notion of social class was a useful analyzer in regard to social inequality. It was easy to connect the economic and social divisions operating in work settings to the social differentiation expressed in other fields of social activities. In fact, under different forms, the class separation underlying economic production was reproduced within all social activities. However, within the current contemporary context, the social class category seems less useful. This is not because social inequality has disappeared. But today its polarization is defined in different terms (Dubet, 2000).

After World War II, the industrialization process was redeployed in a more intensive way than before the economic crisis of the 1930s. Mass consumption increased in an exceptional way and with it a new culture—even a new ethic—of work and leisure emerged (Beck, 1997). This was possible because work conditions improved alongside the transformation of the working class structure. At the end of the 1950s, a new step in the industrialization process was reached, described by some researchers as the coming of a post-industrial society (Bell, 1973; Touraine, 1969). For them, it was as if we had entered a new model of social change, where the incentives of restructuring were driven more by knowledge and organizational principles than by capital. This coincided with the expansion of human services, especially in health and education, which contributed to a reorganization of the occupational system. The workforce was increasingly driven by professional specialization while the traditional skilled activities of the previous era declined. The old industrial economy transformed into a **knowledge economy**, where services took the lion's share of economic activities.

The transformation of the workforce can certainly be apprehended through class relations. However, the class conflicts of the previous industrial era were relegated to the background. It was not an accident that after World War II social relations were more frequently defined in terms of social stratification than in terms of class conflict. At the time, economic restructuring led to an unprecedented expansion of the middle classes. And today, as François Dubet (2009) underlines, 80 per cent of workers are employees. In Europe and North America, the middle classes represent 70 per cent of the society as a whole. Those who are not part of this group are the 20 per cent having the lowest incomes as well as the 10 per cent of those with the highest incomes. When polled, the vast majority of employees mention that they belong to the middle-class category. For them, social stratification—defined as social division between strata of population sharing a similar situation according to socio-economic criteria—is more significant than the former reference to social class.

As mentioned earlier, the description and analysis of social division through a study of social stratification rather than an analysis of class relations does not mean that inequality became an issue of the past. Within the post-industrial society, which is also a mass-consumption society, inequality between social groups has not disappeared but has been reframed with a new vocabulary:

> When the class barriers weaken, you must mark your level by your way of consuming, lifestyle and tastes. It is not enough to inherit a social position; one must still serve it constantly through distinguishing oneself from those

with whom one does not want to be confused; stand out without being overbearing, however, since if the distinction is too pronounced, the mark-down strategy loses its symbolic effectiveness. (Dubet, 2009: 60–1)

Despite what has just been said, conflict and class inequality may be viewed as structural elements of modern societies that are, above all, capitalist societies. Beneath social stratification, class relations remain active even though their expression is modulated through levels of inequality that are less homogeneous these days in comparison to the difficulties faced by the working class of the industrial era. However, these differences are constantly challenged by the fact that Western capitalist societies are also democratic ones. The functioning of democracy requires that equality should prevail, at least in a formal and symbolic plan.

The two faces of modernity—market inequality and democratic equality—are profoundly interrelated. It is impossible to conceive of one aspect without the other. The inequality embedded in market and/or the capitalist mode of production is always criticized by social actors in the name of a formal egalitarian democracy. But as we know, it is very difficult to achieve equality of opportunities as Durkheim conceived it. It is true that the enforcement of democratic principles through redistributive social policies have reduced the more striking expressions of inequality of the industrial society. However, other forms of inequality related to the transforming character of the social structure within post-industrial societies have emerged—particularly in the case of market economies, but also true for more regulated economies existing in Europe. For example, the fragmentation of the labour market that has increased over the past few years has led to greater income disparities. Moreover, relations of domination can prevail over social and cultural terrain that is not necessarily directly related to working conditions. If people feel excluded in the workplace, they can also experience discrimination because of attitudes in regards to religion, sexual orientation, or lifestyle. Indeed, within contemporary post-industrial societies, inequality is increasingly "multiple" (Dubet, 2000, 2009).

On a daily basis, such inequality can be observed in urban neighbourhoods of metropolitan areas even though inequality is not always reflected through social relations toward space. Cities are certainly milieux where "the wealthiest and poorest members of society coexist and interact" (Zuberi, 2010: 110). In that sense, poor and rich individuals constantly communicate and co-operate in many ways: they share public services, and both benefit from the urban amenities that can be part of the excitement related to city life. In fact, it is their simultaneous presence that contributes to enriching the pluralism, the diversity, and the creativity of urban life. Unfortunately, beneath this formal coexistence of members of society sharing the advantages of cultural diversity, urban inequality prevails.

Urban spaces of contemporary city-regions are fragmented and segregated according to the wealth of households. Even though rich and poor coexist, they do so differently, which is why an increasing portion of the population in Canadian metropolises experiences poverty and feels segregated. This is the case for a number of new immigrants but also for a segment of urban Aboriginal communities (Peters, 2010). Single parents and people with work-related disabilities are also vulnerable (Werkele, 2010).

However, it is true that the standard of living in Canada has generally improved over the past decades. For example, the number of single families living in poverty has been significantly reduced since the mid-1990s. In that respect, what happened in Canada was similar to what occurred in other OECD countries. The federal government and the provinces took different measures targeting poverty reduction. But this broad picture does not tell the whole story. When we take a more analytical look at figures, we find that this trend in poverty reduction did not reflect a structural improvement. Welfare dependence is back to 1970 levels (Richards, 2010).

Indeed, we know that according to income, segregation is increasing: "in virtually all of Canada's major cities, the poorest neighbourhoods saw income declines between 1980 and 2005, while the wealthiest neighbour-hoods saw even faster growth" (Tencer, 2011: 1). This is a major concern, especially when we know that in some cities (e.g., Montréal, Québec City, and Vancouver), one-half of neighbourhoods have been affected by income decline.

In a study of neighbourhood change in Toronto, J. David Hulchanski (2007) has shown that between 1970 and 2005 an income polarization within the city was at play. Over a 35-year period the city was transformed by strong disparities expressed through a decline of neighbourhoods with middle-income households in comparison to an increase of neighbourhoods where we find high-income households as well as of neighbourhoods containing low-income households.

Beyond contextual differences, the disparities described and analyzed in regards to the city of Toronto can also be found in other major Canadian cities. However, what is disturbing is less about the disparities per se—although disparities are certainly a matter of concern when policies are defined with the objective of reducing them—and more about the increase in such disparities alongside the development of Canadian city-regions. Unequal income distribution, moreover, means difficulty in obtaining adequate resources, support, and opportunities for achieving a fulfilling life course. It is the enhancement of capabilities, if we borrow the category elaborated by Amartya Sen (1993), that is threatened by this unequal distribution. In other words, in regards to the forms currently borrowed by Canadian urban and metropolitan development, residential mobility became more difficult than ever. The filtering process—whereby older housing becomes available to households with fewer resources as such housing ages, contributing to these households' spatial and social mobility and improving their living conditions—is no longer as effective as it used to be. Households in deteriorated areas of city-regions can no longer move to better or more affluent areas due to their economic situations. In addition, lower-income households living near downtown, in inner-city neighbourhoods where housing costs remain relatively low, are often driven from their apartments by **gentrification** processes that increase property values (see Box 5.1).

Even though the income inequality and socio-spatial polarization that occur in Canadian city-regions do not have the same intensity as what occurred over the previous decades in other countries—if one thinks for example of the poor suburbs of major cities in France (Bacqué and Lévy, 2009) or of many inner-city neighbourhoods in the United States—the same logic is

Box 5.1   A Small Piece of Gentrification in Toronto

Metropolises are known for their cultural diversity. Cities like Toronto fare well in this diversity, which can be readily observed in urban space. Clustering of people of common national or geographical origin is a strong feature of multicultural cities.

Iain Marlow of *The Globe and Mail* (December 21, 2012) has captured the vitality of South Asians' commercial district in Toronto's space. Restaurants and other commercial buildings in what may be called a piece of transplanted India (around Gerrard Street East) are the mark of a community that has adopted Toronto. But there is concern that the commercial avenue is changing and losing what made it so unique and attractive. Gentrification and social integration are at work. One resident, the owner of Sonu Saree Palace, complains that "The new generation, they're not into saris," meaning that young people may select trades or careers other than those of their parents.

Gentrification is a long, almost inevitable process of physical as well as social change in many cities. Some residential neighbourhoods and commercial districts are more prone to gentrification than others: those relatively close to or in the city centre may experience change over long period of time. This is happening in the Toronto area, which Ian Marlow so vividly describes in his article. Old buildings are torn down or will soon be. Some people will make money with such gentrification, while others will look more and more at odds with the transforming surrounding area. Whether a sightseer is strolling in Manhattan, in London, in Toronto, or in Montréal, he or she may easily observe the gentrification process in full swing in some areas, resulting in a patchwork of buildings representing different historical periods and different urban purposes.

involved. Income and social inequality are supporting spatial segregation and aggravating, in return, disparities between social groups.

Furthermore, discrimination remains a complex and insidious process. Statistical variances regarding income do not tell us the whole story. To better understand how inequalities emerge and are reproduced through social relations, a general analysis of social and economic restructuring is required. Normative dimensions are also involved. The priority and advantages given to the dominant cultural model, for example, contribute to protect the influence elites exert on the economic and political systems (Tilly, 2007). Those who do not share the same values or do not have sufficient resources to contribute to the development and reproduction of these values tend to be excluded or marginalized.

At the same time, the shrinking of the working class over the past decades has contributed to the reduction of its cultural universe. By joining the ranks of the middle classes, many members of the working class have had to adapt to a different lifestyle, one that is less homogeneous and less able to support a strong identity in comparison to what was possible previously through their working-class membership. Consequently, when faced with adversity or economic and social hardship, individuals feel more easily excluded. This can help us understand recent urban phenomena, such as the increasing number of homeless in Canadian cities, or the growing number of children living below the poverty line in several major cities. This form of poverty characteristic of current city-regions was less pronounced when the working-class ethos was more effective and able to maintain different channels of solidarity. In light of these last remarks, the multiple forms of inequality we referred to above are then more easily understandable.

The New Social Landscape of Canadian Cities

Inequality and its consequences are only one aspect, albeit a negative one, of urban social and economic diversity. Growing and prosperous cities, like large Canadian cities, can alleviate poverty through market processes and government measures and programs. But there are other characteristics of large cities, and of Canadian cities in particular, that strike urban researchers as well as urban dwellers themselves. It is, in Wirth's term, such cities' social heterogeneity that causes the diversity of urban populations, owing to country of origin, styles of life chosen, or the effect of the division of economic activities. One consequence of this heterogeneity is the clustering in space of groups with common characteristics. In this section we will examine the cultural (or ethnic) and social diversity of Canadian cities and how such diversity creates clustering of people in urban space in what the Chicago School called "natural areas," with the term "social areas" being substituted later on for obvious reasons. Cities are human constructions, the result of interactions between and choices of people and institutions, not due to some natural process.

That the urban social landscape—or socioscape—of Canadian cities has changed importantly since about 1970 is true, but this is far from the whole truth. Canadian cities have always been open to immigration, especially in "gateway" cities, where immigrants concentrated in the past. Although today's immigrants are encouraged to settle more widely—in regions, for instance—some large cities still act as the main gateways. Change in location patterns is slow to happen and, despite government and policy efforts to spread out immigrants, preferred choices of living location remain more or less the same. In a series of publications entitled "Our Diverse Cities," the Canadian Metropolis research network has examined many aspects of the location patterns in large and less large Canadian urban areas.[2] According to this network, immigrants concentrate in some areas while shunning others. They do so for personal reasons, but the wide variety of opportunities large cities offer is a determining factor. Public policy also plays a role: large urban areas offer government services to immigrants to help them find a job and learn one of the two official languages. However, economic and social factors play an even greater role in choice of location because many immigrants seek to settle with or close to people like themselves, where they can benefit from personal and community contacts to better adapt to the host country (Chen et al., 2011).

Over more than a century, immigration patterns have changed substantially, in number as well as in source of immigration (Fong, 2011; Ley, 1999). Immigrant numbers were large in the 1910s and 1920s but dropped in the 1930s and 1940s, only to increase again in the 1950s. A large surge occurred after 1990 (Fong, 2011: 133). The peak immigration number, however, was reached around 1910 when about 400,000 people came to Canada. During the 1990s and 2000s, about 200,000 immigrants moved annually to Canada, and it is believed that more immigrants will come to Canada in the years ahead. If between the 1920s and the 1940s immigrants overwhelmingly arrived from northwestern Europe and the British Islands in particular (close to 50 per cent), after World War II, southern and southeastern Europe provided many of the new immigrants. However, immigration continued from the British Isles (between a third and a quarter of them between 1955 and 1970). Starting in the 1980s, sources of immigration diversified, with a slow but steady rise of Asian immigration (Fong, 2011: 134).

Where do immigrants settle when they arrive in Canada? For the most part, they now settle in large cities, in contrast to immigrants' choices at the beginning of the last century. In the 1910s, for instance, immigrants populated the countryside. Between 2001 and 2006, on the other hand, 77 per cent of immigrants settled in the five largest Canadian cities: Toronto, Vancouver, Montréal, Ottawa-Gatineau, and Calgary (Fong, 2011: 135).

(© Gregory Holmgren/Alamy)

Immigrants to Canada tend to settle in large cities, adding to the diversity of urban areas (Toronto's Yonge Street pictured above).

This settlement pattern is clearly visible in the 2006 Census (see Table 5.1), where the top tier (here urban areas of over 600,000 inhabitants) of the Canadian urban system has changed its social, or cultural, composition markedly over time and has been receptive to important numbers of immigrants. Table 5.1 shows the nine largest Canadian urban areas, in decreasing total population size, and the proportion of immigrants in each city in 1996 and 2006. The Halifax urban area, which does not belong to the top tier (with a population of a bit less than 400,000), is added for "spatial equity" in the treatment of urban data across all regions of Canada.

If the populations of all large urban regions, as drawn by census metropolitan areas (CMAs), comprise between about 20 per cent and 50 per cent of people who have been born in foreign countries (a definition implicit in Statistics Canada's use of the term "immigration status"), Québec City is the one-man (or one-city) out: in 2006, immigrants comprised only 3.6 per cent of its population. Change between 1996 and 2006 was important in Toronto, which saw an increase of 10.7 per cent in immigrants, followed by Vancouver at 4.7 per cent.

Visible minorities comprise an important proportion of urban immigrants in all large CMAs, particularly in Toronto and Vancouver (table not shown). For instance, in 2006 visible minorities in Toronto made up 42.5 per cent of the total population; and in Vancouver, 41.4 per cent. In all other urban areas, visible minorities made up less than 20 per cent of the total population. These demographic and cultural facts have some consequences

Table 5.1 Urban Canada and the Immigrant Population: Large CMAs (2006 and 1996)

Urban Area (CMA)	% Immigrants (2006)	% Immigrants (1996)
Toronto	52.3	41.6
Montréal	20.4	17.6
Vancouver	39.3	34.6
Ottawa-Gatineau	17.9	16.0
Calgary	23.5	20.8
Edmonton	18.3	18.4
Québec	3.7	2.6
Winnipeg	17.5	19.7
Hamilton	24.1	23.3
Halifax	7.4	7.4

Source: Based on Census of Canada. 1996, 2006. *Census Metropolitan Areas Profile.*

for shaping Canadian society, for assimilation or integration into Canadian society, and for the urban cultural and social composition.

One important question that has been intensely researched in urban studies and urban sociology is how deeply immigrants are integrated into the host society; another important question, conversely, is whether they remain in immigrant neighbourhoods for generations. This kind of research may be called ethnic residential patterns or ethnic residential segregation; the latter implies that some degree of the segregation is not voluntary (Driedger, 1999; Fong and Wilkes, 2003; Fong and Shibuya, 2005; Hou and Balakrishnan, 1996; Ley, 1999; Myles and Hou, 2004; Smith and Ley, 2008). Urban segregation studies come from two intellectual sources: first, from the Chicago School model of urban growth and residential patterns; second, from American studies on racial segregation in urban areas (Clark, 1986; Glaeser, Resseger, and Tobio, 2008; Logan, Stults, and Farley, 2004; Massey and Denton, 1988; Taeuber and Taeuber, 1965). The Chicago School model assumes that immigrants, or migrants, wherever they are from, will assimilate in the host society and that their patterns of residential choice will not differ from members of the host society who have the same socio-economic status and family status. For instance, if a migrant group easily integrates into the economic structure, the second generation will live in the same neighbourhoods as others in the same the social and economic group, regardless of where they came from. However, the persistence of ethnic residential clusters in large cities shatters this model of social, economic, and spatial assimilation (Fong and Wilkes, 2003). Moreover, research on immigrants' economic integration shows that the process of integration is not fully reached and that variation between immigrant groups is important

(Ley, 1999). Although this last point is beyond the objective of this chapter, it bears on the problem at hand. If immigrant groups improve their life chances and pass them on to their children, they will more likely follow the Chicago School model of spatial mobility. There is some evidence that this process is under way in Canadian cities, as researchers (Fong and Hou, 2009) have found, although there are important variations among immigration groups depending on the source of immigration and decade of entry. But there are noticeable exceptions. Some immigrant groups may well substantially improve their economic perspectives but may remain fairly concentrated in urban space. This has been observed for religious groups, such as those of the Jewish faith, even over a long period of time (Drouilly; 1996; Guay, 1978, for Montréal). It is, however, difficult to determine whether urban spatial concentration is a choice or a constraint imposed from outside, like soft discrimination in the housing market. Furthermore, if there is a relation between economic conditions and cultural residential patterns, one has to wonder which factor is the cause and which factor is the effect (Chen, Myles and Picot, 2011).

Clustering and Dispersing in Multicultural Cities

The distribution of people in urban space is not random. People express their preferences when they choose one neighbourhood over another. But personal and family preferences are constrained by many other factors, such as revenue, job and school location, community attachment, aesthetic values, and so on. Residential choice is a complex decision that may involve a long search and tradeoffs between aspirations, personal means, and availability and affordability of housing types. The urban social mosaic struck the Chicago School's sociologists (Park et al., 1925), and they tried to explain why people with the same characteristics cluster in the same neighbourhoods.

Eshref Shevsky and Wendell Bell's *Social Areas Analysis* (1955) launched a new phase in the study of urban social differentiation. It gave rise to a long tradition of quantitative research on urban residential patterns in the American city, which was followed by Canadian and European urban researchers. Under the term of *Factorial Ecology* (the study of urban ecological differentiation with the use of factor analysis, a powerful mathematical technique to analyze large numbers of data), this kind of urban research took an even greater quantitative turn and established itself as a solid, quantitative method (Guay, 1978).

This tradition of research has come up with a more diversified picture of urban social areas although this variation is played on a very strong theme. The many decades of research have produced an understanding of the socio-spatial structure characterized by the following points. First of all, many large urban areas are differentiated by three large divisions: a socio-economic status (SES) that captures the variation among a set of variables mainly composed of education, occupation, and revenue; a family status (FS) that separates areas according to stages in the life cycle, i.e., families with young children as opposed to all the others; and different ethnic status (ES) that identifies neighbourhoods according to one, sometimes two, important cultural—and "racial" in the case of American cities—groups that cluster therein. The second characteristic of the socio-spatial structure of urban social areas is the social structuring that is spatially distributed according to some model. The SES is often distributed in zones and, secondarily, in sectors. The FS is, on the whole, zonal in form, with family status increasing with distance from the city centre. In addition, the various ES are composed of clusters of immigrant groups, a large number of which are located close to the city centre in the zone of transition. Canadian researchers (Balakrishnan and Jarvis, 1991: 537) have discovered that up until the 1990s, the concentric model describes Canadian cities well; despite many changes over decades, Canadian cities "have not [deemed] invalid the association found between SES, family size and concentric zones." Let us remember that Burgess's model, although focused on zones, also takes into account sectors, especially for middle-class households, which may cross more than one zone.

There are of course important variations between cities in the United States and in Canada, but this double (social and spatial) representation seems to hold for the industrial city, that is, from 1920 to 1970, before the large influx of immigrants and the economic restructuring of large cities in the 1970s. True, urban researchers have criticized the model, which was deemed too rigid, and have questioned whether the model was in any way universal, at least for the Canadian city (Pineo, 1988).

This line of research is a belated product of the urban development model of Burgess. It is, however, less concerned with zones and spatial development and more with the measure of clustering and of dispersal. The basic questions are whether immigrant groups concentrate, and to what extent. To these two simple questions the answer is clear: yes, immigrant groups tend to cluster in urban space, at least upon their arrival and for the first generation. Once this answer has been given, what is next to explore? Other questions can be raised. Why do immigrant groups cluster and remain clustered? Are they segregated or are they clustered by choice? How is clustering related to economic conditions and the housing market? Finally, do clusters fade with the passing of time, when second and third generations are settled and better integrated economically in the host society?

One answer is to stick to the spatial assimilation model as economic conditions, measured either by income or by a SES index, improve. One may ask whether the conclusion, based on 1961–1981 census data, is still true today (Hou and Balakrishnan, 1996). There is reason to believe that since 1991 the immigration process has changed in many ways. A review of recent data and studies (Mendez, 2009: 103) takes the view that the basic assumptions of the spatial assimilation model, also called the "up and out" model, "continued to hold, albeit with increasing amounts of time reported before the expected socio-spatial outcomes are attained." Some immigrant groups do seem to resist spatial assimilation. Research, for example, has pinpointed that many members of the Chinese community still prefer to live with people like themselves (Myles and Hou, 2004). However, there are various communities of Chinese, and only half of them choose to do so; well-to-do Chinese seem to prefer to buy houses in the same community. But Mendez is not entirely convinced that this resistance to spatial assimilation is robust because some members of this diverse community opt for a suburban living on arrival, without having gone through a transition zone. Moreover, with gentrification and housing improvements in central neighbourhoods, economic integration may not be followed by spatial dispersion from a point of entry, thereby diluting clustering.

Spatial assimilation is a time-dependent process and is, for immigrants, related to the improvement in their economic resources. The cause-and-effect relationship goes that way: from economic and social integration to spatial dispersion (Massey and Mullan, 1984; Massey and Denton, 1985). Two Canadian sociologists have explored this connection in depth in four large Canadian cities: Calgary, Montréal, Toronto, and Vancouver (Fong and Hou, 2009). Critical of the current research on residential patterns that too often focuses on a single generation or on comparing immigrants with the host population (i.e., "whites" in many American and Canadian studies) in only one census year, Fong and Hou set off to test whether successive generations of immigrants differed in their choice of residential neighbourhoods, and whether the assimilation pattern is different according to different groups of immigrants. Unable to use time series data—that is, following some test groups and its members through time—at successive census years, they worked on the data of the 2001 census. They divided the immigrants into four groups: first generation, 1.5 generation, second generation, and third-plus generation. Census data contain items on year of immigrant landing in Canada. If there is a general pattern of spatial dispersal (measures by greater contact with whites in neighbourhoods) for the three studied groups (South Asians, Chinese, and blacks), the trend is less true for the third-plus generation of South Asians (Fong and Hou, 2009: 417). Contacts with whites at the neighbourhood level (census tracts in statistical terms) are also accounted for in each group with less contact with other visible minorities. But the general trend is not sustained over the long run, for "despite the decline [in minority concentration] over generations, the proportions in their tracts of other visible minorities and members of their own group remain high" (Fong and Hou, 2009: 417). Canadian blacks seem to better profit from assimilation than American blacks do as the Canadians' economic integration is converted into spatial dispersal (Fong and Hou,

2009: 417). Finally, third-plus generations do not fare better than second and 1.5 generations (Fong and Hou, 2009: 419).

The authors conclude that the spatial assimilation model is confirmed in large Canadian cities, but only up to a point. A counter-model, called the "place stratification model," posits that some groups may shun spatial assimilation and choose to remain close to their own cultural minority. Selection of place to live is a complex process in which many factors are assessed by residents and members of immigrant communities. In the Canadian studies reported here, there is some evidence that place stratification, or "place selection," is at work despite better economic resources for minority groups that can be converted into location choices closer to the majority group, when other factors such as SES and FS are taken into account. Canadian cities prove to have some degree of social and spatial mobility, although limited on both counts. If economic integration is imperfect, and can be attributed to less education in minority groups—although this has been changing with recent immigration rules—spatial clustering is still a choice and does not necessarily show that discrimination is the culprit.

Cities and Women

There is no doubt that housing and immigration are valuable entry points for understanding the social landscape of Canadian cities. Social diversity is certainly reflected in the ways immigrants and minority communities have settled. Through their ways of inhabiting, immigrants have transformed the materiality and culture of the territory and urban life (Lorinc, 2006); they have introduced cultural differences that are meshed into what is recognized by everyone as the specific reality of Canada's diversity. Nonetheless, we have to keep in mind that, if in Canada, this "diversity is everywhere the norm, its defining characteristics vary by city" (Andrew et al., 2008: 261). In this case, what has to be taken into account goes beyond minority communities; many social actors are trying to be recognized in the social and public space. They think that their distinctiveness should be recognized while not being an object of social discrimination. If integration—through assimilation, for example, with the consequence that the group loses its distinctiveness—is promoted at times, at other occasions these actors prefer to focus on better recognition of their specific differentiation. A tension often prevails between these two courses of action. The way out of this conundrum, as some researchers are mentioning, can be found in the compromise of "differential incorporation"[3] (Peters, 2010: 155). This is what the Aboriginal people looked for. But a tension also existed for women between being distinct and recognizing their differentiation, to take only two examples of actors who had to fight discrimination or exclusion in Canadian cities, especially since the 1970s.

Civic leaders have not always recognized the place of women in the city. Their place is not even fully accepted nowadays after several decades of activism by the feminist movement and despite the fact that identity and differences are increasingly part of the Canadian cultural landscape. Historically, women's access to public space was rejected while political leaders expected that their social life should be confined to the private domestic space (Sandercock, 1995; 1998). This was congruent with a limited and quite male and heterosexual reading of modernity and of the modern city (Wilson, 1992).

The postmodern and poststructuralist turn in social sciences during the 1970s and 1980s contributed a great deal to bring the attention of observers of the urban scene onto the importance of individual actors in reference to their subjectivity and distinctiveness in the production of the social realm. Against this backdrop, gender, defined in relation to a **reflexive project of the self**, is bringing in an original understanding of social and urban problems when related through its "interconnectedness" with other categories of identification (such as sex, class, and ethnicity) (Ryan, 1994). Then, what women put forward was first to combat social exclusion under the diverse and complex forms it can take. But for women it was also important to express different narratives concerning the planning of cities, narratives that considered issues that had been neglected in the past by male planners, including security, concerns for accessibility to the built environment, or the availability of specific services for children (daycare centres, for example).

Of course, women did not await the postmodern/poststructuralist turn for expressing their demands and claims in the face of social exclusion and urban inequality. Their resistance against male values and priorities embedded in planning and organization of city life is much older and can certainly be related to the mobilization of suffragettes in the United Kingdom at the beginning of the twentieth century. These women campaigned for access to equal franchise. At the same time, they struggled for social reforms. A few years later, similar groups of women were active in several Canadian provinces. But, it is also through different social practices of resistance or affirmation of their difference that women took part in shaping the form of and giving sense to urban life. For that matter, women revised the traditional separation that prevailed between public and private spheres. They introduced private concerns regarding the issues of domestic violence and child care into the public domain. They got involved in community development for improving their own situation and those of their fellow citizens (Tastsoglou and Miedema, 2003).

Women have mobilized themselves in different ways under feminism and the women's movement (Dufour et al., 2010). They did that from a series of concerns: fighting for equal rights regarding income distribution and work conditions (Soroka, 1999); combating patriarchal social relationships in the city (Séguin and Villeneuve, 1997); expressing their differences in shaping urban space with another voice (Wright, 2007); or finding new ways of defining solidarity that can reach immigrants (Andrew, 2010). Through these approaches, women "radicalized" the previous conception of modernity. By introducing consideration for subjectivity, sexual differences, and gender, women have struggled with success against discriminatory urban policies (Keney, 1998). This does not mean, however, that women have completely succeeded in achieving a "non-sexist city" (Werkele, 2010). If formal access to the public sphere and political representation is largely accepted in Canada from an institutional standpoint for all citizens regardless of their social, ethnic, or sexual identity, in practice social inclusion remains largely unequal (Bird, 2008). As Caroline Andrew, John Biles, Myer Siemiatycki, and Erin Tolley underline, "fulfilling democracy's promise of political participation, belonging and inclusion requires that we do better" (2008: 269).

Newcomers: Aboriginals and City Life

To a certain extent what is true for overcoming the impediments of social and political recognition of women in urban settings can be transposed to the situation faced by Aboriginal people living in urban areas.

Before the 1940s, few Aboriginal people lived in cities. They mainly inhabited reserves and rural areas even though some reserves were located within or next to census metropolitan areas (CMAs) (Peters, 2010). But since the 1950s, a growing percentage of the Aboriginal population has been engaged in an urbanization process, moving to urban settings: "between 1996 and 2006, the proportion of the Aboriginal population living on reserves in rural areas declined from 53.2 per cent to 46.8 per cent, while the proportion living in urban areas increased from 46.8 per cent to 53.2 per cent" (Peters, 2010: 157).[4] Such an increase does not mean, however, that Aboriginal people are abandoning rural areas and reserves for cities. For them, reserves continue to play an important social and cultural role. Changes are continuously taking place between reserves and Aboriginal urban communities, reflecting through this a "deep ambivalence" towards city life[5] (Lorinc, 2006).

Nonetheless, the presence of Aboriginals in urban areas will keep growing in the coming years. This can be explained by two main factors. First, as has been the case throughout history, cities remain a magnet, especially for young Aboriginals who want to escape the "boredom of the reserve" (Lorinc, 2006: 53). Second, and more positively, urban regions are offering to Aboriginal people, as they do to other Canadians, a series of opportunities in social, cultural, economic, and educational terms that they cannot find elsewhere. For many Aboriginal people, then, moving to urban regions can represent an improvement in their life conditions. Chances of getting a job are certainly better in cities (Lorinc, 2006).

However, half of Aboriginal people in Canadian cities are living below the poverty line as revealed by a study on urban poverty conducted by the Canadian Council on Social Development in 1996:[6] "In 2000, the low income residents of Canada's CMAs were 35 per cent from recent immigrants, 18 per cent from other immigrants, and 42 per cent Aboriginal people" (Heisz and McLeod, 2004: 66, as quoted by Lightbody, 2006: 33). In that sense, it is not surprising to find that Aboriginal people are "overrepresented among the urban poor in Canadian cities and are more likely than the non-Aboriginal population to live in poor urban neighbourhoods" (Peters, 2010: 163).

This reality and its negative impact on urban life conditions have to be replaced in this historical context. Aboriginal poverty is rooted in the colonialism that the members of these communities have suffered since the arrival of Europeans in the Americas. At the outset, in Canada as in the United States, the decision to create reserves was intended to make land available for European settlers and to assimilate Aboriginal people into the European way of life (McCue, 2012). But assimilation did not occur as expected by colonizers. Members of the Aboriginal population, through the affirmative action of their diverse Nations, wanted to keep alive their native culture and traditions. The colonial exploitation of land and resources and the paternalism and dependence that have resulted from it have had negative social and economic consequences for these communities for several generations.

A brighter side to this story is that a "new entrepreneurial spirit" and different strategies of local economic development to empower Native communities are emerging and developing within several Nations (Lightbody, 2006). For instance, implementing social support programs targeting equality of opportunities, especially in the field of education, can help young Aboriginal people complete their curriculum (Deslauriers, Durand, and Duhaime, 2011). Such approaches seem to be a viable alternative to the traditional federal funding programs and activities that were designed exclusively for reserves. From that perspective, Aboriginal culture can positively enhance the cultural diversity of cities, adding to their dynamism and creativity and, at the same time, combating social exclusion and inequality.

Conclusion

We must not confuse social diversity and social inequality. Diversity does not necessarily lead to inequality, and inequality is not an unavoidable consequence of diversity, especially multicultural diversity. There are cultural groups that fare well in large cities and that benefit from the economic and social opportunities that they offer. Others, on the other hand, are not so fortunate. American urban research has been very much concerned with "racial" segregation (particularly of African-Americans), and, since unwilling segregation has remained a political issue, the intensity of research has been maintained. Canadian cities may not be as segregated as American cities, but, as we have shown, similar processes of clustering in urban space are at work. However, there is a positive and a negative source of clustering. People may choose to live with people of their own kind for many reasons, or they may be led to cluster more or less against their own preferences. The two sides of the same coin have to be considered because positive and negative clustering (or segregation) have great impact on policy decisions and on urban planning. Spatial justice, although not an entirely new concern, is on the rise in theoretical urban research (Fainstein, 2010; Harvey, 1996; Soja, 2010). Coupled with problems of urban environmental justice, spatial justice has become a breeding ground for the expression of alternative visions of city life.

Spatial justice is a difficult concept to grasp and to achieve, for total spatial equity may not be possible and justice may be applied to a wide variety of social concerns and problems. In brief, spatial justice is about having reasonable access to urban collective resources, such as public services, urban facilities, clean water and air, and green spaces—all the goods that public authorities provide in an urban context. For instance, in the post-industrial city, all urban dwellers can enjoy drinkable water. Planning the industrial city has solved more or less permanently this problem. But clean air is not available to all, at least in the same amount. There are neighbourhoods that are more exposed to air pollution owing to their closeness to a polluting industry or a public facility, such as an incinerator. Here spatial justice is closely linked to environmental justice. Moreover, public transport may be unfairly distributed across a city. Edward W. Soja (2010) documents how in Los Angeles a protest movement cropped up because of bus routes that did not reach and cross poor neighbourhoods. Planning for spatial justice may be necessary in many instances to reduce urban inequality, and the environmental movement has broadened the issues. Spatial justice is an even greater problem in fast-growing cities of the developing world.

Finally, planning for cultural diversity, as Leonie Sandercock (1998) has insisted on, has become an imperative in all multicultural cities, Canadian ones included. Whether this deeper concern with spatial and environmental justice will lead to a reshuffling of the basic principles of urban planning, which have in the past tended to respond to universal needs and problems, remains to be seen. Nonetheless, over the past decades diversity has certainly contributed to opening up the public debate on alternative options surrounding the choice of an urban and collective way of life (Hamel, 2008).

Questions for Critical Thought

1. How and how far has urban inequality changed over the long period of consolidation of the industrial city and its recent transformation into a post-industrial one?

2. Differentiate between positive and negative urban segregation.

3. Give examples of cultural clustering in your own city. Describe at least one and ask yourself to what extent urban cultural diversity contributes to the urban way of life as you conceive it.

4. This chapter has, in an endnote, taken a strong position in favour of getting rid of the "visible minorities" category in Canadian official (public) documents, such as the census reports. Do you agree? Explain your own view.

5. Give some concrete examples, in your own city or town, of spatial injustice that can be dealt with through proper policies and planning decisions.

Suggested Readings

Andrew, C., J. Biles, and M. Siemiatycki (Eds.). 2008. *Electing a Diverse Canada: The Representation of Immigrants, Minorities, and Women*. Vancouver: UBC Press. The issue of representation remains central to understanding the way inequalities are reproduced in urban Canada. Examining the situation in 11 Canadian cities, the authors of this edited book review the challenges brought in by globalization and immigration that citizens are currently facing or are going to face in the coming years.

Escobar, A. 2008. *Territories of Difference: Place, Movements, Life "Redes."* Durham and London: Duke University Press. Relying on an ethnographic survey about the African-Colombian population, this book addresses local and territorial issues in the face of globalization and environmental challenges. By paying attention to the resilience of African-Colombian activists, Escobar is improving our understanding of social and environmental justice.

Soja, E.W. 2010. *Seeking Spatial Justice*. Minneapolis: University of Minnesota Press. This book is about the Los Angeles city-region from the purview of the city's poorest residents. Relying on the notion of spatial justice as involved in Henri Lefebvre's right to the city, Soja looks at the ways to overcome "the unjust geographies in which we live."

Related Websites

Metropolis
www.metropolis.net
This website promotes "comparative research and public policy development on migration, diversity and immigrant integration in cities in Canada and around the world." Bringing together different research centres from several Canadian provinces, Metropolis is a major research network. It has developed partnerships with "policy makers and researchers from over 20 countries." Information about research results and activities regarding a city's immigration is accessible through the site.

The City Institute at York University (CITY)

www.yorku.ca/city/

> Dedicated to promoting urban research, The City Institute at York University was created in 2006. It is now a dynamic hub for urban research, welcoming several postdoctoral students and visiting scholars every year. The website is useful to learn about seminars and conferences taking place in the Toronto metropolitan region. One can also find information about past and ongoing research on cities.

The Laidlaw Foundation

www.laidlawfdn.org

> The Laidlaw Foundation supports civic engagement, diversity, and social inclusion in regards to community development, the arts, and environmental concerns. It is based on "the process of meaningful, voluntary participation of young people in decision-making and governance."

> Information about the activities and projects supported by the foundation are accessible on the website.

6   Urban Governance and Local Democracy

Learning Objectives

◎ To understand the notion of governance in reference to cities and urban sociology

◎ To understand how governance is shaped by the urban context in which it is taking place

◎ To evaluate the proposals made by the "new regionalists" regarding current issues of metropolitan development

◎ To understand how governance has been implemented in some Canadian cities at the local and metropolitan scale

Introduction

Either for managing environmental problems or to face challenges brought in by globalization, local public authorities are increasingly relying on **governance** when seeking out solutions. Of course, the governance discourse itself is largely influenced by the tradition and political culture specific to the country, or even to the local context where it is expressed. In this sense, issues of governance can certainly not be the same everywhere. Nonetheless, it seems that in all places the reference to governance[1] for solving urban problems has become a requisite.

By definition, a multiplicity of actors is always included in governance processes. In the urban field, generally speaking, governance is a sociopolitical form of contemporary public action open to partnership and negotiation, with the goal of finding solutions along with, ideally, the participation of civil society. In that respect, governance is neither the prerogative of governments nor of political actors. But that does not mean that governments are not involved in the regulatory practices implied by governance.

Governance is a commonplace category of the social and political discourse of the twenty-first century. Yet its meaning remains obscure if not ambiguous (Offe, 2009; Davies, 2011). When we try to capture a problem—or its solution—in terms of governance, we do not necessarily have in mind a specific prescriptive solution. For that matter, it is not a given that we can count on a solution as a proven problem-solving method. Nonetheless, we suggest that beyond these limits governance remains a theoretical pillar upon which we can build in order to better understand the social and political challenges cities are facing. This necessarily implies some clarification.

Above all, governance is a political discourse. It conveys the idea that to deal with current challenges, its emphasis on collaborative values is superior to the one carried on by the notion of "Government," defined as a centralized political authority (Piattoni, 2010). As Claus Offe underlined, "most of the time, governance is being used in contradiction to government understood as the state's competence to rule through hierarchy" (2009: 551). For that reason, the traditional division in democratic theory between state and civil society needs to be profoundly revised. We are no longer facing two completely distinct spheres whose boundaries are established once and for all. In fact, we are dealing with "two separate levels of analysis of a concrete reality in which they are inextricably intertwined" (Blanc, 2009: 217). Governance generally involves a questioning of the authoritarian and bureaucratic model of management, even though the orientation or the finality of its framework remains uncertain.

The successes of urban policies under governance are subject to interpretation due to the quality of co-operation—including power relationships—between those actors. From then on, if citizens who are representative of civil society can be invited to participate in the decision-making processes, what has to be clarified is under what conditions. The presence of citizens does mean that we assist at a "game without losers" as some are pretending. In other words, the presence of citizens is not enough to eliminate conflicts of interests and power relations. In that respect, a large diversity of situations prevails and remains subject to a contextual and empirical analysis.

What have public and private actors learned from governance with respect to the way contemporary societies choose to solve their urban problems? To what extent does governance improve the public and private actors' capacities to solve these problems? Is there a guarantee that thinking in terms of governance instead of government will help bring in original or sustainable solutions? Do social and political actors even have a choice nowadays but to think and act in reference to governance?

These questions invite researchers to consider both the theoretical as well as the empirical dimensions of governance. Consequently, we think it is important to explain how these two dimensions are linked.

The chapter is subdivided in two sections. The first section is dedicated to specifying the notion of governance from a sociological perspective. What are its main sociological dimensions? And what makes consensus in the literature on governance? For that matter, it becomes pertinent to consider the critiques addressed to the notion by many researchers in order to define, in a second step, our own position. We will then explore a possible venue for overcoming these criticisms. Beyond the limits inherent in the notion of governance, we continue to think it can be useful, especially if we define it in reference to a sociological perspective.

The second section focuses on governance as it has been applied to manage urban problems in the North American context, particularly considering cities and city-regions in Canada.

From Government to Governance: A Paradigmatic Shift?

Even though, as we have hinted, governance is a contested notion, the controversy surrounding it has not prevented its use by a growing number of social and political actors (Jouve, 2003). In the academic world, a consensus prevails that governance always includes the participation of non-state actors—coming either from civil society and/or the market—in the management of public affairs. But this does not imply that governance has the same restrictive meaning for popular political discourse. According to Niraja Gopal Jayal (2007), particularly in countries of the economical "south," the notion of governance as referred to by politicians and actors of the civil society takes a much more ideological turn—most of the time in reference to a neo-liberal vision that promotes the private sector's role in society—than in academia. For political actors and managers, governance becomes a recipe with some prescriptive tools—especially when talking in terms of "good governance"—that enable actors to bring in an essential "improvement in government" through processes (more transparency and accountability) and outputs, especially regarding the efficiency and quality of "public service delivery" (Jayal, 2007: 127). From the view of such political and social actors, it would be possible for them to leave aside their conflicts of interests. This is certainly nonsense as well as illusionary (Le Galès, 2002).

The sociology of governance is above all interested in the empirical and institutional configuration of actors and organizations. Sociology focuses on the understanding of social relationships; thus, for sociologists, governance is examined through social transformations, especially those that concern the relationship between state and society (Jouve, 2003; Hajer and Wagenaar, 2003). With governance, private actors—coming mainly from the business community and from civil society—are participating in managing public affairs with the state. As such, a redefinition of roles and actors is necessarily ongoing. That provided, does this mean governance introduces a paradigmatic shift in the study of public action?

A Sociological Perspective

Multiple entry points can be used to better understand the contribution of governance to the public debate about the management of public affairs. At the outset, we agree with several researchers (Jouve, 2003; Lascoumes and Le Galès, 2007; Blanc, 2009) that the notion reflects, in itself, the difficulty of managing complex modern societies through centralized and authoritarian models of government (please refer to Box 6.1). This is why governance necessitates a multiplicity of actors (state and non-state actors) to define and regulate public problems. If, for the time being, there is no satisfactory answer to the problem of regulating highly reflexive liberal societies that are more and more complex—where knowledge is increasing and easily available while, paradoxically, uncertainty is growing—the notion of governance underlines that we can no longer rely on vertical and hierarchical lines of decision-making, as implemented by traditional governments (Hamel and Jouve, 2006). Thus, it is not surprising that governance brings to the fore the shortcomings of governments due to the failure of traditional public policies. Such failures could be related to governments' difficulty in adapting to contextual changes; they resist abandoning or reforming their traditional models of bureaucratic management, models that are no longer appropriate in a knowledge society.

But we should also take into account the flip side of the coin. If the traditional state model is not reliable and if it is less legitimate, an alternative must be found. This is why governance also directs our attention toward new forms of interaction and organization between social, economic, and political actors concerned by the regulation of their respective sphere of activities.

These two sides of the coin are inevitably linked although their repercussions are not identical. The first aspect—the governmental crisis—requires engaging in a historical contextual analysis. The challenge here is to connect past events to the dominant forces in charge of the state in order to reconstruct the chain of changes that brought these forces to power or that has allowed them to stay in a dominant position. The second aspect—the restructuring of action based on multiplying networks (Castells, 1996) as the boundaries between public and private sectors are less stable than ever before—focuses on relations between public and private actors and examines the new conditions of co-operation offered to them. If contextual aspects remain important, they are not quite the same for both categories of actors. The analysis needs to concentrate on institutional constraints and opportunities, given the new forms of co-operation in which actors are involved.

Following these remarks, it remains uncertain if we are or are not witnessing a paradigm shift. A more careful examination of the theoretical scope and the limits of governance are first required. And, in that respect, investigating the notion from a sociological perspective can certainly help.

As Chris Ansel underlines, although no subfield labelled "sociology of governance" exists, "classical and contemporary sociology has much to say about the theory and practice of governance" (2006: 901). According to Ansel, sociological thought has tackled the problems of governance from at least three angles:

Box 6.1

Urban Governance in Retrospect

In order to better understand the way contemporary cities are produced and managed, the notion of governance has proven useful in spite of its biases and shortcomings. At the outset, the notion has been drawn from the literature in economics concerned with transaction costs. But in the field of urban studies, the notion soon became associated with urban regimes—i.e., coalitions able to influence decisions at city hall—defined around various issues, such as economic growth and development as well as the process of regulation involving social, economic, and political actors outside government. Thus, different models of urban governance, more or less open to an active presence of civil society, have been experimented with. Focusing on growth, management, defence of corporatist interests, or welfare, these models give local actors a say in making a difference within a specific national context. In other words, local politics matters and this can be explained by the way governance is being implemented locally.

When approaching the problems of government and/or the processes of governing from the angle of governance, researchers recognize that in advanced liberal democracies, the traditional basis of state power has lost some of its policy capacity. A consensus thus prevails around the fact that "public officials do not enjoy sufficient authority, or do not possess sufficient resources to produce legitimate and efficient policy measures by themselves" (Papadopoulos, 2012: 512). Since the 1980s, the planning and management of cities have relied more heavily on governance processes open to the presence and active participation of public and private networks of actors to achieve tasks traditionally performed by governments. In that respect, governance can be associated with changes in the importance of government. It can certainly be seen as "an alternative to government [as traditionally defined or perceived, we should add] to control by the state" (Hirst, 2000: 13).

These remarks do not imply that the state and its hierarchical authority have completely vanished, however. As David Levi-Faur underlines, "the state remains the pivotal player in establishing and operating governance strategies and partnerships" (2012: 12). Thus, this raises the question as to what shape the current transformation of the state will take. Governance is certainly raising more questions than providing answers:

> While there is much to suggest that this role of the state has changed, and continues to change, democratic government remains centred around the legitimacy of political institutions and the channels of representation, accountability, and consent between these institutions and the polity at large. As long as this remains the case, the issue of how the state transforms to accommodate emerging forms of governance remains a key issue in governance research. (Pierre, 2000: 242)

And this issue of how the state responds is unavoidable.

1. The sources of domination
2. The problems related to social cohesion
3. The specificity of the social world

Along with Karl Marx and Émile Durkheim, Max Weber has contributed more than anyone to research on the problems of governance. When he explored how rationalization has been produced by Western tradition and how it drastically changed the relations between structures and agency within modern societies, he clearly raised the issue of problems of governance:

> For Weber, rationalization was a process whereby "ends" and "means" were progressively clarified and then related systematically to one another. One important consequence of rationalization was the differentiation of institutional spheres—the economy, the political system, society, and religion. And rational-legal institutions like state bureaucracies became "means" to achieve the ends of state, with state officials developing "neutral competence" to serve these ends. (Ansel, 2006: 903)

Building on or differentiating themselves from the comprehensive understanding of society elaborated by Weber, contemporary sociologists have taken different paths to explore the foundations and manifestations of governance. In doing so, they arrived at theoretical perspectives that offer distinctive views. Governance can thus be examined either under the "theory of structuration" (Anthony Giddens), defined as an evolving relationship between actors and institutions; as a "social practice" (Pierre Bourdieu) conceived in relation to the underlying principles supporting regular types of conduct; or as a "disciplinary technology" (Michel Foucault) involved in social control (Ansel, 2006: 904). But there are specialized areas of sociology, such as economic sociology, sociology of organizations, and sociology of networks, that have also brought in original viewpoints on governance by focusing either on the role of private actors, the rule followed by organizations, or the way alliances are connected to channels of influence.

Over the past decades, different specialized fields of the social sciences, including research on governance, have highlighted an increasing preoccupation with the role of the public sphere in the democratization of public policies. For example, in order to "strengthen institutional frameworks of the public sphere" (Offe, 2008: 19), Claus Offe suggests different courses of action. First, he replaces the traditional level of "classical meta-policy"—usually defined in line with a technocratic and top-down definition of problems—with a pragmatic advocacy approach, calling upon the use of new communicative technologies that are open to citizen participation. Second, he emphasizes "cognitive and epistemic rather than motivational and value-related aspects of the political process" (Offe, 2008: 20). The idea is for actors to put aside value conflicts while insisting on policy options. Thus, new frames for communication need to be created. The objective here is to encourage a better understanding of the interaction between actors, as well as to allow for a judicious evaluation of problems. This seems a prerequisite for building consensus about policies or public action. Finally, Offe believes that introducing deliberative procedures for informing political practices that are distinct from the current decision-making process is also required. In other words, the two sides of policy—"analysis and deliberation" on the one hand, and "decision and implementation" on the other—have to take place within a strong public sphere, where the interaction between the two can contribute to providing satisfactory outputs.

Again, all of these aspects are influenced by contextual factors that are part of a historical tradition. But the configuration of political forces in a given environment also needs to be taken into account. Indeed, the common trust required in order for deliberative governance—i.e., oriented toward achieving collective decisions through a rational and equitable conversation among participants—to effectively work implies putting aside traditional and secretive approaches to politics, at least from a critical democratic standpoint (Hajer, 2009). If deliberative democracy always implies "the need to justify decisions made by citizens and their representatives" (Gutmann and Thompson, 2004: 3), this is not necessarily the case with governance, where the focus is usually turned toward the outcomes produced by collective decisions.

Here we come upon the interface between "deliberative democracy" and "governance," which in turn raises concerns about the incidence of governance in regards to political processes of democratization. While governance may involve at times "strategic bargaining" between actors (Papadopoulos, 2002), at the outset deliberative democracy defines social interaction from another point of view. In fact, deliberation always implies conditions that go along with an understanding of the public sphere, driven by institutional arrangements open to justice (Bohman, 2007). Deliberation implies communication that is respectful of the reasons given by citizens and their representatives. If it does not mean that all principles and reasons given by citizens are equally valid, it does mean that to be effective, deliberation implies the acceptance of two normative principles: (1) inclusiveness, favouring the openness of debate to all citizens; and (2) equity, meaning that citizens can co-operate freely and that the weight of their arguments is considered in itself.

On the Criticism of Governance

An elitist theory of politics was dominant in real politics during the Great Depression of the 1930s and after World War II to support growth and reduce social inequalities. In an elitist theory of politics, despite the prevailing democratic representative system, political power remains in the hands of a small group of people who come mainly from major economic sectors and who are able to influence decision makers. This theory, however, started to lose its legitimacy in the 1970s for two reasons. First, social demands were increasingly diversified, following a profound restructuring of the economy and of social relationships, including social relationships toward space. Second, it is the very legitimacy of the state that is now at stake in this restructuring as the state, defined as a strong actor, is no longer in control of the situation as it used to be. This can be explained by the diversity of social demands, due in part to the nature of those demands, but also by a lack of resources.

These factors have consequently transformed the way public action is perceived. The state is no longer considered the sole provider of the public good. As a result, and as mentioned, public action must involve a multitude of actors, both public and private, coming from governments, and/or private businesses, and/or civil society.

The notion of governance has given rise to many criticisms (Blanc, 2009). In the field of international development, during the 1990s, the notion was used as an excuse to expand the scope of international agencies and protect the neo-liberal framework while "criticism of structural adjustment programs proved being very intense" (Fisette and Raffinot, 2010: 8).

By opening the door to an active participation of private businesses in the social and political regulation, many were concerned about the resulting consequences in terms of state capacity to promote the public good. Quoting Jean Leca, Ali Kazancigil (2010: 38) underlines, for instance, that governance means, primarily, a "withdrawal" of the state for the benefit of the market. Thus, the "spirit of governance" would correspond directly to "the invasion of politics and society by the market logic" (Kazancigil, 2010: 40). This perspective has necessarily contributed to undermining the legitimacy of governance in the political arena.[2]

To these critiques, one can add the one that was made some years ago to neo-corporatism, an institutional arrangement where economically dominant actors are invited to take part in processes of social and economic regulation along with the state's representatives. In many respects, mechanisms of governance are similar or can be assimilated to the ones elaborated under neo-corporatist frameworks (Jessop, 1979). Institutional rules set for neo-corporatism tend to favour the best organized and most powerful actors at the expense of representatives of community organizations or social movements. Social actors with fewer resources, then, are disadvantaged in the case of governance, just as they were in the case of neo-corporatism. It is more difficult for representatives of community organizations or social actors to take part in the exchanges and co-operation processes elaborated by authorities. As a result, we can say that governance does not ensure a fair representation of the whole society.

These critical elements thrown pell-mell reflect a number of limitations inherent in the notion of governance, although it has become difficult to deal without governance as governments need to adapt to contextual changes. That is, the difficulties of the notion of governance echo, in different ways, the drastic changes that have occurred in recent years in the relations between the economic, political, and social spheres. In other words, notwithstanding the above critiques, and even if governance does not always coincide with processes of democratization of public management—and, in fact, is often far from those processes—governance does allow us to explore how public action is being redefined while the state cannot bear alone the legitimacy of the public good.

Governing Cities

As we have seen up until now in the book, urban problems are multidimensional; as a result, it is never appropriate to address specific urban problems without taking into account the repercussions a suggested course of action may have on other aspects or issues. For example, when local authorities have to solve a particular problem regarding housing, transportation, or environmental concerns, all of the economic, social, and geographic components of the city are involved and must thus be considered as much as possible when dealing with said challenge.

Nowadays, for urban actors governance is usually taken for granted. Researchers, professionals, and political elites usually refer to governance as something that is part of their cultural mindset. Most of the time, they simply assume that the management of urban affairs has to be treated according to the framework of governance. But it is not that simple: Do the actors understand the same thing or do they all have the same notion in mind when they refer to the idea and practice of governance? Is there a consensus within the field of urban studies regarding urban governance? What about the citizen participation often associated with governance? Does such participation necessarily entail democratizing public management?

The Main Components of Urban Governance

Since the middle of the 1970s, urban processes have become increasingly diversified and fragmented. As the city form is submitted to constant restructuring due to economic, technological, and cultural pressures, the future of city development is difficult to apprehend, and even more so to regulate, if one wishes to overcome the socio-economic inequalities entrenched in city life (Fraser, 1996).

For inhabitants, the experience of living in the current urban reality brings up different problems of livability. Characterized by an ongoing process of change, itself accelerated by the expansion of new technologies of communication—especially within large urban regions—cities are submitted to unexpected challenges. While the availability of information about cities has never been so great, fragmentation and social polarization have risen nonetheless. In other words, if for social actors the possibility of expressing diversity and singularity is easier due to the availability of new technologies of communication, social recognition, and belonging as well as a greater capacity to make choices do not necessarily follow (Bauman, 2001).

Given the complexity of urban problems and, since the 1970s, the necessity for cities to adapt to globalizing forces, governance may be defined as "a problem to solve for public action" (Le Galès, 1995: 89), a view that has been supported by several researchers (Lefèvre, 1998). This position underlines the fact that in order to understand the management of cities, it is not enough to simply look at the relationship between the higher tier of the state and the municipalities. Above all, it is necessary to take into account the interactions between the state and civil society, including the network of economic actors (Le Galès, 1995).

Consequently, the institutional complexities within which cities evolve always inform us of the particular circumstances under which strategic behaviour can be defined. As Hank V. Savitch and Paul Kantor (2002) have shown by comparing 10 cities in Europe and North America, cities *do* have choices and *can* act strategically. To highlight cities' options, we have to consider the series of factors that interact with each other and influence the decision-making process: market conditions, intergovernmental support, popular control, local political tradition, and culture.

If the market conditions remain important everywhere, their negative disposition can be compensated for by intergovernmental support. In other words, when the economy is not at the rendezvous, state investment can take the relay. Of course, cities that experience little in the way of investments or that suffer from poor market conditions and receive little governmental support are more vulnerable than those that do receive a lot of support. As a result, such cities tend to make more concessions to businesses in terms of reducing their requirements in relation to existing regulations. But the tradeoff remains a political choice. It is always possible, even in the face of adversity, not to give way to the lure of rapid local economic development.

The path chosen by municipalities when facing adversity is based on governance mechanisms that differ greatly from one city to the next. There is no one best way to make a tradeoff between contradictory objectives, such as promoting development versus struggling against social inequalities (Le Galès, 2002). The representation of interests and the capacity to build local compromises are thus reflected in the trajectory of each city. But this is also a function of the political leadership as defined by local politics (Haus and Klausen, 2010).

In reference to governance, cities' initiatives are influenced by several factors, including social and racial compositions. However, within Western European countries the initiatives or projects defined by cities for modernizing their public services continue to be supported by the state. Consequently, Western European cities are usually less threatened by global competitiveness than their North American counterparts, especially cities in the United States. If in the United States urban governance is often associated with privatization of public services and public–private partnerships, in Europe the political sphere remains at the forefront of urban management (Le Galès, 2002).

At the same time, we must distance ourselves from an overly simplistic interpretation of the transformations occurring in American cities. Through a thorough comparative analysis of eight American cities, Susan E. Clarke underlines that "market-based institutional orders are not pervasive" (1995: 527). In cities like Seattle, for example, that have what Clarke names "state/ democratic institutional orders" characterized by strong democratic decision processes, citizen organizations play an important role. In other places, like Dayton (Ohio), one can find a decentralized political structure. But Clarke also recalls that beyond the direct role assumed by localities, the federal government has proven to be "a major source of local institutional transformation" (Clarke, 1995: 527). Even when Washington decided to cut federal funding supporting local economic development, in some cities this triggered new attempts toward a renewal of "democratic policy control" from city councils.

Within the context of governance, politicians face new institutional constraints. This is directly related to "a new normative and conceptual understanding of democracy" (Bohman, 2007: 3). They have no choice but to cope with the fact that in the context of the current modernity, increasing pluralism of interests has resulted in the obsolescence of traditional systems of representation. Consequently, participatory mechanisms open to public consultation and to deliberation are now parts of the municipal administrative landscape (Bacqué and Sintomer, 2011). The implementation of such participatory policies and measures for taking the pulse of the population is not only compulsory, but has also radically altered decision-making processes, introducing for political actors on the local scene the constraints of transparency and accountability.

Nonetheless, the transformations taking place in the public scene in relation to the local state do not solve issues of social and political conflict and power. It is not because citizens are now more frequently invited by city councils to voice their opinions on urban projects that they are necessarily in a position to influence in a significant way the future of their cities. Ultimately, those who are able to control the decision-making process remain the ones with more resources. Thus far, what it takes for citizens in general to be capable of significantly influencing decision-making processes has not been defined satisfactorily. Indeed, if we review the literature on participation, at best we find ambivalent interpretation of participatory experiences (Bacqué, Rey, and Sintomer, 2005). This can be explained by the fact that, according to a quantitative assessment, citizen participation is often weaker than expected. Its direct impacts are often quite limited (Rui, 2004), and citizen participation may even contribute to reducing the coherence of public action, at least when evaluated from a republican perspective (Hérault, 2008).

Up to a certain extent, even if the introduction of citizen participatory mechanisms can change the rules of the political game, this does not automatically alter the configuration of power. Despite the rhetoric, when referring to participatory democracy per se, urban governance does not imply an increase in direct democratic control. If, for the promoters of governance, participation can be viewed as a challenge, it remains only one scenario among several other possibilities (Lafaye, 2006).

In light of urban governance, citizen participation has not gained complete credibility (Rui, 2004). In most cases, the resources presented to citizens to give them an opportunity to participate in the planning process are insufficient. In addition, the difficulties that citizens encounter are, in a sense, structural. Because governance does not address the fundamental conflicts underlying urban problems, thinking in reference to governance does not give citizens a better say. In addition to this, conflicts and contradictions are not only defined at the city level, but increasingly are weighted at the scale of metropolitan areas, as was explained in Chapter 4 and as we consider again more closely next.

From Local to Metropolitan Governance

If local citizen participation does not always reach its goals within cities, this is even more problematic on a metropolitan scale. As we have commented previously, urban problems no longer arise exclusively at the neighbourhood and/or city level but increasingly at a metropolitan or city-region scale.

Yet, in most cases, metropolitan institutions are not strong enough— under the purview of legitimate power—to support citizens' social identification and recognition in terms of their capacity to empower themselves. The uncertain character of metropolitan institutions and their lack of resources and legitimacy do not allow social actors to refer to them with much confidence (Hamel, 2005). This can explain why citizen participation has proven to be weaker on the metropolitan scene than at the level of cities or boroughs. Nevertheless, even if its legitimacy remains weak (Lefèvre, 2009), the fact that the metropolitan scale has become a specific political space of its own leads us to rethink the traditional model of analysis of the city—one that used to primarily reflect the concerns of the central city and its prerogatives over those of the suburbs (Jouve, 2005).

For several decades, urban problems, especially in the United States, have been concentrated within inner cities. And for many urban areas, this is still the case due to a conjunction of factors. First, cities are submitted to the competition for economic growth. In other words, due to the pressure coming from an increased international competitiveness, cities are in conflict with one another for attracting investment, companies, and jobs. Second, liberal regulation does not generally direct households in their choice of residential location. And third, in many communities—due to social and political reasons—control and orientation of spatial development has been minimal. The market rules prevail everywhere and the consequences are well known: poverty concentrates in the central districts of cities, where most social problems also take place; urban decay necessarily follows, largely explained by de-investment in these districts or neighbourhoods.

And so the urban dynamic becomes a kind of vicious circle. The poor quality of life that central cities offer to inhabitants—due to, among other things, a lack of resources—encourages affluent households to flee to the suburbs. The consequences are direct in respect of local finance: municipal governments find themselves with fewer resources to meet their obligations in terms of improving the quality of services and infrastructure, which would encourage inhabitants to stay or would welcome newcomers.

This dire situation was clearly underlined by Richard Nixon in his 1970 State of the Union message when he declared, "The violent and decayed central cities of our great metropolitan complexes are the most conspicuous failure in American life today. I propose that before these problems become insoluble, the Nation develop a national growth policy . . ." (Nixon, quoted by Dreier, Mollenkopf, and Swanstrom, 2001: 33). And we know that the state of urban affairs in central cities did not improve afterward this message. As Peter Dreier, John Mollenkopf, and Todd Swanstrom mention, even if Nixon's project could have been promising, it never obtained Congress's approval. After that, the "conservatives have attacked national land-use planning as an unwarranted interference in the marketplace" (2001: 33).

Local authorities have since been struggling to overcome the decaying processes through the deterioration of the urban fabric and the increased poverty affecting urban neighbourhoods. Among the solutions developed, the **new regionalism** is certainly the best-known approach (Orfield, 2002; Savitch and Vogel, 2000; Rusk, 1993). In a very schematic way, we can say that new regionalists have proposed to establish a dialogue at a regional level between central cities and suburbs, in the spirit of governance, in order to support co-operative mechanisms able to face urban issues defined at a metro or regional scale. Among the principles promoted by new regionalists, the most consensual is the following: that the costs of city services that benefit all residents of a region need to be shared by all residents of the region, including those living in the suburbs. New regionalists believe that the dynamism of suburbs cannot exist without that of the central city.[3]

New regionalists thus find it necessary to see urban reality through the lens of a metropolitan interdependence among all the local units that are part of an area. The main urban challenges—sprawl, social segregation, economic decline of inner cities, threats to the environment from urban growth—therefore need to be addressed through co-operation among all the municipalities of a given metropolitan area. In that respect, it becomes necessary to first overcome inter-metropolitan competition. At the same time, one must be aware of the increasing competition between metropolitan regions at a global level (Lesage and Stefanick, 2004). But how can the vision of the new regionalists be achieved in a practical way?

The new regionalist perspective primarily calls upon voluntary and horizontal coordination among key actors to promote regional cohesion for the best interests of the metropolitan region and its inhabitants. Although this principle is in line with the idea of governance, the results are far from convincing. The types of arrangements that occur among municipalities and other groups concerned by addressing metropolitan issues favour, most of the time, the interests of major economic actors (Goldsmith, 2001). As Joel Rast (2006) highlights, for the United States, minority stakeholders—such as African-Americans and Latinos along with other minorities—have not been included in these debates and in the institutional arrangements coming out of such debates.

In the current context of globalization, urban and metropolitan governance goes hand in hand with a process of territorial rescaling, "defined as the remaking or the reconfiguration of land in order to exercise decisional and policy control" (Savitch, 2007: 134). The objective of cities involved in such processes on a metropolitan scale is to strengthen their capacity for action but also to find a way to adapt to the restructuring produced by globalization. "Rescaling" is a geographical but also a political notion, suggesting that change of scale occurs in political regulation. In other words, rescaling is a redefinition of the political order that is at stake. When the new regionalists introduced concerns over metropolitan issues in the 1990s, redistribution of resources by the state gave way to concerns primarily economic in nature.

On a world scale, if national states remain important actors for mediating economic, social, and political relations (Brenner, 2004), their responsibility is often shared with decentralized territorial units but also with supra local institutions, such as metropolitan institutions (like the one that was implemented for the Montréal city-region, as we will see). In this respect, we can talk of an "imbrication of all scales" (Brenner, 2000: 368), which may be illustrated by the strategies chosen by the state and local political actors in the case of Toronto and Montréal.

Rescaling Urban Governance in Canada

At the outset, we have to keep in mind the important difference between American and Canadian cities. In Canada, municipalities are not autonomous institutions as they are in the United States. According to the Canadian constitution, municipalities' authority comes exclusively from the provinces. Municipalities are, therefore, directly accountable to provincial laws, and provinces can always decide to redesign municipalities' territorial boundaries, powers, and obligations. As a result, provinces in Canada have recently been able to reform the municipal system in a prescriptive way, imposing municipal amalgamation, which would have been unthinkable in the United States without the consent of the municipalities involved. In that respect, the cases of Toronto and Montréal are exemplary.

Toronto Amalgamation

The amalgamation of various municipalities to create the "megacity" of Toronto occurred January 1, 1998. Previously, the city was already organized, at a regional level, with a two-tier system of municipal government that went back to 1953. The metropolitan tier was in charge of regional issues (mainly water supply and sewage disposal, solid waste management, social services, and public transit) while local municipalities kept their autonomy in regards to other traditional municipal services. The metropolitan tier brought together thirteen municipalities of the metropolitan area, which were reduced to six in 1967: "The provincial government, which had introduced this momentous and far-reaching model of two-tier governance, saw the opportunity at the time, to use the exploding and rich tax base of the job-rich central city to subsidize development in the suburban areas" (Boudreau et al., 2006: 32).

The decision to amalgamate the municipalities of Metropolitan Toronto was taken by the provincial government in 1997, which was under the control of a conservative party elected in 1995 and defending a neo-liberal ideology (Boudreau et al., 2007). The reason given by the government for imposing such an amalgamation, against the will of a large part of the population of the central city, was to gain efficiency and realize economies of scale at the local level with the objective of reducing taxes. For that matter, some services were totally or partially transferred to the municipality (for example, social housing, roads, and provincial offences courts).

Toronto has been a fast-growing metropolitan region since the middle of the nineteenth century.[4] Such growth never ceased to contribute to expanding the limits of the metropolitan area. If the regional body instituted in 1953—the Municipality of Metropolitan Toronto—then covered an important part of the metropolitan area, this was no longer the case in 1997. In the 1980s, even if the provincial government had created the Greater Toronto Area (GTA) for administrative reasons, this authority did not have any direct political representation. Moreover, the GTA no longer serves as a space of representation that citizens and professionals refer to as the metropolitan region; instead, that territory is the Greater Golden Horseshoe, "the actually meaningful space in which the metropolitan region has to be rethought. The Greater Golden Horseshoe begins to replace the GTA as the operative term and area in which the region is envisioned" (Boudreau et al, 2006: 47). However, this area does not have any formal status at the time being.

It is true that co-operation concerning transportation and school taxes was taking place at a regional level following the amalgamation that created the megacity of Toronto. In 1998, the Greater Toronto Services Board (GTSB) was implemented, bringing together the megacity of Toronto with 24 other municipalities of the area. But the GTSB was dismantled in 2001 after a very

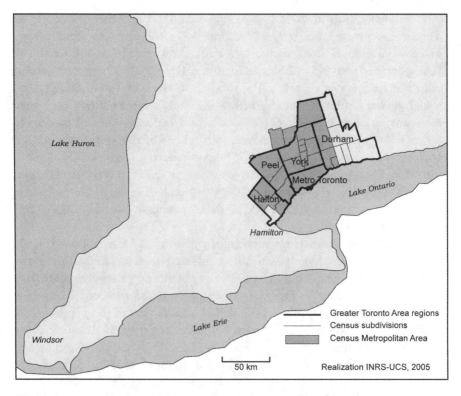

Map 6.1 Greater Toronto Area, Golden Horseshoe, and Municipalities of Toronto
Source: Boudreau, J. et al. 2006. "Comparing Metropolitan Governance: The Cases of Montréal and Toronto."
Progress in Planning 66, p.15.

short period of activity. The state's intention was mainly to plan and manage some services, such as school taxes and transportation, on a regional scale.

Montréal Amalgamation

Compared with Toronto, the Montréal case is, in a sense, more complex. Inspired by the amalgamation process of the "Queen City," the Québec government decided at the end of the 1990s that the management of the whole municipal system needed improvement. Metropolitan areas were thus included in the envisioned reform, starting with Montréal.[5]

As was the case for Toronto, prior to the implementation of the urban and metropolitan reform, a second tier of management also existed in Montréal. Created at the end of the 1960s by the provincial government for solving problems of financing security—and mainly, the costs of police forces for the City of Montréal—the Montréal Urban Community (MUC) brought together the 28 local municipalities on the Island of Montréal. The MUC was in charge of managing the police force, but other services and functions were also added to MUC's charges, such as public transportation, environmental planning, and economic international promotion.

Because the MUC was no longer able to accept the fiscal burden of the central city, by the end of the 1990s the provincial government decided to implement a major reform for the Montréal region in two steps. The intention was to improve the quality and efficiency of public services while also addressing concerns for justice and equity regarding the costs and access to these services.

The first reform consisted of abolishing the MUC and amalgamating the 28 municipalities existing on Montréal Island. That decision led to the creation of the new bigger City of Montréal. But the government's intention was also to update the city management structure. It meant that urban governance would need to be shared with an infra-municipal tier, the borough and its council.

The boroughs were defined from the previous inner suburbs—some of which have been combined—with the addition of old urban neighbourhoods of the former City of Montréal. Twenty-seven boroughs' local councils were then responsible for managing proximity services, which meant that the new City of Montréal had to share municipal responsibilities with these boroughs. Some services and functions are thus managed by the boroughs, such as waste removal, cultural and recreational activities, and local economic development but with coordination at the city level, while other functions, such as fire prevention, are exclusively taken care of by the boroughs. However, the boroughs still remain under the responsibility of the city council. Except for special taxes and expenses, their budget is allocated to them by the city council. Therefore, if the boroughs play an important role in the management of services and infrastructure, their responsibility is secondary in terms of major decisions regarding urban development.[6]

The second step of the reform was to bring together the 82 municipalities of the census metropolitan area (CMA) under the umbrella of the Montréal Metropolitan Community (MMC). The intention was then to establish a strategic authority at the city-region scale for managing equipment and services that are regional in scope—such as the Botanical Garden of Montréal—and to introduce planning for issues whose understanding required a metropolitan perspective, which is the case for international promotion or environmental concerns. This is why the government gave the MMC the mandate of elaborating an economic development plan. The main goal of this document was to define "a strategic vision of economic, social, and environmental development aiming at facilitating a coherent exercise of the Community's powers" (Gouvernement du Québec, 2000: Article 127, par. 1). A first draft of this plan was completed in 2005 followed by a regional comprehensive plan in 2012.

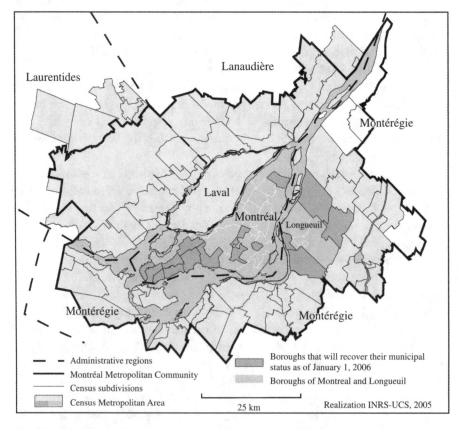

Map 6.2 Boroughs, Municipalities, and Metropolitan Region of Montréal
Source: Boudreau, J. et al. 2006. "Comparing Metropolitan Governance: The Cases of Montréal and Toronto." *Progress in Planning 66*, p.16.

A Comparison of Toronto and Montréal

Urban and metropolitan reforms have not been equally successful in Toronto and Montréal. In Toronto, the stakes were not as high as they were in Montréal as Toronto's economic situation was much better at the time of the reform. More importantly, the decision to impose amalgamation on the local units forming the Municipality of Metropolitan Toronto, in 1997, was less a problem than proved to be the case for Montréal—even though "intense opposition and controversies" were also manifest in Toronto (Boudreau et al., 2006)—because these units had been working together for quite some time. In addition, the Toronto reform demanded the coordination of fewer units. Finally, the municipalities in the Toronto case did not have to adjust to the new burden of a de-amalgamation process, as was the case in Montréal.

In many ways, it was less of a problem for Toronto to integrate municipalities into a common system of management even though in both cities there was dissimilarity between the management culture of the central city and that of the suburbs. But in Montréal, these two cultures were more separate and quite unfamiliar with each other. The new boroughs created from previous neighbourhoods of the former Montréal had quite a lot to accomplish before they could even start to be as efficient as inner city suburbs. Ten years after the reform, more or less serious problems of coordination between the boroughs and the city remain in Montréal, and the economies of scale promised by the reform are still awaited.

In both cases, the reform was conducted with a top-down approach, which largely contradicts the representations and values of governance. Despite this, in the case of Montréal, the Québec government did not restrain itself from making reference to governance even though its strategy for implementing such reform was clearly technocratic (Hamel, 2001).

Urban and metropolitan problems faced by Toronto and Montréal are both similar and quite different. In the two cases, the urban and metropolitan reforms implemented to cope with the cities' problems failed, in different way, to find adequate answers. For Toronto, the clash between urban and suburban values was not addressed by the reform. But the fact that the larger scale of the city-region—the GTA and even beyond—with its environmental and social concerns was not taken care of by the megacity is worrying above all. In the case of Montréal, even though the provincial government and the municipalities have used various scales for redefining the governance of urban and metropolitan issues, they remain caught in a major contradiction, one that has prevailed since the 1960s. On the one hand, from a discursive standpoint, the provincial government seems willing to support the creation of a strong city-region able to modernize its industrial base, to be innovative in the leading sectors, and capable of attracting investments and resources to compete continentally and globally. On the other hand, strengthening the legitimacy and the power of Montréal in the context of a contested federalism—Montréal already represents 49 per cent of the total Québec population and 49 per cent of its gross domestic product—does not receive the consent of the entire political class,[7] to say the least.

As mentioned previously, urban multi-faceted problems can no longer be defined exclusively at a neighbourhood or city level; they are increasingly metropolitan in their scope and consequences. Besides their respective limits, urban reforms in Toronto and Montréal were intended to address issues of urban development specific to these cities in a continental and international context, up to a certain extent by taking into account the metropolitan dimension.

Multi-level governance usually implies taking into account the multiple levels of governing involved in "negotiated, non-hierarchical exchanges between institutions at the transnational, national, regional and local levels" (Peters and Pierre, 2001:132). This is not exactly what happened when the new model of urban governance was implemented in the two cities if we consider at least the relations between provincial and local levels. The top-down approach prevailing in both cases necessarily contradicts the idea of multi-level governance (Piattoni, 2010). Nevertheless, once the new urban systems were in place, their functioning had no choice but to adapt to the requisites of multi-level governance. Processes of de-territorialization and re-territorialization(meaning that these two processes are involved in the state's changing relations to urban areas)—due to the regulation imposed by provincial states—gave way to a restructuring of public action in line with a "multiscalar" governance (Brenner, 2004).

However, as Neil Bradford (2004) has correctly underlined, the Canadian situation is far less developed than what has been experienced since the 1990s in Europe and in the United States with their new focus on urban development. Due to the wait-and-see position of the federal government with respect to urban affairs, a growing mismatch between municipalities and the available policy resources are making things difficult for cities: "given constitutional realities, inter-governmental rivalries, entrenched bureaucratic routines, and Canada's diverse urban landscape, progress in developing multi-level governance will take time" (Bradford, 2004: 44). But it is underway.

This lukewarm optimism relies above all on citizens' active participation in urban affairs. If government's attitudes toward urban governance are going to change in the coming years, an active involvement of citizens will be required (Aubin, 2010). Indeed, citizens' capacity to obtain more resources from the state and new regulations for better governing cities is what will make the difference. The issues are numerous: reduction of poverty in several areas, environmental concerns, improvement of infrastructure, and urban amenities. In the past, the mobilization of citizens at the city level succeeded in bringing concerns about social justice to the forefront, leading to better redistributive policies from the state, especially in regards to social housing and urban services. With the unfolding of the third millennium, urban issues are clearly defined at a metropolitan scale and involve multi-level governance.

Dealing with contradictory economic and social demands at the metropolitan scale, politicians have difficulty mediating the conflicting interests between two opposing visions of development: one in favour of promoting social cohesion; the other, of supporting competitiveness in the global market. But the way out of this stalemate can only be achieved through an active debate supported by fair procedures at different scales of urban governance. If we look more specifically at the case of Montréal, the city was associated in the past with a form of multi-governance that was "quite unstable" (Bherer and Hamel, 2012: 130). With the action of citizens, however, this situation could be on the verge of being transformed under some conditions. One of them would be that citizens resume the spirit of the urban movements of the 1970s and 1980s, which have contributed to the modernization of urban planning and to the democratization of city hall (Hamel, 2008).

Conclusion

After introducing the concept and practices of governance, presenting its main components, and examining some of its concrete manifestations, it is necessary to return to the question raised in the first section of this chapter: is governance bringing in a paradigmatic shift with respect to the study of public action? In the previous pages we have tried to stay as far away as possible from normative dimensions that seem to be recurrent in discourses and analyses of governance in the field of public policy. We have chosen instead to define governance in reference to a research program.

Up to a certain extent, we cannot answer affirmatively to the question of paradigmatic change introduced by governance in regards to redefining public action—because, according to our definition, governance has not yet contributed to rethinking and redefining a new socio-political compromise. Indeed, government has neither the legitimacy nor the resources to regulate urban development satisfactorily. And government fails to achieve the democratizing policies that the new forms of co-operation between public and private actors are targeting. In other words, and to paraphrase Zygmunt Bauman (2000), structural contradictions of current urban development do not dissolve in the "liquidity" of governance.

Modes of regulation that prevailed in the industrial society are no longer effective in twenty-first century societies. The compromise reached at the end of the nineteenth century between the bourgeoisie and the working class must therefore be revised in light of the new social relations that take place within a reflexive modernity, where the diversity of experience by individuals plays a crucial role in political regulation (Wagner, 2008).

In this chapter, we have presented governance from a socio-political standpoint. Beyond the numerous limits inherent in the notion, we nevertheless think that its theoretical implications remain useful to better understand the complexity of social and political interactions involved in public action, which characterize city planning in the metropolitan era.

Questions for Critical Thought

1. How would you define urban governance?
2. What are the main components of governance?
3. Can new regionalists solve the urban problems of our times?
4. Is there a difference between Canada and the United States regarding urban governance?
5. Do you think that, in the field of urban studies, governance is able to carry out a paradigmatic shift?

Suggested Readings

Dreier, P., J. Mollenkopf, and T. Swanstrom. 2001. *Place Matters: Metropolitics for the Twenty-first Century*. Lawrence, KS: University Press of Kansas. London: Edward Arnold. Aware of the current impoverishment process in US cities, the authors of this stimulating book—already considered a classic of urban studies—deconstruct economic segregation at play in these cities and underline the importance of the political issues involved. How do we overcome the decline of central cities in the American context? The solution of "metropolitics," according to these authors, is based on bringing together suburbs and central cities. This is a requisite for combating urban sprawl and sharing resources in order to overcome economic and social segregation.

Le Galès, P. 2002. *European Cities: Social Conflicts and Governance*. Oxford: Oxford University Press. This is an ambitious and well-written book. The author's objective is, above all, to trace the contours and orientations of Western European cities. In that respect, he looks at the relations between the states and their cities. He finds that despite their growing importance, cities remain fragmented. Within the context of globalization and also because of the building of the European Union, cities are facing new constraints and opportunities. Most of the time, cities have succeeded in building compromises between economic development and social and cultural integration. But the forms of governance they produce serve to reveal themselves as quite diverse.

Sancton, A. 1994. *Governing Canada's City-Regions: Adapting Form to Function*. Montréal: The Institute for Research of Public Policy. This is a challenging book because in the face of the dominant urban reformist approach, the author is defending the autonomy of municipalities. Thus, he finds it important to underline the functional capacity of local governments. He also gives a detailed account of the different tier systems of urban governance in Canada. Interested above all in the history of city-regions, the author presents a stimulating comparative analysis of Canada's metropolitan governments.

Savitch, H.V. and P. Kantor. 2004. *Cities in the International Market Place: The Political Economy of Urban Development in North America and Western Europe*. Princeton, NJ: Princeton University Press. The choices made by cities in terms of economic and urban development are not entirely determined by economic factors. Cities do have choices. This does not mean that global constraints do not exist, but some cities have managed to give themselves greater leeway in their choices than other cities have. Why is this so? In order to answer this question, the authors compare in a systematic way 10 cities and their local communities in Europe and North America. They show that public resources can sometimes compensate for market failure.

Related Websites

Hertie School of Governance
http://hertie-school.org

Located in Berlin, the Hertie School of Governance is dedicated to research and graduate training in the field of governance and public policy. In 2005, the school received official state recognition to confer the academic title "Master of Public Policy." Three research clusters are identified: (1) political economy; (2) European and global governance; and (3) organization, management, and leadership. Publication lists and working papers regarding governance and policy issues can be downloaded from this website.

Urban Institute Center on International Development and Governance
www.urban.org/center/idg/about/

The mission of the Urban Institute is to conduct research and assess programs while providing technical assistance overseas regarding policy-making. But the Urban Institute is also committed to continuing training on social and economic issues. Promoting "an integrated approach to local governance and economic development," the Institute supports research and intervention in developing countries. Several research reports and publications are available on the website.

UN-Habitat: For a Better Human Future
www.unhabitat.org/

UN-Habitat is the site of the United Nations agency for human settlements. It has been mandated by the UN General Assembly "to promote socially and environmentally sustainable towns and cities with the goal of providing adequate shelter for all." Several important statements defining the mandate of the organization can be downloaded from the website, such as the Vancouver Declaration on Human Settlements or the Istanbul Declaration on Human Settlements.

7 The City and Urban Planning Models

Learning Objectives

◎ To briefly review the main ideas in urban planning

◎ To assess their use and implementation

◎ To present planning practices in Canadian cities

◎ To present criticisms to dominant planning ideas and practices

---

Introduction

The industrial city represented the epitome of the modern way of life as the industrial revolution represented a huge step in human progress. To announce its demise would be an exaggeration, but one cannot help but notice that things have greatly changed (Xu and Ye, 2011). Conurbations and megalopolises (very large urbanized areas that contain tens of million of inhabitants) have replaced the loosely bounded city of the industrial age.

This chapter will examine the dominant urban planning models of the twentieth century, and compare and assess them. It will discuss how planning models fared against urban reality, and how far they were applied to complex and changing metropolises. Finally, the chapter will examine recent planning practices in the three largest Canadian cities, Montréal, Toronto, and Vancouver, and link these practices to the planning literature.

Urban Planning Models

For the past 150 years, thinkers, professionals, and social movements were very productive in drawing models of the ideal city. This is an ancient tradition, but it sped up with the industrial city. People were dissatisfied with the kind of city that they were living in and that was continuing to develop. Despite improving conditions, criticisms, owing to non-stop urbanization, did not end. On the contrary, by the turn of the twentieth century and even in the middle of the same century, urban models were still proposed and explored by professionals and reformists alike.

An urban planning model or urban model is, first of all, a spatial model. Cities are spatial units, more or less bound by visible and identifiable limits, such as a river, and imposed by political decision. This spatial unit is tri-dimensional, for cities expand three ways: by width, by length, and by height. Buildings, monuments, and infrastructure are deployed in this three-spaced manner, although height is seldom taken into account in urban statistics. Notably, height may be an issue for planning regulations and zoning. When high-rises first appeared on the urban landscape, local governments had to decide where they could be located and built. People didn't want a high-rise close to their houses or fronting a school. **Zoning** was a planning tool very often used—especially in North America, where it was invented—for segregating building types (height, in particular) and function (between residential and industrial, for example) and, in so doing, for segregating social groups with the help of a building code (Scott, 1969; Grant, 2008: 24).

Second, an urban model is often some kind of social blueprint. Whether utopian or pragmatic, forward-looking or craving the past, urban models contain some social ideals or statements. The social dimension may not always be clearly stated, but no model is exempt from a social project.

Third, an urban model has a symbolic function. In distributing people and things in space, at least on paper, an urban model aims at communicating some desirable values and ends. That a city centre should be occupied by government buildings, or financial institutions, or by cultural facilities is loaded with meanings as to what is important, what is vital, and what is central to city life. This is not so different from medieval cities, where the city centre housed the religious, political, and mercantile institutions.

Fourth, an urban model has a double function: solving actual problems and projecting the city in the future. Since city planning is a long-term business, because infrastructure, layouts, and buildings will last for quite some time, urban forms resist rapid change. They show, in Hommel's term (2005), *obduracy*. All planners are aware of this physical constraint. Le Corbusier, for example, was so aware of spatial constraints that the city models he invented were planned to do away with the old city forms.

Finally, an urban plan is, most of the time, a professional invention, whether thought out by an individual or by a team of specialists. Although a particular urban plan can be conceived by an amateur—such as Ebenezer Howard, the founder of the garden city movement—its actual realization is best left to professionals, that is, engineers, architects, and planners.

Urban plans or models are thus multi-purpose endeavours. By ordering space, they partly order social life. The project of ordering urban space is, on the other hand, grounded in some social, economic, and political objectives. The urban models that came out of the industrial city conditions and problems were all conscious and deliberate reactions to unsatisfactory spontaneous developments that led to urban problems,

such as congestion, poor sanitary conditions, and substandard housing. These developments were thought of as less and less natural and
more and more human-made. The reigning positivist philosophy of the
nineteenth century, which believed in institutional and material improvements, proclaimed the use of science and technology to achieve these two
improvements. Whether one belonged to a social movement, to a profession, or even to a political institution, the future could be rosier if people
and institutions adhered to the new spirit of the age. Planners and urban
thinkers were deeply influenced by this dominant ideology. The professionals were more pragmatic than the reformists, but both groups shared
a common vision of the city. Apart from a movement centred on Camillo
Sitte in Vienna and the British Arts and Crafts group, inspired by John
Ruskin, which both had their own international connections, planners
and urban reformers looked not to the past for models and ideas but into
the future (Choay, 1965; Lavedan, 1970). They indeed believed that urban conditions, broadly defined, ought to be better and would be better if
they could understand the situation through surveys; if they could help to
change the political and administrative context and design comprehensive
urban plans. The garden city urban model and its twin regional social city
model—together one of the first comprehensive planning models for the
betterment of the industrial city—are examples of such comprehensive
planning models, meant to reshuffle the urban industrial spatial order for
broad social objectives.

In his intellectual history of urban planning in the twentieth century,
Cities of Tomorrow, Peter Hall (1988) describes in vivid terms the succession of city models: the city in the garden; the city in the region; the city
of monuments; the city of the tower; the city on the highway. These are all
full-scale urban models. Other chapters in his book deal with urban problems and improvements but have no overall conception of an urban plan,
let alone an urban ideal. Let us recall that a great deal of city planning is
problem-related and an immediate response to some need or demand. Not
all planning—indeed, even very little—is about grand plans and comprehensive models. Only true new towns, of which Brasilia (Brazil), Canberra
(Australia), Welwyn Garden (UK), Milton Keynes (UK), and the new
towns in France around Paris, such as Cergy-Pontoise and Marne-la-Vallée,
are textbook examples of planned cities and exceptional achievements,
erected on empty space as actual experiments in "total" planning (Merlin,
1972, 1982).

Urban Models in the Planned Industrial City

The story of the twentieth century's urban planning models is not entirely
new. It is, however, worth comparing the urban models, which is less often

done. Peter Hall's comprehensive book discusses many more urban models, but four stand out (see also Ward, 2002): (1) the garden city model of Ebenezer Howard (1965); (2) the modern movement of planning and architecture of the Athens Charter (see Box 7.1 later in the chapter); (3) the regional movement of Patrick Geddes (1949) and Lewis Mumford (1938); and (4) the techno-individualistic model, more precisely anticipation, of Frank Lloyd Wright (1958).

Each urban model can be linked to a person, to a thinker, or to an advocate, but in reality each is best represented by a school of thought rather than by one or two individuals. The garden city model, developed by Howard, evolved into an international movement (Ward, 1990). Le Corbusier, the high priest of modernism in planning and architecture, is only one representative of a large movement, itself very international. Geddes (1949) and Mumford (1938) did not create an enduring and institutionalized school of thought: they produced very few followers but were instrumental in developing an ecological outlook in planning (Meller, 1990; Welter and Lawson, 2000). Mumford was, in the 1920s, a member of the influential Regional Planning Association of America (RPAA), which may have been the leading think tank on planning at the time. And finally, Wright had many followers, but more in architecture than in planning. His "model" is worth considering, though, for it captured and anticipated leading forces in the American urbanization process and its spatial evolution.

Instead of going into each model in detail, we have highlighted their main differences and similarities in Table 7.1. The models are presented more or less as they emerged in time. The table also includes some criticisms of these planning models, which suffer from being either too abstract or too comprehensive. Jane Jacobs is a good representative of a counter-model *to* planning (Jacobs, 1961), but she is not alone in criticizing planning interventions and models. She belongs more to a school of practices than to a school of thought in that the ideas that she put forward were developed by urban social movements much more than by the intellectual creation of a group of thinkers or planners. True, her *Death and Life of Great American Cities: The Failure of Town Planning* (1961) is a landmark in urban studies and the whole book is addressed to local governments and planners, but it has nourished urban action groups as well as a new breed of urban professionals.

Table 7.1 compares these urban planning models according to four dimensions or organizing principles. Each model has something to say about (a) the ideal spatial form (spatial dimension in the table); (b) the social composition of the urban or regional population (social dimension); (c) the planning process; and (d) the planner's role.

Table 7.1 Twentieth Century Urban Planning Models

Dimensions/ Models	Spatial	Social	Planning Process	Planner's Role
Garden city (E. Howard)	Low density	Co-operation	Highly planned	Reformer and initiator
Regionalism and eco- regionalism (Geddes and Mumford)	Low or medium density	Interregional diversity	Less planned	Generalist, adviser, scientist
Modern movement (Le Corbusier)	High central density; lower density in suburbs	High social differentiation	Highly planned	Visionary, guide, decision-maker
Techno-individualistic (F. Lloyd Wright)	Very low density	Small autonomous communities	Spontaneous and planned	Seer and technician
"Counter-planning" (J. Jacobs)	High density	High urban diversity	Spontaneous and regulated	Technician and participant

The Garden City

Ebenezer Howard conceived his urban model as a response to the advantages and disadvantages of living either in the countryside or in a large industrial city, mainly unplanned, which developed during his time (that is, the end of the nineteenth century, the beginning of the twentieth). For Howard, each living habitat is marked by some "good" and some "bad" or "less good." "Bad" in the countryside are conditions such as "lack of society," "low wages," "lack of amusement," and "no public spirit." Although these conditions are compensated for by some "good"—such as beauty of nature, fresh air, and low rent—they cannot offer what the city has in plenty: social opportunities, amusement, chances of employment, and high wages. (These despite the city's numerous "bad" traits, such as areas of unemployment and slums, "closing-out of nature," "isolation of crowds," high rent and prices, and "foul air and murky sky") (Howard, 1965: 46). The garden city idea would bring together the good of both places while avoiding the bad.

The ideal garden city is a reformed social and spatial city. In it, urban densities of habitations and people are low; the social model rests on a combination of co-operative land ownership and public facilities with private housing and factories. The economic model builds on industries as well as on an agricultural economy. And the train is central in planning the garden city: it circles the city and links it to other garden cities. For Howard, the planning process is best left to professionals who have embraced a double role of social reform and of spatial technician. The garden city is, in sum, a planned city that is preferably erected on unoccupied land.

The Regional City or Eco-regional City

The regional city, or eco-regional city, is not as planned as the garden city. It can be more or less concentrated for Geddes was quite aware that in this "eotechnics" era—the second phase of the industrial revolution centred on electricity, chemistry, and non-ferrous metallurgy—cities could be built almost anywhere. As well, owing to technological developments, they could grow, as they already had, into what Geddes called conurbations, namely as a set of cities that have jointly urbanized (Geddes, 1949). Geddes wanted planning to respect three broad principles: work, place, and people. In arriving at theses principles, he was influenced by continental sociologists and geographers Le Play, Reclus, Ritter, and Humbolt (Hall, 1988). However, Geddes's main contribution to planning was without a doubt his advocacy that there should be no plan without a survey. A civic, or regional, survey is necessary for planners to understand the past and present of a place and to plan the future in respect of a city's continuity in time. A trained biologist, Geddes shared with his contemporaries an evolutionary perspective. Planning might help in bringing about better living conditions—a "Eutopia" as he called it—which was a mindset largely shared by Victorians and positivists alike.

Mumford was an early American proponent of garden cities. He was at the same time a staunch supporter of regional planning in America, being a founding figure of the Regional Planning Association of America (RPAA) in the 1920s. In planning, Mumford is famous for his regional approach and his ecological viewpoint. Regional planning is the proper response to cities that have grown in large conurbations. Plans should not limit themselves to municipal plans but must be conceived in a lager spatial, economic, and social context. The industrial revolution brought people to cities that have grown to large sizes—hence, his support for the decentralized garden city. Planning, therefore, should reflect this important change. However, with respect to spatial planning, Mumford may have been of two minds. On the one hand, he was aware of increasing city sizes but thought that urban growth was unsustainable. Regional planning also meant planning for urban decentralization toward planned garden cities, more or less linked among themselves in regions, each to some degree autonomous or at less distinctive. These regions would have their own ecological base so that they would differ among themselves. A coastal region, for example, differs from a mountain or a prairie region such that planning principles and practices should also be different. Mumford's ecological standpoint is consistent with his regional approach to planning.

However, unlike Howard's, Geddes and Mumford's planning ideals have not been extensively carried out. Geddes did plan cities in Palestine and in India, which lent him some international recognition (Meller, 1990). What may last is the idea that planning must rest on surveys. The planning process remained, however, rather centralized and guided by professionals whose role was scientific, generalist, and technical. For Geddes and Mumford, one aspect that planners should preserve and even promote was diversity, both ecological and social. Mumford and Geddes initiated a regional and ecological movement in planning that inspired, without forming a proper school of thought, planning practices based on designing with nature (McHarg, 1969). Mumford was an early supporter of the Tennessee Valley Authority (TVA) large development projects for they appeared to him to put forward some ecological ideas in the form of ecological restoration. Also, a planned rural electrification was much needed and was lauded by Mumford. The river basin region as a planned area was in need of entering into the modern era (Friedman and Weaver, 1979). TVA was later criticized vehemently, even by Jane Jacobs, for relying too much on large electrical utilities for development, which became a large source of acid rain (Jacobs, 1984).

The Modern Movement
The modern movement in architecture and planning is certainly the most comprehensive and far-reaching model of urban planning. Its history spans many decades but its evolution came to fruition in the 1930s and 1940s— troubled decades to say the least. With the garden city concept, this urban model is the most important contribution of planning ideas to city planning and urban design. Far from being an individualistic endeavour, it was the product of a whole professional corps more and more aware of their own power and skills. In 1942, the modern movement published a manifesto, which Le Corbusier wrote in an imaginative and provoking style (Le Corbusier, 1957).

From the viewpoint of the modern movement in planning, the industrial city has to start a new life. The old industrial city had created lots of problems, in large part because of a lack of planning. Large cities cannot be left to themselves and to every individual motive and decision. A city is also a collective good, to speak in very current terms. The planner is a guide, a visionary, and his or her role in organizing the city functions (work, circulation, housing, recreation) is paramount. Only the planner can see and imagine the whole, and plan accordingly. The modern city is concentrated in its centre, where high-rises rule. It is highly segregated, where work places and industry are spatially differentiated from residential areas. The city is, as is society itself, highly hierarchical; leading functions and offices, such as finance and government, occupy the city centre. Planning is functional although its decisions help to promote a modern way of life. The planner has a great role in guiding society to a better and more harmonious way of urban living.

The Techno-Individualist Model
Finally, the techno-individualistic "model" of Lloyd Wright is much more spontaneous although architects and planners may help in bringing it about

(Wright, 1958). Wright envisaged the already begun spatial movement of the American population as a long-term process of geographical decentralization. People would and should prefer to live in the countryside, but instead of being isolated they would be connected with other people and other places by the car, the airplane, and modern communications systems. For Wright, this was a vision of and for the future, where each family could live on at least one acre of land and connect to the land (a concept he called the Broad Acre City). The planner is not a central figure in this model. True, transport, communications, and public facilities have to be planned, but the role of the planner is limited, although Wright designed himself a plan of his Broad Acre City.

The "Counter-Movement" of Jane Jacobs

The social movements of the 1960s and the 1970s criticized urban planning ideas and practices. Jane Jacobs's ideas crystallized this movement; she was a leading intellectual of a planning counter-movement, so to speak (Jacobs, 1961). Jacobs, in her book on the great American cities, deplored the planning decisions that ruled the first half of the twentieth century and the postwar decades. She argued that there is something basically wrong with planning because planning kills the diversity that arises naturally in large cities. Echoing Wirth, but more positively, Jacobs associated cities with diversity. Indeed, cities are places for the expression of diversity and for spontaneity. All planning risks jeopardizing this diversity as well as, we might add, liberty. If planning is unavoidable in large cities, it should at least be guided by principles leading to and promoting all kinds of diversity: social, economic, architectural, etc. The planner's role should be minimal, avoiding grand plans and, instead, designing regulations that help diversity. Thus, a city is not a work of art or a blueprint for the future but an evolving human and physical entity. In a nutshell, Jacob's conception of the city is organic, whereas many, if not all, urban models tend to be mechanical. An organic city evolves and changes through the combined actions of its inhabitants, whereas the mechanical city is modelled on reproducible parts, thought out by experts.

Planning Ideals and Urban Dynamics

Urban planning models are certainly striking in their diversity. They also circulate and diffuse internationally. Canadian planning is a good example: it was open to ideas and to people from elsewhere (Ward, 1999). Urban models *are* ideals. To what extent they are implemented in practice, however, is worth considering.

If one model, the modern movement, was dominant in theory and in practice, alternative models have always contested its supremacy. The garden city model is, however, an alternative that speaks to another age. Although the model has inspired many realizations, not the least of which was the first generation of British new towns (Hall, 1980a), most of its applications are designed suburbs. Gone are the principles on which the garden city model was built: no collective propriety of land; no self-contained city; no green belt, except in very few cases such as post–WWII London and other large British urban areas; no networks of garden cities into a social city; and, finally, no trends toward a large-scale geographical decentralization.

Viewed from this perspective, the garden city movement appears to have been a failure except that the model was in fact experimented with and applied in many places around the world. Montréal had its own garden city experiment, which in reality is a garden suburb (Choko, 1988). The American Greenbelt town project of the late 1930s and 1940s was a successful experiment but limited in space and time, and in number. In fact, very few Greenbelt towns were actually constructed (Scott, 1969: 335–42). New suburban developments may have borrowed from the garden city model, but they did so very selectively. Low densities, green spaces, some public facilities, not always well developed, have characterized many suburbs, but no one can dispute that such developments have been a limited appropriation of the concept. What does remain from the garden city model is its spatial layout and physical concern for enjoyable living areas; what's been left out is its social goal. But during the twentieth century, cities' physical conditions changed as did their demographic, family, and cultural characteristics. The travails of the industrial city are no longer the main issue.

The regional city model may be a greater challenge to put into practice than the garden city. Although Mumford's prediction about the future of metropolitan civilization has not been fulfilled, metropolises present previously unknown problems. First, the metropolitan government is a difficult issue. The waves of successive amalgamations in large urban areas in Canada are a case in point (Sancton, 2000; Collin, 2002). Although the process was painful, as in Québec, metropolitan governments, whether the result of amalgamations or the voluntary union of individual municipalities, are taking an active part in planning regional infrastructure and services, in strengthening the metropolitan economy, in tackling social issues, and in facing ecological problems such as climate change (Bicknell, Dodman, and Sattertwaite, 2009; Kousky and Schneider, 2003; Robinson and Dore, 2005). The regional urban model had great ambitions for metropolises and conurbations, but it is only recently that political and administrative structures have been put in place to run an effective regional policy. The ecological dimension in city planning has experienced a revival of late, and new currents of thought have partly absorbed its aims in planning, such a "new urbanism" (see Chapter 8).

The Wright's "model" may have had some success, at least in North America, where trends to regional decentralization are moving fast. But new urban areas are created in the process; or old ones, such as Calgary and Edmonton, are expanding. New urban corridors arise in regions long deserted, or in regions where urbanization had been slow and where the typical industrial city had not taken root. However, these various movements are a far cry from Wright's expectation, and, with the rise of new ideas in planning, the spread-out city, decentralization, and urban sprawl are no longer the sole trend, being replaced by a counter-trend, the compact city. Whether the promises of the compact city are being fulfilled is a different issue.

Finally, the modern movement may have contributed the most to city planning and development. Very few grand plans, also significantly called master plans, were applied in totality, but city-centre redevelopments were highly inspired by the modern movement so that planners came to be identified with this movement and with conceptions of city development that have been highly contested by urban movements. Success bred contention in this case, and planners as well as urban politicians had to learn to live with social mobilizations opposing their plans. Québec City is an interesting and telling case. The city and its administration had toyed with grand plans that were later contested by social movements and beaten at the polls. After the 1992 municipal election, a new breed of city officials changed the course of planning and urban policy and moved away from the modernist movement.

Why is there such a gap between the promises of modern planning and urban policy, and the actual interventions? One reason is that modernism tends to start from scratch, from an urban tabula rasa.[1] One of Le Corbusier's most ambitious plans—the *Plan Voisin* for redesigning Paris—does away with much of Paris, leaving on the ground only a few historical monuments, such as Notre-Dame Cathedral. Many of the other city plans he conceived started on unoccupied ground. The modern movement has been successful in such circumstances: new towns could be planned and built according to a model, whether modernist or naturalist, such as the garden city model.

The second reason is that many professionals and planners, not to mention intellectuals and even city officials, came to dislike the industrial city, for very good reasons. Since public interventions, in planning as well as in public health, had been successful, why not move a step further and rebuild huge portions of a decadent city? The solution to slums was clearance and high-rises together with green spaces, which were planned according to modernist principles. Many deplored such constructions for they tended to breed public insecurity. Wide-open spaces are nobody's places, where it is difficult to watch over children.

The third reason is to do with professional confidence and arrogance. The Athens Charter (see Box 7.1) is clear on the role of planners (architects and urbanists, more precisely). They are leaders and guides: beacons, so to speak. They know things that others do not, and their skills can promote collective goods and the common wealth. Planners had the public good in mind and could not understand why they were not given carte blanche, backed by powerful mayors and municipal political parties under the banner of "civic progress."

Finally, in every democratic society there are counter-powers. Planners and city officials' power is counter-balanced by private economic forces and by civil society's power. Visions about the good city may sharply differ in a highly differentiated society. Planners' vision, despite the Athens Charter (the planning profession's manifesto for building a modern city), is only one vision of what good city life is all about. Moreover, inequalities and social tensions nourish conflicts about what to do and what and how to plan. Those who lack urban resources evidently better convey demands for a better distribution of them, such as housing, public facilities, green spaces, and public transport. No planner can substitute himself or herself to people with needs. A paternalistic attitude, congenial to all forms of positivisms, has been fading.

Can a large city change and evolve without a plan (or smaller plans)? Private developers plan cities according to models they draw from the planning tradition, which they adapt to consumers' needs and wants. They can invent new urban models, such as the neo-traditional suburb in all its variety, the commercial centre, and the edge city (Gans, 1967; Gareau, 1991).

Box 7.1

The Athens Charter

Written by Charles-Édouard Jeanneret ("Le Corbusier," 1867–1965), a prominent architect and urban planner of the twentieth century, the Athens Charter is the basic manifesto of the so-called modern movement in architecture and planning. The ideas that are found in the charter were already circulating in the 1920s and the 1930s inside the CIAM (*Congrès internationaux de l'architecture moderne*: International Congresses of Modern Architecture). The CIAM was founded by a group of prominent European architects.

In 1933 CIAM organized its fourth congress in Athens, where the main ideas of the charter took shape—hence its name. However, the charter was not published until 1942 in Paris (Le Corbusier, 1957).

The Athens Charter is a very short document that states the principles of modern architecture and planning needs to be promoted and applied. The manifesto starts with locating the city into its larger region. This means that modern planning must adopt a regional outlook because a city is only one part of a wider regional context. The charter goes on with fierce criticisms of the industrial city and its unchecked growth, which leads to major problems. Not only does such runaway and unplanned growth infringe on nature and agricultural land, but it is also chaotic,

Private developers have also promoted new urbanism (Filion, 2003; Ouellet, 2006). Private developers planned many industrial cities and postwar as well as prewar suburbs. Levittown, a postwar American suburb, is a good example of private planning (Gans, 1967). Indeed, many post–World War II suburbs were built with basic public regulations and large inputs by developers. These developers more or less acted as Hollywood producers: they assembled professional people, listened to their ideas, looked at their financial resources, but decided in the end what was best for the consumers, the buyers of a house or of a commercial building. Their power in shaping the industrial and post-industrial city was and still is huge. Although they have to comply with more municipal regulations, on the protection of the environment in particular, and with broad social directions in urban policy and planning, developers still are important urban actors. The urban regime theory captures the network of interests and relations between private, public, and sometimes civil society actors. Private developers can organize even public consultations on an urban private project, as has been recently shown in Montréal. But there is a downside to urban privatization: the collective good, such as free movement in urban space and the provisions of distributed and equal public facilities, may be in danger of

creating many urban problems in sanitation and public health, in slow and congested circulation, and in lack of public amenities. In view of that, the modern planner is invited to apply rational principles of spatial and social order in order to stop this kind of growth and plan for future developments.

Along with its desire to solve some of the industrial city's major problems, the charter develops an urban conception based on functionality and monumentality. The former means that a city must be divided into zones for different purposes. There are areas for industry, for commerce, for housing, and for public facilities and green spaces. The modern city commands that each area, or zone, is separated from the others. *Monumentality* refers to large buildings needed to accommodate a growing urban population.

The Athens Charter ideas were very influential after World War II, mostly in Europe but also in the Americas, especially in Brazil. Starting in 1954, Brasilia was planned as the new national capital by urban planner Lucio Costa (1902–1988) and architect Oscar Niemeyer (1907–2012). They planned a monumental and functional city along the Athens Charter and CIAM principles.

Contemporary urban planning is less keen on the modernist principles although some are necessarily maintained. Strict zoning needs to be relaxed in favour of mixing functions. Monumentality may be less valued although high-rise buildings continue. Perhaps the Achilles' heel of the modern movement may be that it is too technocratic and expert-driven, with no public input through participation.

losing ground. Hulbert (1994) has criticized the 1980s planning practices in Québec City for relying too much on private developers. He was afraid that a city of private developers might emerge.

Urban planning models may best serve as an inspiration, not as a blueprint. They generate ideas, confront them with complex realities, and test them in a piecemeal manner. However, planners who invented the urban planning models were more ambitious, believing that they could shape city development for the better good. But their ideas were built on an outmoded model of urban governance, which they learned the hard way. Whether city evolution needs one model or a combination of models depends on how one sees city life. If we emphasize a city's diversity and liberty, comprehensive planning and grand plans should be checked by private decisions of urban dwellers. If, on the other hand, we see the city as an experiment in physical and social engineering, then planning is allowed and may even prosper but within democratic bounds. If, however, we understand the city as a common, although diversified, project, then democratic deliberation for the production and distribution of urban resources should be favoured (Forester, 1988, 1999; Friedmann, 1981; Healey, 1997).

Canadian City Planning in Practice

Can models be discerned in the recent planning of large Canadian cities? How far do "ideal-type" models and their linked ethics fit the practice of urban planning in Canada? Is there a huge gap between theory and practice in planning the development of the current, as well as the past, cities? A complete answer, based on historical analysis and an elaborate comparative method, is beyond the scope of this chapter. However, we can have some idea of planning contexts, practices, and choices in looking at the three largest urban regions of Canada.

Stages in Planning the Montréal Urban Region

The evolution of city planning in Montréal has gone through three phases. The first phase, roughly the postwar years till 1970, was built on modernist ideas of city planning. The second phase (1970–1990) showed a large city torn between opposing interests (long-established local communities versus developers, for instance) and aspirations (suburban living versus living in central neighbourhoods, for example). The third phase began around 1990 when the metropolitan government prepared, and later adopted in 2011, a plan to consolidate a new phase of planning and urban policy.

During the first phase of city planning, the Montréal area was open for development and spatial change. The urbanization process accelerated and urban politics and planning had to respond. Grand plans were elaborated, inner city areas were torn down and built anew, renewal operations in older neighbourhoods were carried out, and suburbia developed at a fast pace (Lortie, 2004). Urban planning made way for expressways that led to further demolition and to noise and pollution but also to further development of suburbs.

The first phase planted the seeds for the second phase. Meanwhile, the process of internationalization, the rise of the so-called knowledge economy, and the opening of markets for goods and services battered the old industrial economy of Montréal and sharpened the social tensions. Deindustrialization in Montréal was a painful experience (Lamonde and Martineau, 1992). One could see its effects on the grounds (in the form of increased poverty and degraded urban environments); in urban space; and in people, families, and built communities (Sénécal, Malézieux, and Manzagol, 2002). What had been built during 100 years and more was being destroyed in a decade. What replaced the destruction, however, was neither immediate nor purely spontaneous. If this was creative destruction in capitalist urbanization, it was successful. Government action was needed to help the new economy emerge and thrive. Over two decades, the urban economy was reborn, but the costs were not small in social polarization. If the central city was battered, the suburbs experienced strong growth and enjoyed a much better living space. With the passing of time, suburbia continued to expand and gained in diversity and autonomy.

In the third phase of urban planning (1990 and after), as mentioned, a plan to consolidate a new phase of planning and urban policy was introduced. A recent plan, called the Metropolitan Planning and Development Plan of the Metropolitan Community of Montréal, is an ambitious one that seeks to change the way of planning the city region over the next 20 years. This third phase seeks to integrate sustainable development in planning and ease the social tensions that sprouted in the second phase. This metropolitan plan contains three overarching objectives:

1. Sustainable development becomes a deliberate aim in planning and developing the whole city-region.
2. New infrastructure and transport systems need to be planned carefully and closely integrated to new land and housing developments. This means, hopefully, a more compact city-region, or at least one that is less spread out.
3. The metropolitan community is engaged in promoting and implementing a sustainable way of urban life, which rests on much denser growth and renewal and on the production of what the plan calls "sustainable spaces." The objective of sustainability must be achieved at all urban scales.

The plan draws heavily from new ideas about urban sustainability, new urbanism, denser and more compact cities, land developments linked to transport systems, and an "ecological" urban way of life that some planners, as well as many citizens and politicians, are ready to promote and try out. The plan is of course accompanied by a great variety of measures and programs that will unfold over the next two decades. The plan was adopted in 2011 in spite of opposition and reservations from municipalities at the fringe of the urban metropolitan area, which feared that their own development could be stopped or restricted.

It is easy to level criticisms at such master plans. This plan's long-term view, much needed in planning the urban fabric and the urban infrastructure, remains open to doubt due to uncertainty about the likely evolution of large cities. Planners and municipal governments in the 1950s did not and could not anticipate the deindustrialization process that struck like lightening in the 1970s. Twenty years from now, what will be the urban impact of global warming or of an aging population and demographic stagnation, if the latter occurs?

A second criticism of such plans rests on the considerable coordination between actors and institutions that is necessary to achieve the objectives and to change the content of urban planning and policy. Co-operation will certainly be needed to achieve the broad goal of densification, for this may lead to fault lines between local elected officials. The plan relies on large resource mobilization, financial and otherwise. Some of these resources will have to come from higher tiers of government, while others from pooling local resources.

Sustainable development has greatly influenced the last phase of city planning in Montréal. However, if urban sustainability is a process as well as an outcome, it is certainly a long and winding one, regularly subjected to doubts, criticisms, and the upsurge of new interests, concerns, and aspirations.

The Political Economy and Ecology of Toronto

Toronto's postwar planning history has faced problems similar to those in Montréal, including designing a regional governance system (Frisken, 2001). The postwar boom lasted, under the aegis of a modernization movement, until the end of the 1960s. It was followed by a long phase of public contention, economic restructuring, and the rise of environmental concerns (roughly 1970–1990). According to Stephen Bocking (2011), one can see in the 1960s the roots of social tensions over planning ideals, ideas, and projects. Toronto has now, in a third phase, set its planning principles under sustainable development, given momentum with the publication of the UN Commission on Environment and Development (1987), which popularized the idea of sustainable development. Critics may say that it all depends on what sustainable development means, whether it is a radical idea, or a more reformist one; on whether the environment is a major constraint to ongoing development; or on whether sustainability is a hollow concept. This debate has been going on for decades and, despite governmental adherence to sustainable development, it will likely remain a contentious idea for years to come.

Greater Toronto is a fast-growing urban region, within a fast-growing mega city-region, the Golden Horseshoe. As Bourne, Britton, and Leslie (2011: 236) acknowledge, "Depending on how it is defined, the greater Toronto region is the fifth or sixth largest metropolitan economy in North America and one of the continent's fastest growing mega-regions." It is also spreading out at a fast pace, although regulations, planning, and government restructuring have tried to limit urban sprawl. Being Canada's largest urban region and its most populous regional area, planning its future development is not without impact on the way Canadian planning will evolve. Desfor and Keil (2004) have interpreted Toronto's involvement with ecological preservation and restoration, such as the Don Valley project, as an example of ecological modernization although, because of a contentious politics, the cases studied may more likely belong to political ecology, which stresses conflict over the environment and which ecological modernization tends to play down. In a nutshell, ecological modernization is the process by which the economy and the polity have started to take into account today's ecological problems as very serious and in need of proper responses through policy change, either governmental or industrial. For some authors, ecological modernization can be successful only if leading economies, with the spur of active governments, can tackle the multiple environmental problems. For Desfor and Keil (2004), Toronto, as a prosperous city inside a prosperous province and country and as urged to act by a local environmental movement, could embark on the ecological modernization path or on what others call sustainable development.

Land, ecosystem, and biodiversity protection and restoration are only one aspect of urban planning, which has to deal with many issues at the same time as well as in sequence. Transportation; densification; provision of public services; infrastructure development, improvement, and replacement (and, yes, cost control) are tasks planners and local authorities have to handle. Growth is to be managed. The Growth Plan of the Greater Golden Horseshoe (2006) sets Toronto's growth into a wider context. The Greenbelt Act (2005), a provincial piece of legislation, "declares a large territory of land to be off limits to property developers" (Boudreau, Keil, and Young, 2009: 99). Moreover, there is an urgent need for a public transportation system in large Canadian cities, after years of neglect. If local authorities, planners, and residents want a more desirable and liveable city and if they all want it to be more compact and ecologically friendly, public transportation is a key element in planning for development and sustainability. Other cities have also emphasized transport planning as an urgent issue. They have knocked at the door of provincial and federal governments for resources and help. Toronto may be in the frontline, but it is sharing its place with others.

Regional institutions and metropolitan governance may help to reach decisions on long-term objectives. The merging of cities into wider governance systems (in Toronto, first in 1953 and, more importantly, in 1998 into a megacity) is deemed to facilitate decision-making and pooling of resources. However, tensions may remain between the central city and its suburbs, as well as between the private city (called by Keil, 2002, "Toronto Inc") and the public city.

In the North American continental context, Greater Toronto is a major urban region, owing to its demographic size, its economic clout, and its cultural diversity and dynamism. According to Bourdreau, Keil, and Young (2009), Greater Toronto has recently followed a "neo-liberal model" that is more private-driven than public-driven. However, there is a tradition of "public planning" in Toronto, often under provincial guidance, which the years of contention tried to maintain and expand (Frisken, 2007). The neo-liberal tag attached to Toronto's planning describes only part of the process in the city. The whole region is subjected to more ambitious and public objectives, such as planning for sustainability on a large scale as "extended metropolitanization," where city, region, agricultural land, and nature are all considered (Macdonald and Keil, 2012). Provincial authorities have been leading actors of this movement toward greater regionalization, but one cannot refrain from thinking that regionalization is also the result of years, indeed decades, of **political ecology** from below. However, the planning challenges remain considerable for the sustainability path is a long process, fraught with conceptual difficulties and possible change of fortunes.

The Vancouver Model

Is there a particular planning model in Vancouver? Is Vancouver planned differently, and does the cityscape of Vancouver mean something different to Canadian planners, politicians, and urban citizens? Vancouver is proud of its planning and urban design achievement, and this may partly explain its attraction. "Vancouverism" is the local term to describe this success (Boddy, 2004, 2005; Bogdanowicz, 2006). This term has various meanings, but it chiefly describes **high-density planning**, with public amenities, to which socially mixed housing in new developments can be added. The Vancouver city centre (or "downtown," in North American parlance) is the architectural model of tall, slim housing towers. Other forms of densification, with fewer high-rise buildings, also define the model, such the denser housing developments in False Creek South, opposite the housing towers of False Creek North. However, to what extent is sustainable development, or design, a planning success? And if it is a design success, does this mean that it is also an urban success?

The urban area of Vancouver is regularly placed at the top of the list of the most liveable cities in the world (*The Economist*, 2008). Although there is some subjective judgment in the assessment of what a livable city is, there seems to be some agreement on the criteria used. Shape and landscape are obviously not enough to characterize a city as livable. Social, economic, and ecological factors must also be considered. On the design and shape factors, Vancouver has passed the grade. On other factors, however, there remains a lot to be improved. Housing is not cheap in Vancouver although the Vancouver municipality has done a great deal in planning for social housing. And while the urban region is open to immigration and no entrenched social tensions have come up, homelessness is still a problem in need of solutions. Moreover, Vancouver proper could be a model of planning and design, but what about the whole urban region? There is some reasonable doubt about the "Vancouver achievement" (Punter, 2003). The city may be a physical and architectural success story, but this may hide other problems.

The Vancouver city centre has become the preserve of high-rise towers. These buildings are mostly blocks of flats, and their recent increase may have crowed out commercial and office buildings, which have been moving to the suburbs for some time, providing for the local populations as well as for the whole area. Whether this is an anomaly depends on one's own idea of a large city. We traditionally think of a city as comprising a clearly identifiable centre where business, government, and commercial activities are located. But no large city is made up of only one centre. Most have multiple centres, and this multiplication of centres is brought about by city growth and urban differentiation of activities and residents. If the Vancouver city centre is less and less a thriving business centre—and one need to be careful about this assumption for there has been a new economy on the rise in Vancouver's inner city (Hutton, 2004)—the implication is that it is no longer a city as we used to conceive it. Is the Vancouver model, then, ushering in a new model of city planning, the ultimate "new urbanism" (Boddy, 2004: 19)? It may be too early to conclude, but reading the vast output on Vancouver, we may be inclined to think so.

With respect to city planning, Vancouver shows three problems. First, city-centre dwellers tend to travel by car to the suburbs to do their shopping, where large shopping centres are located. If this is the case, they don't contribute much to urban life and diversity in the city centre. Second, the achievement of the city of Vancouver is not necessarily diffused to the suburbs. Among the fastest-growing urban municipalities in Canada are some Vancouver suburbs, such as Surry, Burnaby, and Richmond, which have witnessed a 10 per cent and over population increase between 2006 and 2011. In addition, even if Vancouver has been planned for sustainable development through regional plans, municipalities remain in charge of land-use planning. The city of Vancouver may excel in high-density planning, but the principle could be lost in translation when it reaches suburbia. Third, a city mostly growing in and around suburbs experiences transportation

Vancouver is characterized by high-density planning.

problems. Planning a public transportation system becomes more difficult and costly since there is no converging point for work, to which many people shuttle everyday. Vancouver is proud to say that, owing to social protests of the 1960s and 1970s, there are no highways criss-crossing the central city, but there are also no proper tramways or underground systems.

However, when all is considered and to be fair to the planning tradition that Vancouver has created in Canada, the Vancouver area remains highly attractive. Growth and immigration numbers are testimony to such a valuation of its living conditions, in particular its geography, its physical amenities, and its cultural diversity (Sandercock, 2004). It is possible that planners, urban designers, and architects had too much say in defining and advertising Vancouver. Other voices, especially its diverse ethno-cultural voices, should also be heard, *urbi et orbi*: inside as well as outside the city's symbolic walls.

Conclusion

Canada's recent urban planning practices show three different and at times similar processes. Montréal has recently played the regional card for planning as well as for economic recovery. Toronto tries to unite two processes, which may appear at first sight opposed: fully participating in the economic opportunities that globalization offers while at the same time planning for greenness and sustainability. But, like Montréal, Toronto has also experimented with regional governance, and not always very successfully. Vancouver, owing to its geographical location and the composition of its population, is open to new trade and investment opportunities in Asia but has selected a model of its own, which is now being exported (Boddy, 2004: 18-19). All three cities have adopted a sustainable principle in planning, although they are all conscious that the ultimate goal may be hard to hit (see Chapter 8).

The social tensions that arose in the 1960s over planning decisions and models of growth, played out in all three cities, will certainly not go away under the aegis of sustainable development. Urban movements in all three cities gained the right to participate in planning decisions. The sustainable development project relies heavily on public participation. If the World Commission on Environment and Development (1987) is right, shifting urban policy and planning toward sustainability is a long shot that needs people in instead of out. This does not mean that social tensions and conflicts will vanish, but an open public debate about urban living conditions, amenities, and infrastructure may ease some tensions. Toronto's new planning practices that Boudreau, Keil, and Young (2009) describe for the 1990s and onward are better described as private advertisement than as public participation in planning decisions.

Finally, let us take up the claim made earlier (Chapter 3) that urban planning is an instrument of the creation of large cities as socio-technical systems and landscapes. If we look at the urban planning models, we can readily see that all urban thinkers devoted some thoughts to technology in cities. Whether it is the garden city model or the regional model, technologies are crucial elements of the urban way of life and for urban growth and development. One of the twentieth century's crucial technologies of mobility is the car. If many urban planning thinkers, such as Mumford and Jacobs, were critical of the car's ubiquity, others, including Le Corbusier and Wright, wanted to accommodate the city to the car and not the other way around. Wright's anticipation even makes room for the airplane as a means of linking "broad-acre" cities. Over the course of the twentieth century, other transportation technologies came to embody characteristics of city life and the economy. If the nineteenth-century city was confronted by the sanitation question, the twentieth-century city was confronted by the mobility question, just as the twenty-first-century city will be confronted by the ecological question (see Chapter 8). During the long period when the industrial city was being planned, questions were not tackled or in some cases solved outside technology and socio-technical systems. Urban planning was and still is a strong agent of "technicality." Even though planning models were rarely followed or wholly applied, they have served as reference points, as ideas that inspired decisions and actions.

The idea of urban sustainability took roots and, as we have shown, appears to be applied a bit differently in the three largest Canadian cities. High-density building in the city centre is Vancouver's preference. Toronto, on the other hand, is concerned with sprawl and with its environment. But if growth cannot be stopped, it can be oriented and contained by a green belt. The metropolitan community of Montréal wants sustainable development in all its forms. But Montréal also stresses that intensive land-use development is necessary since the city-region is growing modestly. Moreover, the regional economy still needs to be repaired although it has lately been rising from its ashes (Shearmur and Rantisi, 2011).

This whole period of public investment was in large part directed to the production and distribution of buildings, infrastructure, collective facilities, in brief to technological artefacts, most of them large, complex, and expensive. The period has reinforced the industrial socio-technical system, already put in place in the nineteenth century, to a point where negative feedback in the form of pollution, environmental degradation, noise, congestion, and so on set in.

Questions for Critical Thought

1. Compare the leading models in urban planning.

2. Explain the gap between urban models and urban realities.

3. What lessons do you draw from 50 years of planning in large Canadian cities?

4. Do you agree with the statement that cities are one of the most important human inventions?

Suggested Readings

Bourne, L.S., T. Hutton, R.G. Shearmur, and J. Simmons Eds. (2011). *Canadian Urban Regions: Trajectories of Growth and Change*. Toronto: Oxford University Press. Although it is not a book about urban planning, it is highly relevant to problems and opportunities faced by Canadian city-region planning. This book gives the social, economic, cultural, and political context in which planning decisions are made. The book contains an overall review of the change and challenges of Canada's metropolitan areas, and looks more closely at particular city-regions: Montréal, Ottawa-Gatineau, Toronto, Calgary, and Vancouver.

Grant, J. (Ed). 2008. *A Reader in Canadian Planning: Linking Theory and Practice.* Toronto: Nelson. Jill Grant has assembled a valuable reader on Canadian planning in all its aspects. Nothing is left behind: ideas, practices, ethics, challenges, even planning errors are presented by a great variety of authors, including practitioners.

Hall, P. 1988. *Cities of Tomorrow.* Oxford: Blackwell. This is without doubt an outstanding book on the intellectual history of urban planning in the twentieth century. Peter Hall is much more concerned with the object of planning than with planning theory and ethics. For him, urban planning is an important contribution to the well-being of urban dwellers. Urban planning as social reform could well summarize Hall's own intellectual standpoint.

Ward, S.V. 2002. *Planning the Twentieth-Century City.* New York: Wiley. Ward's book is a valuable addition to Hall's, covering the same period and the same subject matter. But it is less an intellectual history of planning than a history of what urban planning has achieved in the century. Another merit is its comparative perspective, centred on the "advanced capitalist world."

Related Websites

Canadian Institute of Planners
www.cip-icu.ca
Since 1919, the Canadian Institute of Planners/Institut canadien des urbanistes has been dedicated to promoting planning in the organization of space and in the wise use of resources and the environment. It publishes the professional and academic journal *Plan Canada*.

American Planning Association
www.planning.org
The American Planning Association, founded in 1935, is a leading professional association for urban, regional, and environmental planning. It publishes the professional and academic *Journal of the American Planning Association* (JAPA).

Global Planners Network
www.globalplannersnetwork.org
Formed in 2005, the Global Planners Network adopted in Vancouver in 2006 a declaration on Reinventing Planning. Working with national planning associations and UN-Habitat, the network is concerned with rapid world urbanization and its ensuing problems on urban living conditions. It is a strong promoter of sustainable development, which cannot be achieved without sustainable urbanization.

8 Cities, the Environment, and Sustainable Development

Learning Objectives

◎ To briefly present sustainability

◎ To discuss "smart growth" and "new urbanism" as responses to the current problems of large cities, in particular to sprawl and its consequences

◎ To show how and why large Canadian cities are more and more engaged in climate change policy

◎ To compare measures to reduce greenhouse gas in some Canadian cities

Introduction

The industrial city and the suburbanization process that developed out of its expansion have produced a series of new urban or, rather, metropolitan problems. Urban sprawl—the expansion of city limits over larger and larger space—became an issue much later (chiefly in the 1980s, at least in Canada), but its root causes have long been at work. Suburbanization is nothing new when cities grow wider and bigger (Brugman, 2009). New areas are developed and built over with commercial, industrial, and residential functions. Moreover, changing lifestyles, economic prosperity, and politics have to be considered as sheer numbers and land occupation do not tell all about the dynamics and problems of a city. When people are wealthier, they tend to consume more dwelling space and the individual house, including its surrounding area, remains a preferred choice for many households and families (Fortin and Bédard, 2003). On the other hand, an aging population may choose a smaller living space and a more central position in an urban area. Economic opportunities, such as low interest rates or affordable housing due to technological innovations which lower the costs of building, may lead to a greater consumption of urban space and urban dwelling. All of these factors have some impact on city growth. The larger Canadian urban areas are not contracting and are instead expanding, at least for the time being (Bourne and Simmons, 2003).

Sprawl may be a loaded term, often masking a negative value judgment. The term is difficult to define and, in the planning profession, it has become for many a trend that should be curtailed and even stopped. Some researchers have explored the significance of high and low urban density in North America (Newman and Kenworthy, 1999). In Canada and the United States, older urban regions are denser whereas newer ones tend to be less dense. Sprawl has been perceived as an evil whereas compact cities are seen as a virtue because sprawling cities consume more energy, more land, and more resources. With a growing environmental awareness, current city forms and developments are open to this environmental criticism.

This chapter will explore the changing urban conditions with respect to two particular social concerns: the environment, or nature more broadly, and sustainable development. It will analyze how these ideas have some bearing in urban change and planning. New planning ideas have tried to tackle the issue of the environment and sustainability in large urban areas. They are called "smart growth" and "new urbanism" and they represent planning's way to adapt the city to environmental change, local as well as global. The chapter will end with a discussion on how some Canadian urban regions are responding to climate change, a truly global phenomenon.

Cities and Nature

What is the relationship between cities and nature? If all agree that cities are part of a larger environment, does it mean that they can be considered a special kind of habitat? On the other hand, is a city, whether large or small, an **ecosystem**? The term seems inapplicable to cities for they are the exact opposite of a natural environment: they are heavily built and nature is a very small part of their landscapes. However, research has tried to think of cities in ecological terms (Hough, 1995; Pickett et al., 2001). There are two such conceptions: (1) cities as areas comprising particular ecosystems, and (2) cities as whole ecosystems. Ecosystems are structural, functional, and spatial units. They are composed of a variety of species that interact among themselves and have physical and chemical elements. Cities comprise some specific and particular ecosystems: a pond, a lake, a park, and a wetland, enclosed in an urban area, are all within-city ecosystems (Coutard and Lévy, 2010; Müller, Werner, and Kelcey, 2010). These are, however, fragmented, on a small scale, and often unrelated to other natural systems.

Can we think of cities as whole ecosystems? Yes and no. As natural ecosystems, cities are systems that process energy and materials; they house different animal and plant species. A city is, however, much more than energy and material cycled and recycled, much more than structure and differentiation of species and habitats in an evolving (blindly) process operating according to Darwinian principles. It is a human construct, perhaps the most complex construction humans have ever made. A city is better described as a socio-technical system than as an ecological system. However, the composition of an urban "ecosystem" is quite different from any other type of ecosystem for human beings are a unique "species" whose constructions have nothing to do with other species. A sociologist would not be happy with identifying cities with ecosystems, although other disciplines may find ground to look at cities from a bio-ecological angle. The crucial question is not whether cities are ecosystems but whether they contribute to general sustainability or not, and whether they are themselves sustainable (Rydin, 2010).

The environment and sustainable development are not interchangeable. Sustainable development is a much broader idea than environmental protection for it also includes social equity and economic efficiency. The purpose of sustainable development is to choose a development course where these three dimensions, also called pillars, are no longer opposed but are made to work together in various practices, policies, and decisions (Guay, 2004; Mancebo, 2006). Some authors prefer the expression *sustainability* to *sustainable development* to emphasize that all development is predicated on a sustainable environment (Clark, 2007). (See Box 8.1 for a further discussion of these concepts.) A sustainable environment, or a sustainable ecosystem (the term *ecosystem* tends not to include human beings

Box 8.1

Sustainable Development and Sustainability

Sustainable development (SD) has been much talked about for the past two decades. The idea of SD first appeared around 1980 in national and international documents and writings. It may be seen as an intellectual outcome of the environmental movement of the 1960s and 1970s. The environmental movement has been critical of the kind of growth chosen by postwar economies and societies and has stressed that there are ecological damages to economic growth. Industrialization, science and technology, and the developing international economy have all been processes conducive to environmental degradation and problems although nations and the international community wholeheartedly embraced a growth path. But offering criticisms without offering an alternative program may be self-defeating. And while there were radical programs for changing the development track in order to preserve nature, such as social ecology and deep ecology, most were too demanding and perhaps impossible to achieve in a foreseeable future.

Sustainable development was, to many, a proper response to growth leading to environmental degradation on a world scale. The 1970s and the 1980s were a gloomy period, not only from an economic point of view but also from the environmental except as agents of transformation and degradation, whereas the term *environment* does include them), means that an environment's resources, its integrity, and its "health" are maintained in the long run (Waltner-Toews, Kay, and Lister, 2008). Legislation on sustainable development takes this long-term imperative into account. For instance, the Canadian Federal Sustainable Development Act defines sustainability as follows: "the capacity of a thing, action, activity, or process to be maintained indefinitely" (Canada, 2008: 2).

By what means and policies can cities attempt to achieve sustainable development? Smart growth and new urbanism are broad programs of urban development to this end. But specific policies to confront global environmental change, such as climate change, at the urban scale can also take the path of sustainable development.

Smart Growth as Acceptable Growth?

At the urban scale, growth has enriched many social groups and provided affordable housing and public goods for a large part of urban populations. But growth still seems to be needed since not all needs and aspirations, such as food, shelter, education, and jobs, have been satisfied (World Commission

perspective. As a result, many people were looking for a comprehensive and reform-oriented idea or project. Sustainable development, as defined in 1987 by the United Nations World Commission on Environment and Development (WCED), came to be seen as a credible "world project" of changing the nature of growth in order to take more care of the environment. The WCED defines sustainable development as the responsibility to use nature and its resources in a manner that promises that future generations will not be deprived of the same benefits. It stresses the intergenerational responsibility with respect to the environment and its resources. The WCED is not against economic growth; on the contrary, it is pro-growth albeit different growth because there are so many basic needs that are not being fulfilled, particularly in developing countries.

Most people cite this definition (based on basic needs and generational responsibility) of the WCED, but they forget to add that the commission believes that there are barriers, or limits, to reach sustainability—mainly cognitive (scientific and technological) and institutional ones. In a hefty document called "Agenda 21" (for the twenty-first century), ways to implement and to achieve sustainable development are suggested, targeting countries and their policies. The document contains hundreds of recommendations in its 40 chapters. Since sustainable development is about thinking globally but acting locally, some municipalities are engaged in Local Agenda 21, a process by which sustainable development is promoted and implemented at the local level. Most active Local Agendas are found in Europe.

on Environment and Development, 1987). If economic growth is still an imperative, is urban growth necessary? It depends on what is meant by urban growth. If it refers to dynamic cities that overcome the de-industrialization period, that open themselves to new global opportunities, that invest in new technologies, and that attract members of the creative class (Florida, 2003), then growth is not only acceptable but also desirable, at least for many urban citizens. On the other hand, if urban growth means doing things the old-fashioned way with respect to planning and urban policies, consensus may break down and traditional policies and decisions will have to be rethought and redesigned for the construction of **creative cities** (Scott, 2006). Is smart growth an intelligent and creative response to urban growth and city problems? Writers interested in creative classes and cities are not too keen on the spatial and physical aspects of cities and the evolution of urban forms.

What are the key elements of smart growth (Filion, 2003; Ouellet, 2006; Smart Growth Canada Network, accessed July 2013)? In a nutshell, smart growth is contained growth. It is a struggle against sprawl in so-called urban development. But to be against something is not the best rallying cry. Smart growth must be *for* something. Two schools of thought may clash here. The first, an heir to the limits-to-growth perspective, will plead, like good Malthusians, for stopping urban growth, in particular in the form of urban sprawl, because there may be no other choice. From this perspective, smart growth is not so much a choice as it is an inescapable constraint; the need to adapt is often a need to limit. This way of thinking is not dominant in urban policy and planning, and has not, so far as we know, found strong professional and political support. The second school of thought emphasizes the positive side of turning away from urban sprawl and adopting smart growth. It argues that urban sprawl consumes resources and investments and that a denser and tighter city created by smart growth will lead to various gains, including economic ones. Moreover, if compact cities are accompanied by public transport, then air pollution, noise, and greenhouse gas emissions will be reduced. Also, smart growth may render people less dependent on the car and more dependent on their own biological means of transport and on less polluting technologies, such as the bicycle. Health improvement may follow. Finally, a more compact city may lead to a greater sense of community, the loss of which has plagued many urban neighbourhoods, as predicted by Wirth (1938).

Smart growth, then, is the plan. What is the reality? Large Canadian cities have adopted more or less unknowingly, and often tepidly, a smart growth approach. Toronto was an early leader (Filion, 2000, 2003). Vancouver was not far behind, or even ahead (Alexander, 2000; Alexander and Tomalty, 2002; Curran and Tomalty, 2003), and Montréal, in planning new urban developments, has broadly referred to smart growth principles.

Calgary, Québec City, and Ottawa, which may have been the true pioneer, are also initiating policies and actions along a smart growth path (Ouellet, 2006; Guay and Hamel, 2010). However, can all the new urban planning policies be considered sustainable development?

To be considered sustainable, urban policies and projects must meet three broad criteria: (1) to respect and protect the ecological integrity; (2) to act with economic efficiency; and (3) to foster and promote social equity (Guay, 2005). It would be presumptuous to conclude that current policies and urban projects all fall under the banner of sustainable urban development. For instance, the federal government and the provinces have recently embarked on large infrastructure investments. The programs and their guidelines are less animated by sustainable development than by other reasons, such as providing jobs, avoiding crumbling infrastructure and ensuring public security, not to mention a latecomer—as a stimulus policy in the economic recession (Guay and Émond, 2010). Also, compared with European cities, Canadian cities are trailing in adopting **Local Agendas 21** and in adopting an urban sustainability charter for municipalities to follow their European sisters (see, however, a statement of intention by the Federation of Canadian Municipalities, 2005). Although there are signs that mindsets and actions may be changing, there is still a long road toward sustainable urban policies and practices (Grant, 2006). Smart growth may be more amenable to a Canadian policy network, federal as well as provincial, that values growth in the context of globalization and believes that large Canadian cities should be active actors in the globalization process (Wolfe, 2003).

New Urbanism and Sustainability

If smart growth remains strongly economic, new urbanism is strongly "urbanistic." This planning innovation emerged in the 1980s when a diverse group of professionals, planners, architects, and urban analysts, sensing a change in attitudes of urban residents and seeing problems in the "natural" evolution of large urban areas, were concerned that urban spatial trends may be neither sustainable nor wholly desirable. Not only do growing cities consume space and resources, but they also invest heavily in infrastructure to sustain their growing pace. All of this is costly, and many trends in space occupation are wasteful. When public finances are tight, ideas may emerge to design means to spare land and investment in infrastructure. In this context, the idea of a compact city—or compact neighbourhoods, more appropriately, for the new urbanism—took root.

Post–World War II cities were planned very differently from one another. In Europe, governments were involved in planning, owing in part to postwar reconstruction needs (Hall, 1980a). But North American cities, and their new developments in particular, were less planned and left more to private initiatives. Planning, then, was often limited to regulating private decisions. When it came to large public investments in infrastructure and broad public policies, such as social housing, however, planning was called for (Hodge and Robinson, 2001). True, new large-city redevelopments and renewal were more planned and under the control of local governments or higher-tier governments. But the ruling philosophy was that housing, commercial, industrial, and office buildings were best left to the marketplace. Regulations ensured that local nuisances were avoided or minimized, despite planning ambitions by some professionals and officials for greater public involvement (Wolfe, 1984).

One of the greatest characteristics of the past 60 or so years of urban development is the consolidation of suburbs following the basic layout of individual housing, roads for the private car, commercial centres, and some public spaces in the form of recreation facilities and green spaces. This pattern, planned by nobody in particular, came to represent a way of life, the aspiring "urbanity" of a growing middle-class (Fishman, 1987; Jackson, 1985). Some planners, such as Americans Clarence Stein and Clarence Perry, helped to define some of its features, but many new suburbs were left to the interaction between developers and the consuming families and households. With the emerging environmental movement and the concerns toward nature and the environment, including the built environment, the relationship to space and resources was gradually redefined. In this context new ideas were formulated: Can cities consume less space and offer other forms in which urban life can be expressed? Can they be planned differently? Is a rethinking of planning models, either private or public, necessary?

The new urbanism school of urban planning thought so. The movement is a professional movement as was the previous *modern movement in planning and architecture* that dominated a large part of the twentieth century. The new urbanism movement had some resonance in official circles and local governments. Built around a small group of architects and planners whose professional practices were chiefly private, it gained some public recognition in public planning (Ouellet, 2006). But its supremacy as the leading planning model was disputed by the smart growth school of thought as well as by other conceptions and representations of urban life.

Like the smart growth "movement," new urbanism's origins are diverse. Concerned with new issues, such as the protection of the environment, the economic and environmental costs of urban development, and a more or less acknowledged longing for a sense of place and community, the new urbanism movement was built around a set of principles that ushered in, at least according to its proponents, a new relation to urban space and, as is often the case with urban planning and architecture, new relations between people. The basic ideas of new urbanism are the following:

- Walking should take a greater role in urban mobility. The car has relegated walking to short distances and as a secondary mode of mobility. The modern movement has been so obsessed with traffic congestion and with efficiency of goods and people movements that it has downgraded walking in urban space. But walking has many virtues. Indeed, when cities and neighbourhoods are planned to give a greater role to walking, health and environmental benefits are reaped. Moreover, people-walking may lead to social interactions; a greater sense of community could develop as a result.
- New urbanism promotes greater density and deeper diversity of people and buildings. The modern city has segregated the urban functions in almost exclusive zones of industry, commerce, and residence, with the consequence that car mobility became a necessity. This postwar planning ideal is best seen in the building of suburbs following World War II.
- A town or a city should have an identifiable centre and some identifiable peripheries. Although this principle is promulgated by the modern movement, as expressed in the Athens Charter (Le Corbusier, 1957), new urbanism is a reaction to the overall suburbanization trends from the 1970s and onward. This trend saw suburbs urbanized, with one or more centres of commercial and administrative activities, while at the same time the city centres lost their attraction and started degrading. While a large part of urban planning and decisions in the 1980s and 1990s was a strong public response to this trend, city centres lost their feathers and their historic role was not entirely regained, in many, although not all, Canadian cities, at least along the traditional functions and vocations (Guay and Hamel, 2010).
- A challenge to the compact city, denser and more diversified, is transport and mobility. As a result, the idea of transit-oriented communities, in the planning of new urban developments, is promoted (Laliberté, 2002). But the model can as well be applied to older communities that have lacked proper public transport systems in the past. Where the train and the tramways are structuring infrastructure in urban space, other modes of mobility, such as the bicycle, can be accommodated.
- Finally, new urbanism also pursues broader objectives, such as environmental sustainability and improvement of urban life through planned communities.

There are a number of criticisms of new urbanism (Garde, 2004; Ouellet, 2006). For some, it is a marketing strategy. Since new urbanism communities are often privately developed, its leading thinkers have a vested interest in emphasizing its merits while muting its limitations. Moreover, new urbanism communities are chiefly for the rich or the middle class and are rarely for the poor and the degraded central city neighbourhoods, despite some experiments in central city developments. Finally, new urbanism may be a concept with limited applications outside American and Canadian urban regions. European cities are denser and more diversified. They have been more publicly planned and the housing market has long been state oriented or state supplied. Despite these reservations, however, new urbanism concepts and ideals remain strong and fairly diffused.

With respect to smart growth, new urbanism appears local and less ambitious in scale and scope. Smart growth is a long-term strategy for urban development and planning that makes sense only at the regional level. While American states, such as Maryland and to some extent Oregon, have adopted the smart growth concept (Filion, 2003), new urbanism, by contrast, focuses on local interventions and mostly on new urban fringe developments. It is also more spatially oriented and less economically driven. However, both seem to agree with sustainable principles, and new urbanism, with its emphasis on livable communities, permeates the smart growth project (Curran and Tomalty, 2003: 11). As well, there is some overlapping between smart growth and new urbanism, but the two conceptions as a basis of "new planning" do still differ as one is an economic project with "urbanistic" implications while the other is an "urbanistic" project with economic implications.

Cities and Climate Change

Global environmental change is certainly a new reality, at least with respect to climate. For the past 10,000 years, the Earth's climate has been stable, with small peaks and troughs in temperature but nothing compared to an ice age (Archer, 2009: 64). Although there are large variations between the poles and the tropics, human ingenuity has allowed us to cope with differences in temperature, moisture, wind, and other environmental conditions.

If cities have in the past, and in the industrial era most noticeably, learned to solve some of their own environmental problems, they now are enmeshed in a much larger context. Local problems are not entirely out, but global problems are massively in. Two are worth considering, namely climate change and biodiversity loss. Climate change is truly a global problem but with many and diversified local impacts. Biodiversity loss is chiefly a local problem, but, when repeated hundreds or thousands of times, its consequences are truly global.

What can cities do to contribute to the general effort to solve these two problems, or at least to not contribute to their growth? Let us limit our inquiry to climate change since it is the most discussed problem and since the biodiversity debate and policy tend to focus, understandably but in part wrongly, on non-urban areas and on non-urban "ecosystems," although the Millennium Ecosystem Assessment (2003) takes urban habitats into account.[1]

For some time, at least in Canada, which is different from Europe, large cities were not much concerned with climate change. A survey of Canadian municipalities has shown that municipal official respondents thought that climate change was a policy concern for higher tiers of government and that they did not have the resources, specialized knowledge, or expertise to properly deal with the problem (Robinson and Dore, 2005). However, with the passing of time and probably spurred by an international movement for cities' involvement in climate change action, municipalities in Canada and in the United States gradually became leaders on climate change policy (Kousky and Schneider, 2003: Bulkeley and Betsill, 2003). Why this change of heart? Have they acquired more resources to fight global warming, or have they become more aware of and sensitive to large cities' impact on the climate? Both reasons played their part, but the change may also be due to national governments' reluctance to adopt a strong climate change policy.

Federal Government Response

Canada has signed and ratified the United Nations Framework Convention on Climate Change (UNFCCC) and the Kyoto Protocol. The UNFCCC (1992) and the following protocol (1997) were instruments for fighting climate change—more precisely to stabilize the world climate, which is predicted to warm—at the international level. Canada has not been a good international citizen for it has done very little to respect its international engagements. Two other "villains" among developed countries, Australia and the United Sates, have not ratified the Kyoto Protocol. Each seems to have its own reasons for not going along with other nations and, as demanded by the Kyoto Protocol, in reducing, on average, by 5 per cent (based on 1990) their own **greenhouse gas (GHG)** emissions. In the case of Canada, the increase of GHG emissions has been an important issue since the signing of the Kyoto Protocol in 1997. By the end of the first decade of this century, the emissions had grown by about 25 per cent compared to 1990, substantially higher than in the United States (Québec, 2008). It is no wonder, then, that a Canadian plan is still forthcoming and that the regulatory framework on offer is deemed unsatisfactory (National Round Table on the Environment and the Economy, 2007).

There are many reasons, or factors, why the Canadian federal government has had problems in getting out a national plan on climate change, despite some attempts in the past, such as the so-called Green Project (Murphy and Murphy, 2012). One reason is that energy and natural resources are under the jurisdiction of provincial governments. Energy use and policies are highly diversified across Canada. Québec, Manitoba, and British Columbia, for example, rely heavily on hydro power to produce their electricity whereas Alberta, Saskatchewan, and, to a lesser degree because of nuclear power, Ontario abundantly use fossil fuels (oil, coal, and natural gas) to generate their electricity. Greenhouse gas emissions thus vary significantly among provinces. Moreover, the industry has not been forthcoming in the promotion of a national climate change plan. The industry in general, although not all businesses, is afraid of potential production cost increases due to policies aimed at reducing GHG emissions. For instance, a carbon tax will bear heavily on some industrial sectors, the electricity-generating and natural resources sectors in particular, and less on others. Some provincial economies, although not all, are dependent on resources extraction and energy production and may be adversely affected by climate change measures, whether regulatory, fiscal, or market-based. The industry has tended to advise not doing more than the American government with respect to climate policy for fear of losing their competitive advantage to American companies since they operate in a continental economy. Unlike in the United States, in Canada one cannot factor in a strong and active counter-expertise on climate change, led by some scientists, industrial actors, and a conservative movement. True, there is, in Canada, a small group of scientists calling themselves Friends of Science who are highly critical of the whole thrust of climate change science and policy, but their influence and impact are negligible. Moreover, some polls show that Canadians, despite regional variations, are concerned with climate change, are ready to make sacrifices through tax and prices increase, and would like the Kyoto Protocol to be respected, although now it is much too late.

In analyzing why the federal government has been reluctant to embrace sustainable development, some Canadian researchers (Toner and Meadowcroft, 2009) think that there are political and administrative factors against environmental policy innovation in Canada. The structural factor, which has to do with the structure of the federal political system, encourages partisan negotiations, which are often detrimental to compromise and responsible policy making even in a social democracy such as Canada. The cultural factor explains why the federal government is chiefly focused on the economy and on people's welfare and less so on the environment. Recent and past history of the federal government has shown that its role has mainly been focused on promoting economic growth across Canada and equalizing the social conditions among the provinces. The federal public service is, according to Tonner and Meadowcroft, somewhat more conservative on policy innovations. This administrative factor hinders a clear embrace of sustainability. Whether it is sustainable development or climate change policy, a whole set of reasons converge to limit the federal engagement in innovative environmental policies.

Cities Lead the Fight

In what has long been a policy vacuum at the federal level, cities—as well as provinces and states in Canada and the United States—have begun to fill the gap (Selin and VanDeVeer, 2009). In the absence of a strong national policy, what factors explain why cities take on the climate change policy agenda? Have the same citizens who accept timidity at the national level become intrepid in the cities they live in? Are local forums more prone to discussion and debate over the environment? Is the sample of local politicians a new breed of decision takers, more daring and less constrained by tradition and less afraid of negative public reactions? Are local politics more consensual than national politics? Or is climate policy at the municipal level a means to build political capital for local politicians? The answers to these questions are far from being straightforward. It is true, as Anthony Giddens has observed (2009), that a great deal of the climate change debate has been about costs, undesirable changes in lifestyle, constraints, and, on the whole, less freedom to enjoy, at low cost, modern technology goods, such as the car, the use of electricity, and so forth. A change of discourse seems to be called for. Have cities found a way to make acceptable local sacrifices by transforming them into benefits? If so, why have national governments not followed the same path and emphasized the benefits that can be gained with a strong climate policy? People cannot be so different when they vote locally as when they vote nationally.

Let us suggest three reasons for this difference between cities and national governments, at least with respect to Canada: first, public participation in policy issues is, in general, much stronger at the local level than at the national level. Indeed, the public participation movement has, in large part, started in cities and municipalities. The 1960s and 1970s urban movements for more public input into urban policy and projects have created local conditions for a stronger and ongoing public participation on local issues (Guay, 2005). Public participation is now recognized in planning legislation and practices. There is a culture of participation as well as of debate on planning issues and decisions. For two decades following World War II, large cities were submitted to some sort of experiment—whether it was controlled or not is another issue—called urban modernization in the guise of urban renewal, infrastructure development, transport and housing policies, and so forth. As a result, local associations and groups came to criticize and oppose local decisions. The urban movements were not only opposed to a lot of projects, but they wanted to contribute inputs to urban policies and planning decisions. In many large Canadian cities, the political landscape changed: it was more open to "social democratic" ideas and policies about what a city should be. In Québec City, in Montréal, in Toronto, and in Vancouver, "left-wing" politics were experimented with and pursued for some years, leading to important shifts in planning decisions. A sort of balance was struck between economic interests and other social interests. Québec City is a good example (Guay and Hamel, 2010; Mercier, 2002). Over a period of two decades starting at the end of the 1980s, Québec City's centre was transformed not according to plans and ideals of a "growth coalition" but according to plans, ideals, and visions of a more balanced group of interests. Local politicians learned to better respond to this diversity of interests.

The second reason for the difference in the ways that cities and national governments deal with climate change policy is to do with what cities have to offer and what cities provide to their citizens. A non-policy, or a weak policy, on climate change at the federal level seems to have no impact in the short run. People, except for environmental NGOs and climate scientists, would not press themselves to pressure their representatives to adopt a strong climate change policy. Moreover, and here Canada is still a revealing case, *benefits* are spread out whereas large *costs* may be concentrated on a few social actors. If a carbon tax were imposed, people would not take it smilingly, and strong economic interests—such as fossil fuel producers and large consumers—may revolt. In sum, this is in the nature of politics: costs seen, but benefits (a cleaner environment tomorrow) unseen. Yet it is possible that in an urban context benefits as well as costs are visible. Fossil fuel consumption in using cars for urban transport is seen as increasing pollution just as increasing the public transport supply can be seen more directly in the present as well as in the near future: cleaner air, less noise, less congestion.

The third reason for the differences in the ways that cities and the national government deal with climate change is that municipalities are the chief agents of planning decisions although they do share some decisions with higher levels of government, such as transport and housing policies. Urban planning decisions can make great strides in fighting climate change. Public transport policy and infrastructure change are major actions to reduce GHG emissions. Many "adaptation" actions are related to spatial planning, urban as well regional. Flooding, for example, caused by climate change, can partly be controlled through land-use regulations. In a warmer climate, urban hot spots can be a health risk for many people. Proper planning measures, such as increasing vegetation and green spaces, can alleviate the problem. These decisions are highly visible. People can see for themselves some of the impacts of an urban policy.

Mitigation Measures and Adaptation Measures

The UNFCCC has defined two types of action necessary to achieve the goal of stabilizing the climate system: (1) measures "to mitigate climate change by addressing anthropogenic emissions by sources and removals by sinks of all greenhouse gases not controlled by the Montréal Protocol" and (2) measures "to facilitate adequate adaptation to climate change" (United Nations, 1992, article 4.1. B). *Mitigation measures* are, to put it simply, actions taken now, or very soon, to reduce the current level of emissions. *Adaptation measures* are to anticipate what the future will be and to prepare communities and people for a warmer climate and all of its impacts.

If the mitigation measures and policies have dominated international and national debates over the best way to stabilize the climate system—and the 1997 Kyoto Protocol is a mitigation agreement—adaptation actions are looming in the policy future. Québec's action plan (2006–2012), the federal regulatory framework, and many provincial plans, weak or strong, try to address the issues of reducing greenhouse gas. Adaptation measures, however, trail behind mitigation measures. Whereas policy-makers seem to know what the options are in mitigation action, adaptation is a less developed policy action despite the IPCC message and analysis that we should prepare more consistently for a warmer climate (IPCC, 2007).

Thus two types of measures, decided in tandem, are needed to face climate change. What actions have cities preferred and chosen? Some authors have suggested classifying urban policies with regard to climate change according to whether they are self-governed, governed through enabling, governed by provision, or governed by authority (Alber and Kern, 2008: 6; Bulkeley and Kern, 2006). *Self-governed actions* are ones where municipalities and local governments can decide on the areas they control and are responsible for what are the best measures for themselves. *Governing through enabling* means that, through education and advice, urban citizens are prompted to change their behaviours. For instance, campaigns for energy efficiency, for waste reduction, and for recycling waste products lead people to behavioural change. *Governing by provision* refers to the public sector buying goods and services that are "climate-friendly." *Governing by authority* is more in tune with what governments are expected to do: impose legislation and regulations on activities and on people' choices. For instance, transport policy to limit urban car use is an authority-governed type of governance. However, it may also belong to the provision type of governance because governments may impose certain regulations on manufacturers for energy efficiency. In other words, there is some overlapping between governance types, and one can expect that effectiveness in climate policy should rely on combining two, three, or all types. Advice and publicity campaigns to reduce each urban citizen's impact on climate may be ineffective if not accompanied by strict regulations and alternative options to the car.

These different measures effectively come into play when we consider that all large Canadian cities have recently produced a Climate Action Plan (CAP). Such plans can be divided in two types: (1) a corporate type that deals with how the municipality is going to reduce its own emissions of greenhouses gases and (2) a larger plan that aims at engaging other stakeholders in the Climate Action Plan, such as businesses, households, and other public institutions, to constitute a sort of whole community, or whole area, plan. GHG reductions vary accordingly. Community-wide objectives are more difficult to reach than in-house objectives because the former plans are dependent on decisions made by a wide variety of social actors and organizations. These decisions can be helped by different measures governed by provision, enabling, and authority. Self-governed measures may come rather easily, but they only concern municipal organizations, buildings, and activities that municipalities are responsible for. However, whether the measures are self-governed or not, urban authorities have to act in the four main sectors of activities as identified by researchers: energy, transport, waste, and urban planning and land use (Alber and Kern, 2008: 6).

Following are a few examples of urban objectives on climate change:

- Toronto wants to reduce its GHG by 6 per cent in 2012, 30 per cent in 2020, and 80 per cent in 2050. The base year is 1990. In other words, the Toronto community and Toronto municipality are determined to more or less respect Canadian engagements in the Kyoto Protocol and, in accordance with the best scientific estimates, plan to reduce by a large amount (80 per cent) their greenhouse gas emissions. Among large Canadian cities, Toronto seems to be in the vanguard.
- The City of Montréal plan is less ambitious. It aims at reducing the GHG emissions by 20 per cent, based on year 2005, but this policy applies only to the city's activities and buildings.
- Vancouver distinguishes between its own corporate objectives and the community as a whole. The former is more ambitious whereas the latter is more modest. While corporate Vancouver (activities pertaining to and buildings belonging to the municipality) intends to reduce its GHG emissions by 20 per cent (base year 1990) in the years to come, the city is much less forward-looking for the community as whole, planning only a 6 per cent reduction in 2012.

Large cities, as we can see, are following the spirit of the Kyoto Protocol even if the federal government has abandoned it. In this regard, such cities are in tune with Canadian public opinion, which prefers sticking with the Kyoto Protocol rather than opting for a plan adapted to the Canadian context. Things have changed since the 1990s, when the Canadian municipalities were much less active on the climate change issue. All of the large Canadian cities participate in the initiative of the Canadian Federation of Municipalities. This participation may act as a stimulus for each of them.

Most of the urban plans and measures are concerned with mitigation, the first term of the UNFCCC's equation on combating climate change and stabilizing the Earth's climate. Adaptation measures (as of 2009), however, are far from being as developed as mitigation measures. Toronto is again at the forefront (Toronto, 2008). Vancouver has also examined how the whole urban region can prepare itself for a warmer climate and has set up a working group on climate adaptation. Other large cities and urban regions are concerned with planning for adaptation, but they have only recently discovered that the problem concerns them as well. Adaptation is at times subsumed under a sustainable development plan, as in Ottawa and Calgary.

Not much is known about why cities choose to prepare a plan, whether there has been a large public consultation and whether progress has been made. True, some cities publish yearly reports of where they stand, but nothing systematic and comparative has been carried out. Likewise, even less is known about why and how urban authorities decide to prepare such plans. And little is actually known about other local actors: how they participated in the plan development, whether they agreed wholeheartedly, or whether they were reluctant to be associated with the plans. Indeed, a sociological analysis of climate change policy-making at the urban level is missing.

It is more and more obvious that climate-change policy is a stepping stone in sustainable development. Some cities have already acknowledged that no progress on the path of sustainability can be made if the climate-change issue is not factored in. When the climate-change issue reached the international polity, the problem was couched in terms of a challenge for all of humanity. The idea of sustainable development played the same card: "There is only one Earth"; "Our Common Future." Worries were about ecosystem integrity for when ecosystems are damaged, there may be grave and irreversible impacts on human activities, health, and well-being. While scientists, policy-makers, and environmentalists tried to convince people, governments, and the industry to reduce GHG emissions, opponents and policy-makers started to calculate the costs of and climate-change policy's impacts on economic growth. Economic considerations took over, even dwarfed, ecological concerns.

The more the global debate and controversy over climate change penetrated all institutions and all nations, the more the climate-change debate switched to focusing on differentiated impacts of a warmer world. Coastline and delta populations will be affected overwhelmingly (Stern, 2009). Arid regions of the planet will most likely become dryer and if developed-world cities and agriculture may not be spared by a changing climate, at least— and in contrast to developing-world populations—they will have greater means to adapt to a warmer world. As a consequence, the global debate turned to equity and to justice concerns, as shown internationally since the Johannesburg Summit and the recent conferences of the Parties at Copenhagen and Cancun on climate change. If large Canadian cities are moving along the adaptation path in their urban governance, they will have to be more concerned with equity and with **environmental justice** issues (Adger et al., 2006).

In Search of the Sustainable City

The World Commission on Environment and Development (WCED) devoted a whole chapter to urban challenges (1987, chap. 9). While a great deal of its analysis and recommendations were addressed to cities in the developing world, some ideas were highly relevant to the already developed world cities. For instance, the WCED highlighted the environmental problems of developed cities that consume, because they are richer, a lot of energy and resources and, through sprawl, valuable agricultural areas. It also pinpointed that social housing in many countries is ineffective, both private and public, because of its poor quality. But one relevant criticism for this section of our chapter is that the quality of urban infrastructure remains poor and in urgent need of improvement and restoration, and that new infrastructure have to be thought out anew. Finally, the focus on cars in planning policies has led to pollution, noise, and congestion, which are the usual complaints about the difficult co-existence between the car and the city. Agenda 21 contains a long chapter on human settlements, in which large cities in the developed countries have some work to do to be on the sustainable development path.

Sustainable development is composed of three broad principles: (1) ecological integrity, (2) economic efficiency, and (3) social justice. All are constantly reaffirmed in the official literature, including the Canadian act on sustainable development, and in provincial legislation on sustainable development (Canada, 2008; Québec, 2008). Social justice and economic efficiency are strong reasons to act in urban areas. Many infrastructure are provided for economic benefits, such as roads, motorways, ports, and airports, but others are provided for personal and social benefits, such as clean water and waste disposal. Public transport is planned and provided for both purposes. In order to achieve sustainable development, the three objectives must be met and must guide policy-making. Although many cities claim to aim at sustainable development, examples of cities that have already reached this stage are scarcer. Urban sustainability has, in various fashions, revolved around three main points: (1) "to reduce the external footprint"; (2) "to make the city more liveable"; and (3) "to make the suburbs more sustainable" because "suburbs are the least efficient component of an urban concentration" (Bugliarello, 2006: 25).

Are there examples of sustainable cities? Perhaps not, but some new urban developments are progressing in that direction (McGranahan and Satterthwaite, 2003). Experiences in ecological planning have been achieved in some European cities, such as Freiburg, Germany, a case well researched and talked about, and in new developments in Sweden and the Netherlands. Some are rehabilitated industrial zones (Dumesnil and Ouellet, 2002). European municipalities adopted, in 1994, a charter on local sustainability, called the Aarlborg Charter (European Conference on Sustainable Cities & Towns, 1994). In particular, these municipalities want to do their part in fighting climate change, which can be achieved in many ways, but a change in transport policy is a key element. Moreover, some cities, such as Stockholm, have embarked on the protection, restoration, and improvement of urban biodiversity by enlarging urban parks and connecting them. In so doing, they have created, although it seems at first sight contradictory, an "urban biosphere" (Dogsé, 2004; Platt, 2004).

Urban restoration ecology, and restoration ecology for that matter, encompasses a large set of practices and is helping to bring back nature in cities (Gross, 2010; Jorgensen and Gobster, 2010). Gross has observed that citizens' organizations and stakeholders were often instrumental in the rise of ecological restoration, in particular in cities. But the scientific approach has moved in, developing **restoration ecology** as opposed to ecological restoration, and has given scientific foundation to the practices. However, some examples show that scientists, planners, and citizens can co-operate in bringing about restoration projects. For instance, Gobster (2001) has studied the interactions between stakeholders in the restoration of Lincoln Park in Chicago. Gross (2010) has on the same project concluded that Lincoln Park has been successful because stakeholders have been able to take into account nature's response—which he calls ecological surprises—to human action and to accept that not everything is known about the environment and the ecosystems—which he calls "non-knowledge." In short, in projects of ecological restoration, ignorance has to be factored in; as well, openness to surprises leads to better planning and social acceptability. Examples of ecological park restoration in cities are accompanied by sister projects of urban river renewal in Canadian cities, including in Toronto (the Don River) and in Québec City (the Saint-Charles River), where some aquatic and banks restoration has been achieved and is still under way (Québec).

There remains a lot to be accomplished on the sustainable development front. But policies and practices are changing and seem to be changing for good. Once a city is redesigned in a more compact way, is better able to control sprawl, and is investing heavily in public transport, it will be difficult to undo what has been done. There is, as Hommels (2005) has aptly described, "obduracy" in urban systems, in other words, physical resistance in the urban form, at times on top of social resistance. The goal of achieving sustainable cities is similar to the goal of achieving, one-and-a-half centuries earlier, the livable industrial city. However, the urban challenge today is compounded by rapid urbanization worldwide and by the expansion of large cities in the developing world, where economic, social, and environmental problems are tightly linked and much harder to tackle and solve (Myllyla and Kuvaja, 2005). The urban sustainability challenge is surely worldwide but also highly differentiated depending on cities' location in the world system and their stages of development. A unique vision of the urban sustainable future may not be warranted even though the three principles of sustainable development must be upheld.

Conclusion

This chapter explored the pathways to the sustainable city. Sustainability and the sustainable city are responses to modern society's and industrial society's relationship to nature, a relationship that has, partly, gone wrong. As a result, models and practices have been designed to move urban planning and policy in the direction of sustainable development. New urbanism and smart growth are heralded as the best way to achieve urban sustainability. But these models show limits, and criticisms have been levelled at them. Climate change has become a new and major policy issue for large Canadian cities. Although municipal authorities were at first reluctant to enter this policy arena, they have embraced it for reasons that have to do with how cities work. Canadian municipalities have also produced policy statements, but they are only at a preliminary stage; a great deal of work remains to be done. For example, a closer connection with the biodiversity issue is needed.

Finally, we can ask whether the technology city of the twentieth century lost all links to nature. Receding nature in large cities has been a long and consistent historical process, but cities, like people, cannot totally escape from nature. The habit of conceiving and defining cities as socio-technological systems may no longer depict the true nature of what the sustainable city should be. In the context of global environmental change, cities may be better thought of as social, technical, as well as ecological systems, in which the services provided by nature, such as clean air, pure water, a stable climate, and biodiversity, are valued, protected, and restored when urban ecosystems are damaged (Pincetl, 2010).

The chapter has been about planning challenges and about broad ideas for change. Smart growth, despite its limits, foretells a story of long-term and large-scale change that can be closely linked to climate-change policies in large urban areas. New urbanism can best operate at a small to medium scale for it focuses on new urban developments and urban neighbourhood planning. Both planning ideas can be seen as technological solutions (re-designing urban form, planning public and private transport, providing for green and blue spaces, etc.) to a host of environmental problems. But cities cannot be changed overnight. They have their own momentum, to use a physical metaphor, and change is often more incremental than radical. What to do with the existing urban forms and objects, with an old stock of housing, with the current layout and facilities already built and in use? In order to reach some sort of sustainability, urban policies should also be about retrofitting the technologies and objects in place (Biello, 2011).

The housing stock, for example, can be greatly improved not only by new urbanism projects but also by preserving and retrofitting what is already on the ground. The federal program—if and when it is maintained—to improve the energy efficiency of old houses and buildings may, in the long run, go a long way toward promoting urban sustainability. Not only will the urban buildings and infrastructure consume less energy but they will also remain in use, and less material will have to be disposed of. This may help reduce the ecological footprint of large cities, that is, the amount of matter and energy consumed by urban dwellers and by the urban way of life. This of course does not preclude radical technological change in energy systems, and in using and recycling material. Policies of urban sustainability, however, open the door to many incremental changes that may include a variety of technological changes, both old and new.

Questions for Critical Thought

1. Why are large sprawling cities now seen as a problem?
2. Why is an ecosystem approach to cities of limited use?
3. What are the main problems of current cities in the developed world?
4. Why have large Canadian cities decided to act on the climate-change issue?
5. What are the barriers, social or otherwise, to a sustainable city?
6. Would you say that urban retrofitting (of houses and buildings, for instance) is a better way to promote sustainability than new urbanism and smart growth? Please develop an argument that takes into account technological change.

Suggested Readings

Boone C.G. and A. Modarres. 2006. *City and Environment*. Philadelphia: Temple University Press. The book is a broad view of the city and the environment. Ideas such as healthy cities and green cities are explored. Green spaces and parks are modern planning tools.

Hommels, A. 2005. *Unbuilding Cities: Obduracy in Urban Socio-Technical Change*. Cambridge, MA: MIT Press. This is an interesting analysis of the urban form and the constraints of space and of built infrastructure on planning options and change.

Mol, A.P.J., D.J. Sonnenfeld, and G. Spaargaren, 2009. *The Ecological Modernisation Reader: Environmental Reform in Theory and Practice*. London: Routledge. The book seeks to understand what ecological modernization is all about. The great variety of papers is introduced by leading exponents of the ecological modernization thesis.

UK Sustainable Development Commission. 2009. *Prosperity without Growth? Transition to a Sustainable Economy*. Retrieved from www.sd-commission.org.uk. This report is worth reflecting on. New paths to prosperity are explored. Although cities are not the central issues they should be, they are nonetheless a part of the sustainability challenge.

Related Websites

Smart Growth Canada Network

www.smartgrowth.ca

This is a national organization, founded in 2003, promoting smart growth and change in urban planning and governance toward sustainability across the country "through education, research and capacity building strategies for the broad range of decision makers." Implementing smart growth and sustainability is the network's overarching goal.

United Nations Environment Programme (UNEP)

www.unep.org

UNEP is an international organization that focuses on understanding global environmental change and exploring avenues to sustainability.

International Human Dimensions Programme on Global Environmental Change (IHDP)

www.ihdp.unu.edu/

Linked to many global research programs on the environment, the IHDP focuses on the role played by human societies and activities in changing the global environment. Research explores how the Earth as a system, or system of systems, can be "governed and managed."

9   Globalization and the Urban Way of Life

Learning Objectives

◎   To understand whether the urban way of life is changing in the context of globalization

◎   To define and discuss the globalization concept

◎   To examine the idea of the global or world city

◎   To assess urban strategies in the context of globalization and post-industrialism

◎   To describe the urban divide in the global urban South

Introduction

We cannot understand cities and their recent evolution without looking at the process of globalization. Although a complex social phenomenon, globalization is the broader context in which cities, in particular the city-region, are more and more defined. The three pillars of urban sociology—urbanization, urbanity (a way of life), and urbanism (urban planning and urban materiality)—which serve as guiding principles for the whole book, are undergoing great transformation under the process of globalization.

The purpose of this chapter is to analyze recent urban evolution in the context of globalization. The chapter is divided into four sections: (1) the process of world urbanization; (2) the meaning of globalization as a complex process and as a representation of a changing world; (3) the meaning of the global city; and (4) the features of the global urban South/global South. The chapter will conclude by asking whether an urbanized world will necessarily be a more sustainable and just world. Topics already examined, such as compact cities, urban concentration, and new models of urban planning are all relevant to determining whether the urbanizing world is on the path of sustainability and urban livability. To reach these two objectives, some conditions have to be met and public action has to be set in motion.

An Urban World in the Making

For the first time, the world has become truly urban: more than half the population is now living in cities, and many people live in large and very large ones (see Table 9.1). Moreover, the twentieth-century city has shown large increases in some basic numbers (see Table 9.2). Let us comment on some trends leading to an urbanization of the world that is linked to an all-around globalization process.

Table 9.1 Urban Population Change: % Urban Population by World Regions

Region (total)	1950 (2,518,600,000)	1975 (4,068,200,000)	2000 (6,070,600,000)	2030 (8,130,100,000)
World	29.1	37.3	47.1	60.8
Africa	14.9	25.3	37.1	53.5
Asia	16.6	24.0	37.1	54.5
Europa	51.2	66.0	72.7	79.6
Central and South America	41.9	61.2	75.5	84.6
North America	63.9	73.8	79.1	86.9
Oceania	60.6	71.7	72.7	74.9
Developed Countries	52.5	67.2	73.9	81.7
Developing Countries	17.9	26.9	40.5	57.1

Source: United Nations: *World Urbanization Prospects*, 2003: Retrieved from www.esa-un.org/unep/

Table 9.2 The Twentieth Century Growth Pace

Indicators	Multiplication Factor
World population	4
% Urban population	13
World economy	14
Industrial production	40
Energy consumption	16
CO_2 emissions	17
Water use	9
Ocean fisheries	35
Land irrigated	5
Land for food	2
Forests	0.8 (−20%)

Source: McNeill, J.R. 2000. *Something New Under the Sun: An Environmental History of the Twentieth-Century World*. New York: Norton, 360–61.

Over the last 50 to 60 years, the world has urbanized rapidly. In 1950 less than 30 per cent of the population lived in cities. By the year 2000, that number increased to close to 50 per cent, and during the 2000–2010 decade it did reach the 50 per cent mark. Projections show that the urbanization process will continue unabated and that by 2030 60 per cent of the population will live in cities. Continents each followed their own pathways to urbanization, however. Europe and North America urbanized early, as was shown in Chapter 3, with more than half their population duly urbanized by 1950. But Europe lagged behind North America: in 1950, 51 per cent of the European population lived in cities compared with close to 64 per cent of the North American population. Although at the end of the nineteenth century Great Britain was an urban society, other European countries, notably in Eastern Europe, had a fairly large rural population. Oceania, thanks to Australia and New Zealand, was in 1950 highly urbanized. And South and Central Americas were also on a sustained urbanization path. In Latin America countries, cities were built almost from scratch during the colonial period. As well, a long tradition of urbanization is clearly visible in the colonial past of many New World countries (Bairoch, 1985: chap. 26). On the other hand, Asia and Africa started their urbanization process comparatively late. Although both continents had long-standing cities and, for some countries including China, India, but also the Arab countries and Iran, a glorious urban past, rural living was still in 1950 the dominant way of life, with a rate of urbanization barely over 15 per cent. The United Nations projections indicate that both continents will be fully urban (at least half the population living in cities) by 2030. Finally, if the urbanization rate of developing countries will be over 80 per cent by 2030, the developing world will eventually catch up, reaching 60 per cent by 2030.

Large cities (those with over a million inhabitants) were for many centuries mainly a developed world phenomenon. London, Paris, Berlin, Vienna, all centres of empires, or New York, Chicago, and Tokyo, with their own "internal empires," ruled the urban world and more in economic, political, and cultural terms. The future, however, may be quite different with very large cities coming from the global South (identified as the set of all developing countries as opposed to the developed North).

The "global South" is an expression encompassing different realities. Despite its wide diversity of situations, cultures, and economies, the global South is nowadays taken as a key actor in world trends and decisions, problems, and challenges. Not all countries in the global South fare the same. Many representatives of this global South, which includes other countries in addition to those in the southern hemisphere, are developing and urbanizing very fast. For instance, John Friedmann (2005) and Terry McGee (2007) have described the urbanization process of recent China: four to five "mega urban" regions are taking shape in China, each containing some 80 to

100 million people. These regions are capable of accommodating rural areas and agricultural activities in their midst to form some kind of town and country model on a scale Ebenezer Howard would never have dreamed of. In India, similar processes are taking place, where larger urban areas are transforming themselves into mega urban regions although their recent

---

Box 9.1

China, an Urban Society

China is an old urban society that has experienced many changes in pace and extent of urbanization in its long history. Recently, though, its urbanization has been accelerating. Under the communist government of Mao (roughly between 1949 and 1979), there was a strong anti-urban bias. Development would come from the countryside, and cities were often seen as living off the rural people. This conception is found in some classical Marxist writings about the relative importance of cities and rural areas. But on the whole urbanization was checked only for a period. There was a secular movement toward city life because cities offered a variety of ways of life and a diversity of goods, jobs, and other benefits, such as education and culture. Because they are large and more diversified, cities breed greater productivity in economic activities. Geographically, urban areas are concentrated in the Eastern part of China, and this pattern is centuries, if not millennia, old (Wu and Gaubatz, 2013: 310).

At the end of the European medieval period (fifteenth and sixteenth centuries), China was a highly urbanized civilization (the term *civilization* is more appropriate than *society* because of the geographical and demographic size of China). When the Western civilization embarked on its many revolutions (scientific, industrial, democratic, and geographic), China stagnated and missed these revolutions, in particular the industrial revolution, which started there timidly only at the end of the nineteenth century (or perhaps even the beginning of the twentieth century).

During a large part of the twentieth century (1911–1949), China witnessed periods of turmoil, which were not always conducive to a strong urbanization and a strong urban society and economy. However, after the Maoist period, China chose, in the 1980s, to industrialize at a very fast pace and to develop its economy more or less according to some market principles. At first it was hoped that this industrialization would take place chiefly in the countryside, with the small and medium-size cities the focal point of the double process of urbanization and industrialization. But the dynamics of industrial development prefer large industrial plants and large cities.

Nowadays, China has an urban structure and hierarchy that are built around enormous urbanized regions, where rural areas are intermingled with large urban areas and where the population reaches the hundreds of millions. The main corridors of urbanization are the following: in the South, the Pearl River area with Guangdong as the urban centre; in the North, Beijing is the urban node of a long

growth rate has stabilized, even declined (UN-Habitat, 2008/2009: 20–1). These two countries do not necessarily represent things to come for all developing countries, but they do indicate a trend, or a wave, of the future. The megalopolis, no longer the sole preserve of developed countries, is spreading widely across the globe.

urban corridor leading to the coast; in the Centre of China, Shanghai, the economic capital of the country, is the centre of a very large corridor of urbanization; and finally, the interior of China has an urban corridor centred around the large city of Chongqing (Wu and Gaubatz, 2013: 119).

China's cities are not particularly environmental paradises, to say the least. There have been internal and external criticisms of urban environmental management. However, Wu and Gaubatz (2013: chap. 11) pinpoint that, in part owing to urban protests, urban environmental policy is no longer avoidable, in particular related to air and water pollution.

(© Nikada/iStockphoto)

Shanghai, an important metropolis, is in one of the main corridors of urbanization in China.

If New York, Tokyo, London, and Paris have, in population size and economic clout, led the world during most of the twentieth century, most of them will be surpassed by cities in developing countries at least in demographic terms (see Table 9.3). Already by the beginning of the twenty-first century, only three cities of the developed world (Tokyo, New York-Newark, and the Los Angeles region) were among the top 12 largest cities by population. And the United Nations projects that by 2025 only Tokyo and the New York area will remain in this megacities club. The fastest growing urban areas are on the whole coming from emerging economies: China, India, Mexico, and Brazil. Other fast-growing cities come from countries that are not yet considered emerging economies but that may prove to be so in the future, such as Dhaka, Bangladesh; Karachi, Pakistan; and Kinshasa, Democratic Republic of the Congo. But, as we have already stressed, numbers are not all. The urban picture is much more complex, contrasted, and nuanced, with light, dark, and twilight zones as in many good paintings.

Not all of the recent urbanization process has taken place in the big (1 to 5 million), large (5 to 10 million), and megacities (over 10 million), according to UN-Habitat (2008/2009: 18). In Africa, small cities grew rapidly between 1990 and 2000; in India, cities of all sizes have grown at about the same rate, that is, between 2 and 3 per cent on average annually. In the developed world, however, it is the largest cities that have grown the fastest.

Table 9.3 Growth of the Largest World Megacities, 2007 and 2025

Megacity 2007	Population (thousands)	Megacity 2025	Population (thousands)
1. Tokyo, Japan	35,676	1. Tokyo, Japan	36,400
2. Mexico City, Mexico	19,028	2. Mumbai, India	26,385
3. New York-Newark, US	19,040	3. Delhi, India	22,498
4. Sao Paulo, Brazil	18,845	4. Dhaka, Bangladesh	22,015
5. Mumbai, India	18,978	5. Sao Paulo, Brazil	21,428
6. Delhi, India	15,926	6. Mexico City, Mexico	21,009
7. Shanghai, China	14,987	7. New York-Newark, US	20,628
8. Kolkata, India	14,787	8. Kolkata, India	20,560
9. Buenos Aires, Argentina	12,795	9. Shanghai, China	19,412
10. Dhaka, Bangladesh	13,485	10. Karachi, Pakistan	19,095
11. Los Angeles-Long Beach-Santa Ana, US	12,500	11. Kinshasa, Democratic Republic of the Congo	16,762

Source: UN-Habitat, 2008/2009. *State of the World's Cities*, p. 6 - www.unhabitat.org/pmss/listItemDetails.aspx?publicationID=2562.

How does the world urbanization rate compare to other significant rates of growth? Historian John R. McNeill (2000: 360–61), in his environmental history of the world in the twentieth century, has compared rates of growth of different indicators (see Table 9.2). The world population has grown by a factor of 4 over the past 100 years whereas the urban population grew by a factor of 13. If the world economy grew by a factor of 14, it was, by a wide margin, surpassed by industrial production (40 times). Meanwhile, land cultivated and irrigated grew at a much slower pace: 2 and 5 times, respectively. The energy consumption grew by a factor of 16, and the greenhouse gases emissions by about the same factor (17 times). These numbers draw an interesting picture of the world we have built. It is an urban world where electricity, a great technology of the last century, informs us where we live and where we will, in all likelihood, be living in the decades to come.

Globalization and Globality: Process and Representation

The globalization of the world is an ongoing process. For some, globalization is an economic process spurred by advances in technologies of information and communication. For others, it is basically a political process brought about by international institutions in which the states play a leading part but are forced to cede some of their power to international agencies. And for others, there can be no globalization if there is no cultural process of seeing the world as a whole, as a shared planet, as an environment shared by a common humanity.

These understandings and partial conceptions of globalization point to a complex, manifold process. Although the world of today may be just a little more globalized than the world at the end of the nineteenth century, as some authors have recognized (Bairoch and Kozul-Wright, 1996; Held et al., 1999), this does not mean that today's globalization is not unique or special. What is, thus, particular to today's globalization? It is obvious that technology has been greatly enhanced over the past 100 years, that economic exchanges have increased immensely, with new nations taking part in the international market, and that an international political order has been in place since the end of World War II. But there is nevertheless a feeling of something new today. David Held and his co-authors have explored at great length the globalization process. They define it in the following terms:

> A process (or set of processes) which embodies a transformation in the spatial organization of social relations and transactions—assessed in terms of their extensity, intensity, velocity and impact—generating transcontinental or interregional flows and networks of activity, interaction, and the exercise of power. (Held et al., 1999: 16)

This comprehensive definition highlights the relationships between space and social relations, as well as the changing nature of transactions among human societies and among human beings. Moreover, according to this definition, flows of goods, people, and ideas—this is implied more than explicitly stated—have accelerated, have deepened, and have intensified. In a short but well-crafted book on globalization, especially for its contrasts between the ideal and the reality of globalization, sociologist Malcolm Waters defines it more succinctly, albeit not less meaningfully, as follows: "A social process in which the constraints of geography on social and cultural arrangements recede and in which people become increasingly aware that they are receding" (Waters, 1995: 3). Waters' definition adds something decisive to the globalization process, which may be the key element distinguishing the end of the twentieth-century process from that of the end of the nineteenth century. The globalization process is also cultural, expressing itself as an awareness of receding constraints of space and distance. "Awareness," however, is a difficult idea: how can one know if people today are more aware of what is going on in the wide world? One has to rely on proxies. Mass communications that have more or less defined part of the last century and the mobility of people, as Urry (2007) has insisted, may help us understand how people today are more aware of belonging to a common world than people were in earlier centuries.

Globalization that takes into account the mental or cultural process is referred to by other authors as globality. Robertson (1992: 132) defines *globality* as "the consciousness of the (problem of the) world as a single place" or "the world as a whole." In a very different vein, Manfred Steger (2003: 7) uses the term *globality* "to signify a social condition characterized by the existence of global economic, political, cultural, and environmental interconnections and flows that make many of the existing borders and boundaries irrelevant." His definition does not depart from that of other authors except for separating process and conditions. He goes on to say that "the term globalization should be used to refer to a set of social processes that are thought to transform our present social condition into one of globality" (Steger, 2003: 8). Steger even speculates that "it is conceivable that globality might be transformed into something we could call 'planetarity'—a new social formation brought about by the successful colonization of the solar system" (7–8). Whereas Waters and Robertson stress the cultural process of globalization, Steger insists on the new social condition where many processes converge to contract space and distance and accelerate flows and interconnections.

What were and are the pathways to globalization? Robertson (1992) and Shumel Eisenstadt (1986) have emphasized the role of religion toward a more global world. The great religions of the world, which emerged in what Karl Jaspers called the axial age—an idea later taken up by Eisenstadt—were vectors of a globalization process that was never truly universal but that nevertheless spanned large areas of the world. What religion created is a common community of believers united under a common doctrine, a set of practices, and, sometimes but not always, a common organization. These communities were, in principle and under rules of conversion and adhesion, open to all and spread across space and beyond frontiers. Such communities had in a sense contracted space and geography by setting up a virtual common group that was never definitively closed and whose frontiers remained flexible.

Empires of the past were also means by which globalization occurred. Many people, countries, and continents were gathered under one rule in the European empires of the sixteenth to the twentieth centuries. The sense of belonging to a common political organization was not always very strong, but a sole domination was pressed upon very different groups of people. Awareness of sharing a common destiny was certainly more ingrained in the elites than in the various people brought under a common dominion.

Commerce and economic exchange also led to forms of globalization. Drawing from the historian Fernand Braudel, Immanuel Wallerstein (1974, 2004) has used the term *world system* to characterize the capitalist and European process of economic globalization. In this particular process of globalization, Wallerstein stresses the international division of labour and of surplus accumulation in the core countries living off, so to speak, the resources, natural as well as human, of a vast periphery. States are distributed according to their position on the economic scale. This process is not only economic but also political. Core states are much more effective at dominating over the whole system than are states at the periphery although the latter may be more brutal toward their own people.

Science and cultural modernity, based partly on liberal and democratic values and on the idea of continual progress, is another aspect of the globalization process (Drori et al. 2003; Huff, 2011). This modernity may be called a cultural globalization based on the belief that the natural world can be explained in its own terms and that science will become the dominant if not the sole representation of what the world is and how it works.

If, however, we accept Held's and Waters' definitions of globalization, we have to accept that past experiences of globalization were limited because they did not create a sense of belonging to only one world or only one Earth. The environmental movement of the twentieth century was instrumental in creating a sense of being in a common world, not only natural but also social and political, as it became clear that the Earth's environment was fragile and that concerted action was necessary to face environmental degradation (McCormick, 1989).

What role is there for cities in this globalizing world? There are two ways by which cities can be part of this world: (1) as actors on the international stage—for instance in participating as political actors on policies and actions on the climate-change issue—and (2) as individual actors in the economic and financial arenas. The two kinds of actions do not fully overlap because cities involved in specific global issues, such as the environment, are much more numerous than cities that are able to influence the direction of the world economy.

The Global City: Meanings and Examples

The idea of the global city came up on the urban research agenda in exploratory papers written and co-written by John Friedmann (Friedmann, 1986; Friedmann and Wolf, 1982). Friedmann was not the first to sense that some large cities had moved to a higher stage of development and influence, and that they entertained connections with other cities and parts of the world. Before him, Peter Hall (1966) had examined the role played by London and New York in the international political economy. These two pioneers started an urban research program, which, as we shall see, was very much concerned, if not obsessed, with international urban hierarchies. Although there is nothing wrong with hierarchies, focusing too much on them may hide other important processes taking place in globalizing cities.

The focus on hierarchy and the leading role of a city in a non-national economy are partly due to Braudel, who has studied the evolution of European capitalism from the fifteenth to the nineteenth century (Braudel, 1979). Although Braudel did not use the term "global city," he may be thought of as the inventor of the concept. In presenting the history of the European making of capitalism, Braudel singles out successful world economies, each dominated by a large, leading, and coordinating city. When the world economy spanned the Eastern Mediterranean area, Venice was the leading city where capital could be accumulated for international trade. Afterward, when Western Europe dominated the world economy, Antwerp, Amsterdam, and London were, in succession, on top of the world trade and exchange. In Braudel's conception, there is no world economy without an important city leading it. However, Braudel adds that leading world-economy cities may not be leaders in all aspects of social life. For instance, Venice was the leading economic city, but Florence was the culturally inventive city of the period. When London's reach was, in the second part of the nineteenth century, wide and deep in a world economy much larger than Venice's, Paris was the leading city in the domain of the arts, while Vienna dominated in the domain of philosophy. Braudel introduced different rhythms and specializations in his concept of world economy, which may be more accurately termed "city economy" for it was through the actions and decisions of these large cities that the "wheels of commerce" were activated.

The most-often cited books on globalization generally eschew the part cities play in the globalization process. The term "world city" or "global city" has only recently been used, but it has diffused rapidly. According to Peter Hall (2006: 23), Patrick Geddes, a keen observer and analyst of cities throughout history, coined the term "world city" after having coined the word "conurbation." There is some hesitation as to which term best describes the role of cities. John Friedmann uses "world city" more or less as Braudel used the term. But Sassen and followers of her point of view prefer "global city." The two terms may, for all practical purposes, be used interchangeably although not all agree (Ghorra-Gobin, 2009). Just as economists distinguish between the world economy—the sum of all national economies—and the global economy—the part of the international economy that is governed by large firms and financial institutions that have a truly global reach—some urban researchers like Sassen have adopted this usage.

Friedmann launched a more or less new urban research agenda on world cities in key papers in the 1980s (Friedmann and Wolf, 1982; Friedman, 1986). The period is significant. The twentieth century moved through marked phases, from openness to closeness, from internationalism to protectionism. The postwar years were open to international process and exchange but basically were years of national reconstruction and development. But since national building and construction were not, as opposed to the 1930s, shut to international exchanges in all theirs manifestations, globalization expanded dramatically so that by the 1980s a new world had taken shape. Since globalization is a comprehensive process, cities were also caught in the movement. This is the context in which Friedmann and others sought to understand the causes and the implications of globalizing cities.

The process of globalization as applied to cities is manifold. Global cities are governed not only by economic processes but by other factors that have important local implications on the urban way of life. Friedmann and Wolf (1982), in their world city hypothesis, identify some basic changes. The methodology followed by the two authors is close to the ideal-type conceptualization that is found in sociology, in the footsteps of Max Weber, and in many social sciences. The economists' idea of the market can be thought of as an ideal type, a sort of abstract or pure theoretical idea of something that does not exist empirically. The concept of community that anthropologists refer to is also an ideal-type construction. There is of course no single community but, rather, a great variety of communities. But social scientists rely on the concept of community, which is much more than a definition, in order to understand concrete groupings of people. The same can be said about the global city ideal-type: its conceptualization is necessary to grasp concrete and empirical global cities.

The World City

Friedmann and Wolf set out a comprehensive research program where economic restructuring is the cornerstone of the whole process of city globalization. Economic restructuring takes different forms. Although transnational corporations and financial institutions are in the lead, government services are also part of the restructuring process: "they are concerned with the maintenance and reproduction of the world city, as well as the production of certain items of collective consumption, such as the planning of transport systems, education, urban parks and sanitation and so on" (Friedmann and Wolf, 1982: 320). Technological changes, in transport and communications most notably, are an essential spur to the globalization process.

Social and physical restructurings are no less crucial to the globalization process and to the formation of world cities. Transnational elites are taking shape, identifying themselves less with their respective national countries and more with their jobs, their insertion in the **international division of labour** and their wealth, and consumption patterns (Sklair, 2001). But an important underclass is also emerging, numbering, in the estimation of Friedmann and Wolf (1982: 322) 10 to 40 per cent of the labour force. Immigrant workers flock to world cities for the economic opportunities they can find. The physical restructuring is characterized by the growth of very large urban areas forming urban fields, defined as "a pertinent economic region of having a radius of about 60 miles" (Friedmann and Wolf, 1982: 323). But the internal structuring of world cities is very unequal. Using Los Angeles County as an example, Freidmann and Wolf show how population growth rates of its different communities or sub-areas differ from -7 per cent to +233 per cent (Friedmann and Wolf, 1982: 324). These changes have implications for urban dwellers, often negative, but the authors observe that there are no equalizing mechanisms to respond to such contrasting rates of growth.

Political conflicts, another important process, are a consequence of these many restructurings. Struggles emerge over public resources and economic opportunities as parts of the urban areas separate more and more one from another. Without getting into details, restructurings, again led by the economic forces, raise difficult problems for urban planning. Here the authors revert to pieces of normative advice:

> Territorial planners must grasp the essential nature of these conflicts and the contradictions, which underline them. It is here that they must make their interventions, furthering progressive forces in their attempt to withstand the dissolution of life spaces into a vast economic space controlled by capital. (Friedmann and Wolf, 1982: 327)

The authors go on the advisory pathway for urban planners (Friedmann and Wolf, 1982: 330–1). They seem to believe that planners can do a great deal to limit or erase the new urban contradictions through a "partisan planning" ideology to assert "territorial interests over those of transnational capital" and "within the territorial context, the interests of the working class both as a whole and into several factions" (Friedmann and Wolf, 1982: 330). Whether planners have adopted this recommended style is an empirical question.

The merit of Friedmann and Wolf's essay is that it paints a likely picture of a world city. They often use Los Angeles as an example of a world city generating many internal problems. In contrast to the Chicago School, the Los Angeles school of urban studies is far from being optimistic. But can the model be generalized? Have all world cities in formation followed the LA pattern? The clear answer is no. Although every major city in the industrial world has gone through a deep process of restructuring, not all have gone the LA way, with due respect to the LA School's thinkers. One would be hard pressed to compare Vancouver, Toronto, or even Montréal, which has lacked imagination in many of its recent developments, to the bleak state of Los Angeles as described by Friedmann and his urban co-researchers. Moreover, is it true that Los Angeles is showing the features Friedmann and Wolf's set forth in their hypothesis? Recent studies disagree (Erie, 2004).

Their essay is time-dependent. It was written at a difficult time in the American urban history. But just as Chicago's development was not the path-breaking example other industrial cities were going to follow, Los Angeles is neither the world city model in its "eutopian" format nor in its "dystopian" outlook (Davis, 2006). It is perhaps worth stressing again that there is no universal city, whether industrial, technological, ecological, or global, and that all cities are different and to a large extent unique, even though ideal-typical models are useful to understand processes of change in the urban way of life and in the urban fabric. In the same way, no planning models are universal although planners do need abstract references in order to plan effectively.

Ranking of World Cities

A second paper by Friedmann (1986) set urban research on a different path, one that was embraced by Saskia Sassen (1991, 1994) and Peter Taylor and his research team (2004). Without turning his back on his previous analysis, Friedmann became concerned with ranking world cities. Again under the influence of world-system theory, which structures the world into core, semi-periphery, and periphery countries and regions, he separates core regions and core cities from semi-peripheral regions and cities. No city from the periphery can be described as a world city. In order to build a world ranking of cities, Friedmann relies on the economic restructuring he has previously explored. World cities, still his favourite expression, are marked by a high concentration of some economic activities that are essential to the working of the world economy. Transnational corporations' headquarters, banking and financial establishments—in both their social and institutional sense—business services, such as legal, accounting, and advertising services, transport and communications services and facilities, and some government services are control instruments in the world economy. They constitute the selection indicators for world city ranking. This idea of control and command is borrowed from Sassen, who more or less defines global cities as control-and-command systems of the world economy.

World cities form clusters of core and semi-peripheral cities. And within each broad category of core and semi-peripheral regions there are primary and secondary clusters. London, Paris, New York, and Tokyo are members of the first cluster of primary core world cities. Moving down the hierarchy, Brussels, Milan, Toronto, and Sydney are members of the secondary cluster of world cities in the countries of the developed world. Countries in the developing world also have examples of primary and secondary world cities (Friedmann, 1986: 72). Examples are Sao Paulo, Singapore, Mexico City, and Seoul. The author reaffirms that similar processes of restructuring are occurring in these cities although at different rates and paces of change. Friedmann is very much concerned with the spatial and social divisions that these cities show. Finally, in a graph of connections among cities (1986: 74), he shows that, inside this urban world system, subsystems emerge. There is an Asian subsystem centred on the Tokyo-Singapore axis; an American subsystem based on New York, Chicago, and Los Angeles and linked secondarily to Toronto and Mexico City; a European subsystem that links London, Paris, the Rhine valley, Zurich, and the Dutch Randstad (Friedmann, 1986: 72–3).

Planning Consequences of Global Cities

Sassen has delved more deeply into this urban research program. In her books on global cities and in her many papers (1991, 1994, 2000), she pushes forward the world city hypothesis. Although she prefers "global city" to "world city," her analysis is much influenced by Friedmann—or is it the other way around? Both authors started this exploration at about the same time. Sassen bases her interpretation on the same political economy perspective and uses more or less the same quantitative and qualitative indicators of what constitutes a global city. She also is much interested in world city ranking, arriving at slightly different hierarchies, but not by much. Moreover, she is concerned with internal differentiation in global cities and the new planning imperative although she has, as has Friedmann, left the field open for research.

The planning consequences of global cities have been thoroughly studied by other urban researchers (Newman and Thornley, 2004; Savitch, 1989; Savitch and Kantor, 2002). Hank Savitch and Paul Kantor compare urban redevelopment processes and politics in many large and global cities in Europe and North America. They look at urban regimes, internal urban dynamics, the local culture, and the role of social groups and individuals, such as mayors, and ask whether urban development and placement on the international scene are converging. Their model, aiming at explaining outcomes, takes into account driving variables, such as market conditions and intergovernmental support; steering variables, such as popular control and local culture; and the process of negotiation leading to planning decisions and urban redevelopment strategies. They observe two broad and opposite types of outcomes, together with a hybrid model in between. One model is a social-centred development; the other, a market-centred development (Savitch and Kantor, 2002: 48–9).

Their comparative study ends up by asking whether all restructuring cities follow the same trajectories. Large cities may all be under the same forces of globalization and post-industrialization, as Savitch likes to say, but the combination of people, processes, and plans are rather specific to each city. For instance, New York, Paris, and London redeveloped and more widely internationalized in the 1970 and 1980s, but the social forces leading to the choosing of policies and plans were very different in each city (Savitch, 1989). In New York, for example, private investors, supported by the municipality, steered the whole process. In Paris, the process was much more technocratic and state-directed, whereas in London, the redevelopment of Covent Garden was steered by a strong civil society movement, even though planners and their principals would have liked a different outcome, that is, perhaps one less traditional (preservation of low-rise buildings and cultural activities, together with small specialized shops) and more modernist in style. Planners did, however, have success in the Canary Wharf development in the former eastern dock area.

Despite a common background of globalization, in which some may think that everything seems to converge, Savitch and Kantor are much more reserved than other researchers. After studying many industrial cities in the process of conversion to post-industrialism in the context of globalization, they conclude the following:

> Cities have choices, those choices vary with differential resources, and they are not without constraint. But they are nonetheless choices that can be applied. And most importantly, urban choices are not immutable, but capable of expansion, construction, and modification. Or to put the emphasis somewhat differently, cities are not mere leaves in the wind of internationalization, but political entities that in many different ways shape economic outcomes. (Savitch and Kantor, 2002: 347)

So much for the converging thesis of globalization, which Waters (1995), among others, is very skeptical of. Savitch and Kantor believe that there is a historical precedent to such multiple post-industrial processes and refer to Karl Polanyi, who, contrary to Marx, saw the industrialization process not as a converging movement in which an abstract and impersonal market would dominate and politics would recede, but as a much more varied historical process where nations make choices and where politics interplay with market forces.

Global cities ranking is still an active business in the world city research program. Peter Taylor and his research team have gone the furthest in developing international hierarchies (Taylor, 2004). Unsatisfied with traditional rankings, Taylor sees them as lacking for these hierarchies are based on attributes and not on connections and links between world cities (2004: 36–9). An attribute might be, for example, the number of transnational corporation headquarters whereas a connection, or linkage, is the number of goods or services, such as flights, being exchanged between two cities and more, and connecting two or more cities. Building on an elaborate set of indicators, Taylor and his team develop their own ranking that is not so different from other rankings. Of course, there are movements up or down in the hierarchies, but on the whole the same global cities appear at the top. With his idea of subsystems within a large system, Friedmann had already anticipated that the global cities network is far from being flat.

An interesting outcome of Taylor's research is not only that cities network in the global economy, but also that they are economically important inside this global political economy. As nations can be measured in gross national product terms, large cities can also be measured and compared in **gross urban products** (see Table 9.4). This urban measure can itself be compared with countries. The international economy has for a long time been structured around nations, in which cities of all sizes were subservient to the national economy and politics. Now, we no longer can avoid taking stock of the demographic and economic weight of large and very large cities. For instance, Tokyo's gross *urban* product is much bigger than Canada's gross *domestic* product for a population slightly less than Canada's. Indeed, only four *nations* produce more than the city of Tokyo: the United States, Japan as a whole, Germany, and France. If New York were a nation, it would be in sixth place in the economic league of heavyweight nations. With size comes economic weight but this depends heavily on whether a city belongs to the developed world or is inside a developing country. Even so, Mexico City has a gross *urban* product the size of Israel's gross *domestic* product. These data are 10 years old, but they give some indication of the increasing importance of large cities and megacities. Whether this will gradually lead to a greater political autonomy for such cities remains to be seen. However, we have seen in Chapter 8 that cities can make alliances and strike deals in the international climate change policy arena. Their role on many issues is expected to grow alongside nations.

Table 9.4 Comparison of 10 Top World City's Economic Weight and 10 Top Nations (in Billion US$, 1997)

City and Urban Area	Gross *Urban* Product	Nations	Gross *Domestic* Product
1. Tokyo	1,443.8	1. United States	7,641
2. New York	829.2	2. Japan	4,651
3. Osaka	628.7	3. Germany	2,341
4. Los Angeles	457.4	4. France	1,534
5. Paris	361.4	5. Italia	1,192
6. Nagoya	291.3	6. UK	807
7. Chicago	273.6	7. China	731
8. San Francisco	213.9	8. Brazil	731
9. Washington/Baltimore	212.1	9. Spain	573
10. London	208.9	10. Canada	560

Source: GaWC and Taylor. Retrieved 19 May 2011, from http://globalcities.free.fr/hierarchie. Used with permission of the author.

The Global Urban South: Growth and Inequality

Is there such a reality as a coherent "global urban South"? The phrase is often heard (and we discussed the term earlier in the chapter) but less well understood. The term supposes that there are common trends and features and problems among a great variety of cities located in different continents. If our overall assumption that there is no universal city is true, it makes less sense to speak about a global urban South as if the cities it contains share a common history and destiny. This is obviously not the case, for a very large city, such as Dhaka, is very different from a city like Sao Paulo or Buenos Aires. Again, it is worth repeating that numbers are not all.

As we have seen in Table 9.3, the United Nations projects that, by 2025, only two megacities of the developed world will be members of the top ten megacities of the world. In half a century, the largest cities moved from the industrial North to the developing or slowly developing South, a process Paul Bairoch has described as urbanization without industrialization (Bairoch, 1985: chap. 30). However, with many emerging economies in the global South, urbanization is more and more linked, although not everywhere, to economic growth. China and India are the prime examples, but many more countries nowadays aspire to material enjoyment and economic development. And since 1985, according to UN-Habitat (2010/2011: 28), economic growth closely follows urban growth. In a sample of countries selected in Asia, Africa, and Latin America, after a divergence in the 1960–1980 period—the reference decades of Bairoch's analysis—the two growth rates converge and the urbanization rate is only slightly higher than the economic growth rate.

Does this have some impact on cities in the global South? The United Nations agency UN-Habitat has for some years documented the state of the developing world cities. The most recent publication (2010/2011) pleads for "bridging the urban divide." It acknowledges that social and spatial divisions are deep and hard to eliminate. For Friedmann's world-city hypothesis, social and spatial divisions are consequences of the globalization process, at least in first-world global cities.

Spatial and social divisions previously existed in large cities of the developing South (Sjoberg, 1960; Le Goix, 2005). Has globalization accelerated those divisions? On some measures, there may be improvements, but on others, urban living conditions haven't improved much. The UN-Habitat 2010/2011 report observes that slum reduction—a visible indicator of inequality in living conditions—is moving in two opposite directions:

> Over the past 10 years, the proportion of urban population living in slums in the developing world has declined from 39 per cent in the year 2000 to an estimated 32 per cent in 2010. And yet the urban divide endures because in absolute terms the numbers of slum-dwellers have actually grown considerably, and will continue to rise in the near future. (UN-Habitat, 2010/2011: xii)

This measure of social and spatial improvement—for slums are a socio-spatial habitat—although significant, is not enough to evaluate whether the global urban South is on the right track to reach the objective of bridging the urban divide. UN-Habitat examines the internal divide using a well-known and tested measure, the **Gini index**, adapted to urban populations. The index, or coefficient, measures the level of inequality among people in a country or, less frequently, inside urban areas. It varies from 0, perfect equality, to 1, perfect inequality, where all the income or wealth as an alternative measure is held in only one hand, which is a very unlikely outcome if not impossible. UN-Habitat has over the years acquired some experience in calculating urban inequalities. The computations are run on a database of individual cities across the world: 94 cities in 47 countries, with additional data (68 countries) at the national urban level (UN-Habitat, 2010/2011: 74). UN-Habitat focuses its analysis on three large regions of the world, namely, Latin and Central America, Africa, and Asia although Eastern Europe is also taken into account. Data are based on two types of measures: income and consumption, or expenditures. National statistical offices prefer one or the other according to experience and to how they expect people to respond to data-gathering on what they earn and spend.

The following discussion and presentation of data is selective and focuses on countries and cities that are deemed to be relatively important actors on the globalization scene. For instance, data and indexes on cities in China and India, Brazil and Mexico will prevail over data and measures from other developing countries in trying to understand how the global urban South affects and is affected by globalization. If all countries, and their largest cities, are influenced by globalization, some also take part more substantially in the process than others do. Cross-sectional data are much more abundant than longitudinal data so that the direct effect of the process of globalization over time is difficult to pin down. Nevertheless, these data are indicative of some of the consequences of being part of a globalizing world.

Inequality in urban areas is nothing new; it may be as old as cities themselves. Because of its greater diversity and heterogeneity of people and activities, all with different capabilities, opportunities, productivity, and luck, one may expect that urban inequality is an intrinsic feature of cities and of large cities in particular. Moreover, in the footsteps of Simon Kuznets, economists have long observed that income inequality tends to increase with economic growth because growth in a market system does not reward people equally (Kuznets, 1966). Inequality increases in the takeoff phase of development to decrease, on the other hand, later on. The curve evolves, with the passing of time, into a bell-shaped form when inequality regresses with income growth.

Cities and countries can be divided into six categories of inequality by using the Gini coefficient, mentioned earlier. The two categories under a Gini of 0.40 are considered of low inequality. Above the coefficient of 0.40, called the "international alert" threshold, the remaining classes are all very unequal and politically sensitive. Very few countries and cities are located above a Gini index of 0.60. For instance, among a sample of 57 countries in developing and transition regions, only Namibia, Zambia, and South Africa have an urban Gini coefficient (measured in income) over 0.60 (UN-Habitat, 2010/2011: 63). Many South American countries show an urban divide between 0.50 and 0.599. Some, such as Argentina, Brazil, and Chile, are well connected to the new world economy. On the other hand, China's urban divide is relatively low, as is Vietnam's. Both have, since the 1980s, entered the world economy.

On the whole, the urban divide is stronger in the African and South America countries, and less so in transition countries of Eastern Europe; the Asian countries lie somewhere in between. The good showing of transition countries can be explained by remnants of a socialist economy and redistribution system—China and Vietnam may also be included—whereas the conditions in urban Africa and urban South and Central America can be explained by sluggish economic growth, weak labour markets, weak states, and specific historical processes, such as military regimes, lack of democracy until recently, and, on the whole, institutional failures (UN-Habitat,

2010/2011: 64). Different measures or samples show these same character-istics and, if the problems are not addressed, trends may set in that will be hard to reverse.

Looking at individual cities that aspire to play a role in the world economy, the coefficients are somewhat revealing (see Table 9.5). Johannesburg is at the top of the selected list with a Gini index of 0.75. Among large cities of the global South, it may be in a league of its own. Mexico City and Sao Paulo fare a little better, but they are well above the international alert—Brasilia, the capital of Brazil, also shows a rather high Gini index of 0.60. South China cities are high on the index, compared with other aspiring Chinese world cities. Shanghai and Beijing are relatively less unequal, with coefficients of 0.32 and 0.22 respectively.

The figures in Table 9.5 do not give a complete understanding of what globalization can do on urban social and spatial divisions. However, time-series data are scarcer. UN-Habitat has provided some indication of change. For instance, between the 1990s and the 2000s, if the urban divide of Johannesburg was reduced by 4 per cent, or 0.03 on the Gini index, and in Sao Paulo by 11 per cent, Mexico City saw an increase of 7 per cent in the index, meaning a greater urban inequality (pp.76–7). Trends and char-acteristic reflect various shades of the urban divide, even in the context of globalization. Societies and cities react differently to universal processes and are able to act, or fail to act, when faced with the same conditions and forces. The LA school, of which Friedmann is a close ally if not recognized as a full member (Dear, 2003), may have exaggerated and universalized too quickly some consequences of globalization because the School was too theoretically driven and was not sufficiently open to particular situations.

Table 9.5 Urban Divide (Gini Index, Income-Based) for Selected Cities: Various Years around 2005

City	Gini Index
Johannesburg, South Africa	0.75
Mexico City, Mexico	0.56
Hong Kong, Special Administrative Region of the People's Republic of China	0.53
Ho Chi Minh City, Vietnam	0.53
Sao Paulo, Brazil	0.50
Shenzhen, China	0.49
Hanoi, Vietnam	0.39
Shanghai, China	0.32
Beijing, China	0.22

Source: Based on UN-Habitat, State of the World's Cities (2010/2011), Figures 2.2.7 and 2.2.8. www.unhabitat.org/pmss/listItemDetails.aspx?publicationID=2917, p. 73, 75

Conclusion

Globalization and globality are two closely linked social phenomena. One is concerned with material and institutional processes; the other, with culture and a world view. Neither a definitive nor an accomplished state, globalization is instead an ongoing movement that may be as important as modernity. Globalization is of course a product of the modern world; the combination of actors and factors that the modern world helped to bring about are fully acting out in a new space-time frame (Giddens, 1990). Economic and technological factors are driving forces, but universal ideals of modernity are as well. There are no wide social movements without deep social representations; they interact with each other to create the "global modernity" we all live in. That this modernity is called by Beck (2009) a second modernity and by Giddens an advanced modernity misses out an important dimension: a global world in the making may not be a break with the modern world, but it creates new conditions that have probably, despite reservations to the contrary, never been confronted by human beings.

The global urban South is, in policy and governance terms, a huge problem that can be converted into a huge challenge (Léautier, 2006). Problems are social and spatial, as we have seen in the urban divide discussion. Problems are also technological, for there is a crying need to improve urban dwellers' conditions, a development path not too dissimilar from what the industrial city had to choose more than a century ago. As well, there are ecological, or sustainability, challenges in the global urban South, which are similar to those of the industrial city but also very different because climate change transforms many of the environmental cards local actors have to play with (Bicknell, Dodman and Sattertwaite, 2009). And finally, there is a political and governance challenge that the UN-Habitat continues to insist on, as do many other international institutions.

In the same way that Northern post-industrial cities redefined themselves by setting up regimes or mixes of urban actors and stakeholders, cities of the global South can choose a direction for greater equality and productivity. Under the title "Five Steps to an Inclusive City," the UN-Habitat report (2010/2011: 150–65) suggests ways to reach this goal. These steps are as follows:

1. *Cognitive*: measuring progress
2. *Institutional*: building more effective institutions
3. *Intergovernmental*: building new linkages with higher tiers of government
4. *Mental*: developing a clear, comprehensive, and sustained vision of inclusiveness
5. *Distributional*: spreading out equitable distribution of opportunities

To these steps are attached levers, such as promoting cultural diversity and urban cultural activities; improving the quality of life; political inclusion;

and education, to name the main levers (UN-Habitat, 2010/2011: 156–72). This seems an ambitious program, but it is one that is within municipalities' reach. The report gives room to numerous experiments taking place in cities across the global South. Urban planning and public participation in plans are crucial elements for inclusiveness, for political engagement, and for improvement of urban conditions. The report laments that urban plans are often outdated or too ambitious, and not sufficiently attentive to local conditions and to people's needs. Having a clear vision of where cities want to go or what they want to achieve does not have to be over-optimistic. Examples are cited where municipalities overcame their own institutional barriers and set themselves on a path of reducing the urban divide and of improving living conditions, especially for the poorest. Cities do have choices and should not dither in their determination to change.

The "good life" is a philosophical idea that modernity deeply believes in and strives to make happen and that most people aspire to. It may be a long process. But globalization, which is often perceived as negative (Held and McGrew, 2002), may in fact be an opportunity to modernize the city in a sustainable way and be more responsive to people's needs. Indeed, in a recent book, Edward Glaeser (2011) announces the "triumph of the city," and it is true that cities have always been linked to civilization. Peter Hall's monumental historical book, *Cities in Civilization* (1998), shows how much we owe to city dynamics. Glaeser does not disagree. He believes that large cities are, often contrary to what some believe, the way to the future for they can be sustainable by becoming more compact and more inventive. As Robert Park has said, "cities are the natural habitat of civilized man." Can they also be the "natural" habitat of ecologically sensitive human beings? It is a great challenge, one that international reports, while not ignoring it, seem at times to downplay. Climate change may hit many cities in the global South and create new ecological and climatic inequities. An urban eco-justice agenda is clearly needed.

Questions for Critical Thought

1. Distinguish between globalization and globality.

2. What criticisms can you address at the world city hypothesis?

3. Do urban strategies and developments in post-industrial cities converge or diverge? Explain why.

4. What conclusions can you derive from an examination of the urban divide in the global South?

5. What can be done to reduce this urban divide?

6. Can Savitch and Kantor's conclusion on the post-industrial city help us to understand the urban challenges in the developing South?

7. Is a sustainable urban future possible? If no, why? If yes, what conditions may help to bring it about?

Suggested Readings

Glaeser, E. 2011. *The Triumph of the City*. London: Macmillan. Building on Jane Jacobs and inspired by her idea on the wealth of cities, although with important differences between the two writers, Glaeser advocates urban concentration and the urban way of life as a way to increase both economic productivity and ecological sustainability. Optimistically, he believes that cities can solve most of their problems with sound planning, but not too much, a dynamic market, and a vibrant civil society.

Held, D., A. McGrew, D. Goldblatt, and J. Perraton. 1999. *Global Transformations: Politics, Economics and Culture*. Stanford, CA: Stanford University Press. This is one of the most comprehensive textbooks on globalization for advanced undergraduate and graduate students. The discussion of the phenomenon is pitched at a high level, but a close reading is very rewarding. Emphasis is on the economic and political dimensions of globalization. The authors are also keen to espouse a historical perspective.

Newman, P. and A. Thornly. 2011. *Planning World Cities: Globalization, and Urban Politics*. Basingsoke, UK: Palgrave Macmillan (2nd ed.). There are no cities without planning, no world cities without planned urban development. Problems are not the same whether one is in a developed world or in a developing world. Problems of transport may be universal, but housing, water supply, job opportunities, and clean air are very specific to every city. There is no proper planning without open and transparent governance, which is a challenge in many large cities.

Sassen, S. 2001. *The Global City: New York, London, Tokyo*. Princeton, NJ: Princeton University Press (2nd ed.). Saskia Sassen is a leading author on global cities. In this monograph, she gives a comprehensive picture of top-of-the-league global cities. She emphasizes the command and control capacity of these three global cities, adopting a flexible political economic perspective.

Taylor, P.J. (2004). *World City Network: A Global Urban Analysis*. London and New York: Routledge. This book on city networking is methodologically sophisticated. Taylor and his co-researchers have gone very far in trying to understand how world cities are connected and why. It is not an easy read, but very rewarding.

Waters, M. 2001. *Globalization*. London and New York: Routledge (2nd ed.). Less dense and less comprehensive than the book by Held et al., it is nevertheless an interesting discussion of globalization. Waters emphasizes the gap between what theory and theoreticians say about globalization and what the reality still is. Globalization is an ongoing process. Whether the outcome, in all its manifestations, is unavoidable remains an open question.

Related Websites

UN-Habitat
www.unhabitat.org

UN-Habitat is the leading international organization on world urbanization and cities in the developing world. It produces reports of high quality, containing data analysis and policy recommendations. UN-Habitat has conducted comparative research on urban inequality in developing countries, from which the data in this chapter are drawn.

The World Bank Group
www.worldbank.org

> The World Bank is an international organization created in 1944 to promote world development. It helps in planning and financing large development projects, such as dams and infrastructure, in developing countries. It is not only a financial institution but an expert on many aspects of world development. The World Bank has been criticized for focusing almost exclusively on economic growth, but it has, since the 1980s, been much concerned with environment and governance issues. It publishes comparative data on world development, and many policy briefs and reports.

Globalization and World Cities Research Network (GaWC)
www.lboro.ac.uk/gawc/

> GaWC is a leading research centre on world cities with many international connections. It is based in the geography department at Loughborough University, UK. GaWC focuses on the study of interconnections among large cities, which was neglected by many world city researchers, and uses complex indicators to propose rankings of world cities.

Conclusion

This book explored the contribution of sociology to understanding cities and the urban way of life. It is no exaggeration to say that cities are perhaps the most complex and useful of all human constructions. They are complex because economic specialization and social differentiation deepen. Modern city life "makes an individual incomparable to another, and each of them indispensable to the highest extent" (Simmel, 1950 [1903]: 409). Individual choices that people make about jobs, housing, recreation, and mobility are of course not without constraints of resources and without structural opportunities, but they remain basically without an overall design. On the other hand, there are no cities without some sort of planning, a concerted action of different powers or authorities. In the past, religious, military, and political elites could "plan" some parts of the city they inhabited according to their own needs and aspirations. Although various elites still exert influence and power over a city's structure and functioning, cities have democratized and have become an open space for many actors. Not all actors, however, are endowed with the same resources, power and influence, authority, and prestige. It is in this sense that we think of a city as a collective product.

Cities are also useful in the sense that the social division of labour is promoted in their midst, which leads to greater productivity, growth, and goods offered. From Adam Smith to Jane Jacobs, this economic value of living in cities has been acknowledged. Along with economic opportunities, cities also offer cultural and intellectual diversity. They are often associated with civilization because of their capacity to create and diffuse new ideas, whether scientific, technological, artistic, or institutional. However, some have questioned whether there may not be a limit to a city's size and population. From Plato's *Republic* to Howard's *Garden City*, city size has been debated. Between 30,000 and 50,000 city dwellers seem to have been recurrent ideal numbers. Plato wanted to limit city size so that citizens could fully participate in public life. Howard wanted to limit the size of city, both demographically and spatially—the idea of a Green Belt, circling a city of some dimension and limiting its development, finds its origin at that time—because he thought that only a city of limited size could offer the advantages of the countryside, as well as those of the city, without the negative elements of each.

There are great books, but there are also great themes of sociological inquiry. Modernity is a major subject of sociological investigation. We have set urban sociology in an understanding of the modern world, the world that emerged gradually without an overall (planned) design, in order to build on three major transformations: the scientific, the industrial, and the democratic revolutions, which between the seventeenth and the nineteenth centuries defined what modernity is and what modern cities are.

In the first two chapters, we investigated the tight link between sociology in general and urban sociology in particular. The relationship is very close, and, even though sociology has become specialized, urban sociology is still very much about where, why, and how waves of change unfold in cities. Whether we talk of governance, globalization, or sustainability, cities—and especially large cities or metropolises—are where many innovations and new intellectual movements are taking place. Whether these innovations are social movements, institutional arrangements, or technological infrastructure, cities are often their testing ground.

A proper, fully developed urban sociology took time to unfold. The field of study took root in the 1920s in Chicago, but across the Atlantic there were also investigations of city life and the urban way of life. We may recall that Simmel was a pioneer in asking if there was and is a particular urban mentality. He influenced Robert Park, one of the founders of the Chicago School of urban Sociology. At about the same time, the Durkheimian school of sociology, under the research program of social morphology, inquired into the physical and spatial conditions and forms (morphology) of society.

The postwar years saw a revival of urban sociology, which had lost its innovative thrust in the 1940s. Sociology was no longer alone in studying cities and shared its intellectual interests with many disciplines, such as geography, history, economics, and anthropology. Urban sociology was further transformed by the urban studies of the 1960s. Moreover, the industrial city of the North was no longer the sole interest of these urban studies: cities developing in the South also became the subject of inquiry.

And then urban studies became global. Starting in the 1980s, the "sociological eye" (Everett Hughes's expression) moved to global cities and to cities in a globalizing world. Not all cities are truly global. Nonetheless, many cities of different sizes and in different places can play the global card. In so many ways, these cities are linked and related to a world much larger than the one they used to develop in. By focusing too much on leading global cities and their hierarchy, however, urban researchers such as Saskia Sassen and Peter Taylor may have missed important aspects of cities' action in a global world. For instance, cities of different sizes form alliances and networks in order to promote urban sustainability and also to coordinate actions on the climate change issue.

We had to limit our inquiry to the last two centuries of urban history. During these 200 years, as modernity changed so too did cities change. Or is it more appropriate to say this the other way around: as cities changed, so modernity changed? Note that we tend to use *cities* in the plural form for there are no similar cities, as we have repeated over and over again. After long periods of slow urbanization, cities grew rapidly in the wake of industrialization. Historical cities were also transformed by the Industrial Revolution. The end result was an urban environment, highly artificial but also partly natural, that has become problematic. The nineteenth-century industrial city's history has been painted as an urban problems period. People living in this environment were quick to understand that something had to be done. Various professional, social, and political movements tried, with some success, to respond to these difficult times and dire conditions.

The industrial city was transformed by a growing economy and by many at first tepid but gradually warming interventions by governments. Both local and national governments became more active and planned for large infrastructure, or urban technical networks, that improved city life in the long run. Planning was a major element in this transformation. And although planning history tends at times to emphasize the ideal, or utopian, strand of urban planning, many planning decisions are very practical indeed. Roads, green spaces, water supply, transport systems, and communications systems all have to be planned. They mobilize many actors and institutions, resources and people, ideals and ideas. Some planning is a private operation, such as communications systems, and, at first, electricity generation and distribution, but many planning operations are generally under public responsibility, such as water supply and the provision of green spaces. The industrial city evolved into the "technology city," in which many of the urban problems of the former were solved, so to speak, with technology. In so doing, a new socio-technical system emerged to which urban planning contributed more than some are ready to grant. Mobility and its technologies were important and even essential components of the urban socio-technical system of the first modernity, to use Ulrich Beck's phrase.

However, by the last third of the twentieth century, the first modernity's city was under stress. Its ecological footprint, measured by all the resources needed to sustain its activities and its material urban way of life, was great—too great. The problem was no longer limited to some environmental conditions; instead, it was the overall urban way of life that came to be under scrutiny. With the rise of sustainable development, it was clear that, if sustainable objectives were to be achieved, cities and large cities would have to do their part. Smart growth, new urbanism, and urban sustainability were intellectual references to redefine what cities are and should be. The technology city brought about by the first modernity had reached its limits and engendered many ecological risks, such as climate change, and stresses on natural resources.

Meanwhile, the urbanization process was going on and gathering momentum. The world became urban at the beginning of the twenty-first century, when half the world population lived in cities. Moreover, very large cities grew out of existing cities and the urban challenge became truly global. Cities are enmeshed in networks of global activities where the economy rules. But cities are much more than just economy; they are political agents;

they foster creative and cultural environments; and they are the breeding ground where civil society can express itself.

Urban governance is a contested issue in all cities. Faced with mounting urban problems, the industrial city's governments were slow to react and to act decisively. It took urban movements to force them to change and to start coordinated interventions to improve city living conditions. It is no wonder that many planning conceptions are utopian for they compensate for inaction on the part of public authorities. But pressing needs forced local governments, with some help from higher-tier governments, to do something. Urban planning was at last recognized as a key element in governing and structuring cities. The Athens Charter was one of the leading intellectual moments defining planning as an agent of change in modern city. One is tempted to call this moment (from approximately 1930 to 1950) the "planning moment." Planning conceptions have oscillated between two poles: the City Garden conception and the Athens Charter conception although some aspects, such as green spaces, of the former are included in the latter. But both came to be criticized, notably by Jane Jacobs, whose influence on urban planning ideas is important. Jacobs was, in a nutshell, concerned about planning as a force of urban destruction, not only physical but also social. Modernist planning was set to eliminate traces of the past and to quell functional diversity. Jacobs pleaded for greater diversity and spontaneity, for greater private involvement, and for citizens' inputs. She was described as a liberal and a laissez-faire urban theorist. While there is some truth to this criticism, critics miss her important message that cities are not industries and that, if creative destruction is good for the industrial economy, it may be bad for city life. Too much of modernist planning is destruction, replaced by new, built creations that are not always improvements, as opposed to technological progress in industry.

Urban governance is not just about planning and social movements although both are necessary. Governance structures and institutions have changed a great deal over a century. When Geddes coined the term "conurbation" to describe how many cities evolved together, forming large and very large continuous urban regions, he had no idea, or only a foggy one, that this implied thinking anew the political and administrative organization of local authorities. City-regions of many million people demanded forms of government and decision-making adapted to this reality. But the twentieth century saw contested attempts at designing metropolitan structures with strong powers to manage and plan the whole area. What we frequently observe today are double structures: local municipalities overlaid by a regional structure that is more often administrative than political. The "political metropolitan moment" is still to come and, if recent history is any guide, it will not arise easily.

Now, perhaps, the greatest challenge for cities and city-regions is environmental. Sustainable development is not only a matter for national governments and the international community. Since sustainable development is about thinking globally and acting locally, cities and municipalities are part of the movement. Too much talk and public debate have been about urban sprawl and expanding cities over natural, agricultural, and forested land. Hectares of land taken over by urban constructions radically change the ecosystems' structure and functioning, imposing a largely artificial environment. Although urban areas are not entirely devoid of ecological features, these are less dominant in an urban environment. New research, however, has rediscovered the ecological nature of cities. Plants and animals are adapted to this kind of environment, but what stands out is the human-made nature of the urban environment. The sustainability challenge, then, is twofold. First of all, the urban world and its large cities have to restore some sort of balance with nature by saving nature as much as possible and by limiting, even diminishing, cities' ecological footprints. However, in a rapidly developing and urbanizing world, solving this problem is a very long shot. Second, urban planning has to make more room for nature inside the very artificial urban environment it designs. The planning of parks, green spaces, and blue "flows" (i.e., streams and lakes), which belong to the traditional planning toolkit, will not be enough. More has to be done if cities want to do their part to restore and increase biodiversity.

A last challenge pertains to governance, participation, and social equality. Various social movements have fought over urban conditions, facilities, and infrastructure. Not all urban dwellers enjoy the same urban resources. In cities of the global South, urban inequalities are deep and entrenched. Progress is slow and raising the urban poor out of poverty is a great challenge, although there *are* means to alleviate poverty and improve conditions, according to the United Nations Human Habitat. Many of the solutions are in the hands of local governments. They may, however, need to set in motion an administrative and political "revolution" in order to face this challenge.

In sum, urban sociology looks at cities from a variety of angles: economic, technological, political, cultural, and, increasingly, environmental. The city itself may be seen as a total social phenomenon: rich, diversified, multifaceted, highly complex, and made up of people, institutions, material construction, and technologies, all interacting among themselves. And it is out of these interactions and productions that socio-spatial orders emerge and are shaped.

Glossary

census metropolitan areas (CMAs) The largest units of data collection in the Canadian census that pertain to large urban areas. The term *CMA* has recently been replaced with *urban centre*.

citizen participation Direct or indirect engagement of social actors in the public sphere trying to influence national, regional, or local policies. Such a presence can be defined in reference to different type of mechanisms more or less open to the recognition of citizens, defined as social and/or political actors.

city-regions Recent organizational and spatial forms taken by urban phenomena on a metropolitan scale.

colonial towns Towns or cities that arose during the French and British colonial periods in Canada, i.e., from the founding of Québec City (1608) to Confederation (1867). European colonies everywhere were to a large extent dependent for policy, trade, and government on the colonial powers, which were France and England in the case of Canada.

conurbation The spatial organization of the process of growth and urbanization of a set of cities, at first unrelated, which gradually become closely linked to form a very large urban entity.

creative cities A term used in urban and planning studies. It stresses the innovative capacity of some cities to produce news ideas, goods, and services. According to Richard Florida, creative cities attract talent, technology, and tolerance. They are conducive to innovation in all its forms and to economic prosperity.

deliberative democracy A model of democracy that can be distinguished both from the republican—characterized by the capacity of the state to define and represent the common good—and the liberal model—where legislation is established for containing the extension of state power against individual rights. The deliberative conception of democracy relies on rational exchanges among equal citizens and suggests the implementation of favourable conditions for their participation in public reasoning.

democratization The process of influencing public decision-making for the benefit of citizens. A political regime is democratic "to the degree that political relations between the state and its citizen feature broad, equal, protected, mutually binding consultation. Democratization then means net movement toward broader, more equal, more protected, and more mutually binding consultation . . ." (Tilly, 2007: 59).

ecosystem A fundamental term in ecology and biology. It appeared in the 1920s and 1930s in the scientific literature and is now widely used in biology as well as in environmentalism. It is defined as a structural and functional unit. Ecosystems vary in size and diversity. The boreal forest, for example, is a very large ecosystem, whereas a pond is much smaller.

environmental (in)justice An expression recently being used to describe how people and communities are differently affected by environmental problems, such as air and water pollution. People living in a neighbourhood where air pollution is widespread may have their health threatened. Since pollution of many kinds is not distributed evenly, environmental injustice may occur. Social mobilizations under the banner of environmental justice have been organized in many large cities. Environmental justice therefore means a necessary public action to right wrongs.

gentrification The process of transforming run-down neighbourhoods into higher-grade ones due to an influx of wealthy households, causing the displacement of former residents.

Gini index/coefficient A widely used measure of inequality that usually measures the inequality of people's income (or wealth) at the national level. The measure varies between 0 and 1: a coefficient of 0 means no inequality at all, or pure equality; and a coefficient of 1 means that one person or one family has all the income. Applied to urban dwellers or their family, the Gini index helps to describe a state of inequality, and to measure progress in social redistribution or deepening of inequality over time.

global South/global urban South Refers to all developing countries as opposed to developed ones (or the North). "South" is a misnomer—not all developing countries are in the southern hemisphere—but it has been adopted by international agencies and by urban researchers as well. Indeed, many developing countries are in the northern hemisphere, such as India and China, while some countries in the South are highly developed, such as Australia and New Zealand. The two expressions convey the meaning of common conditions. The "global urban South" refers to all cities in the developing world that have some

common problems and conditions, where, for instance, inequality is strong or living conditions are in need of large improvements.

governance The mechanisms for dialogue and co-operation generally elaborated by state administrations for giving different categories of actors—i.e., state, market, or civil society—the possibility to articulate their interests and for arriving at collective decisions. At odds with formal top-down approaches to decision-making, these mechanisms are introducing changes in the state's traditional mode of action.

greenhouse gases (GHG) A variety of gases emitted in the atmosphere that act as a reflecting shield to increase the temperature in the atmosphere and at the Earth's surface, much as a greenhouse warms the surrounding air. Water vapour is one of the main GHGs that is naturally produced by the Earth's energy system. Some potent greenhouse gases, such as carbon dioxide and methane, are naturally produced but are also added to the atmosphere due to combustion of fossil fuels. The increase of these gases leads to global warming, which is a gradual increase of the temperature of the Earth's atmosphere and oceans. Global warming induces many changes on the Earth. If some regions are becoming warmer, others may cool—hence the expression "climate change," which takes into account many changes, all created by GHG emissions. Scientists predict that the Earth will warm by 2 to 5 degrees by the end of the twenty-first century. Climate varies naturally, but scientists believe that the current warming is induced by human activities.

gross urban product The economic output of large urban areas, or city-regions. In some cases, the largest urban area of a country may have a disproportionate share of the whole country's economic output.

high-density planning More people and buildings per hectare or in a neighbourhood.

human ecology The transposition to human organizations and settlements of the science of ecology, which was first elaborated in biology and natural sciences.

integration In general, associated with two different meanings. The first one underlines the process whereby individuals are part of a social system. The second refers to the system as a whole, or systemic integration.

international division of labour A global division of work and economic production that has developed along with increasing international and global economic exchanges. Some countries specialize in some kind of economic activity, for example, financial services, whereas others specialize in another kind, such as light manufacturing. The international division can occur in whole economic sectors—mass clothing is an activity mostly done in Asia—or between different parts of a process of production. For instance, some car parts are manufactured in developing countries where they cost less, while research and development (R&D) remains in the developing world.

knowledge economy An economy where knowledge has become one of the main factors of economic growth. The growing importance of knowledge for economic development has contributed to the restructuring of systems of production.

Local Agendas 21 The local (or regional as opposed to national and international) implementation of the principles of sustainable development. It is a process based on public participation and long-term planning for urban or regional sustainability.

megalopolises Since the second half of the twentieth century, mainly because of the impact of globalization, cities have been increasingly transformed in large urban areas, taking the shape of city-regions or even mega-city regions. Jean Gottmann (1961) was among the first to use the term for describing the "Urbanized Northeastern Seaboard of the United States."

metropolis For early sociologists like Simmel and Wirth, a notion referring to the great cities of their times. Nowadays it is sometimes used as a synonym for *city-regions* or *metropolitan regions*.

metropolitanization The shape taken by urbanization in the late twentieth century in major cities, contributing to their development at a metropolitan scale, changing the nature of traditional cities.

mitigation and adaptation measures Two types of measures to face climate change. *Mitigation measures* aim at eliminating or reducing the causes of current warming by reducing the emission in the atmosphere of GHG. *Adaptation measures* mean that, since climate change is likely, people will have to adapt to a warmer world. Many measures will be needed to ease the effects of a warmer world, and warmer cities in particular.

modernity ". . . The belief in the freedom of the human being [. . .] and in the human capacity to reason, combined with the intelligibility of the world, that is, its amenability to human reason" (Wagner, 2012: 4). The term also corresponds to a historical era characterized by a break with traditional values and models of social organization.

new regionalism Inspired first and foremost by governance, contrary to old regionalism, which was defined through state reform to planning and management with the creation of an encompassing and authoritative tier for decision at a metropolitan scale. New regionalism also relies on the normative claim that suburban vitality of urban peripheries cannot be achieved without the support these suburbs should give to central cities for renovating their infrastructures.

new urban sociology A sociological research program elaborated at first by structuro-Marxist sociologists during the 1970s to reconstruct urban sociology by taking into account the contradictions of capitalism in advanced societies.

planning, urban planning A set of practices that aims at organizing important aspects of urban life. It became a profession during the twentieth century, with its training programs in universities and its representative organizations before governments and the public. Planning has focused on the spatial organization of economic and social activities; it distributes buildings, facilities, infrastructure, parks, and green spaces in a city. Planning is generally a public responsibility, but new private developments are also planned according to principles of distributing constructions and amenities in urban space.

political ecology Can be defined as conflicts over the environment and its resources. Conflicts may take many forms: group or class conflicts over land tenure; conflicts between a local community and the state or an international corporation over some local environmental resources, such as forests or fisheries; or conflicts over urban resources, such as green spaces.

postmodern critique A critical approach to modernity expressing skepticism over the metanarratives elaborated by modern thinkers linking emancipating social utopias to technological progress.

postmodern urbanism A reaction to the ideas elaborated by modernist visions of urban design; relies on a critique of modern architecture and city-making. Practitioners have suggested new orientations for improving the "physical landscape" of cities, increasingly taking into account local cultures.

professionalization Founded on three requirements: (1) advanced training, such as medicine, law, and engineering; (2) the application of general knowledge (scientific basically) to cases and concrete situations; and (3) the exclusive right, granted either by the state or the market, to perform a set of practices. When we say that planning is professionalized, we say that planners learn general scientific principles in a university or a technical school, such as a school of architecture, and that they apply these principles to a variety of situations. They chiefly work for public organizations, but may also work for private developers and engineering firms. If the training of professionals is scientific, the application of knowledge in concrete cases needs other skills, such as judgment and innovation.

reflexive project of the self The capacity of individuals to define and achieve their biography in connection to their singularity: "A person with a reasonably stable sense of self-identity has a feeling of biographical continuity which she is able to grasp reflexively and, to a greater or lesser degree, communicate to other people" (Giddens, 1991: 54).

restoration ecology The set of decisions and practices to re-establish the health and proper ecological functioning of a degraded environment, such as an urban park or an urban river. Many urban rivers used in the industrial era for heavy transport and as a garbage dump have been restored. They have found a new life and are now open to recreational purposes.

scientific (or rationalistic) mentality Concepts that are of wide use in sociology. Max Weber (1864–1920) was the sociologist who most emphasized that modernity is a long process of rationalization, which means that social activities are organized according to some general rules that are applied to all actions and decisions in a particular field. For instance, businesses carefully calculate the use of resources in production; they have developed accounting and engineering methods to allocate them efficiently. Government administrations have developed a set of rules dealing with recruiting and promoting their members based on merit. Science is a strong rationalizing method of understanding the world.

social democracy A form of governance that favours co-operation between large social actors and institutions. For instance, in labour relations, in order to avoid recurrent conflicts, social democracy sets up a process of regular if not permanent negotiation between unions, businesses, and the government. Social democracy also came to mean greater social protection of all citizens irrespective of their personal capacity to pay for some services, such as education, health care, old-age pensions, and other social rights. The financial burden is supported by all through taxes.

spatial justice The issue of justice in relation to urban development relies on conflicts of interests and the capacity to solve these from equity principles. The distribution of social benefits in relation to the city varies due to the location of activities but also to the configuration of power in society.

sprawl The growth pattern, based on low density and land marketing, characterizing the development of metropolitan areas or city-regions since the 1950s in most parts of the world.

suburbia, "urbia," metropolia Collective terms comprising different types of urban areas. Although there are many types of suburbs, they nevertheless tend to differ from the central city on at least two counts: the predominance of low-density housing and of the residential function, although the commercial function (shopping centres) is integrated to the suburbs. Suburbs are generally greener than central cities, although green spaces and parks are not lacking in some central cities, such as London, Paris, New York, and Montréal. "Urbia" and "metropolia" are neologisms copied on suburbia. They both tend to capture a certain spatial form and a certain way of life.

total social phenomenon An expression coined by the French sociologist Marcel Mauss (1872–1950) to describe particular social phenomena where all aspects of social life are enacted. His classical example is the gift exchange in some societies, which is an economic transaction, but at the same time is a social, political, and religious event.

upward social mobility A form of integration in society supported by the chance of advancing to a better position on the social ladder. This can be observed, for example, through the economic and geographical mobility of inhabitants having the capacity to leave an ethnic enclave for a middle-class neighbourhood. Some researchers make a useful distinction between "forced" and "empowered" mobility: "There is nothing empowering about forced mobility between countries, regions, cities or intra-city, nor in the difficulty of moving out of a ghetto. Mobility is empowering when it allows free social contacts as well as improvement of life chances" (Body-Gendrot, Garcia, and Mingione, 2012: 366).

urban creative destruction Is an expression invented by the economist Joseph Schumpeter (1883–1950) to capture the fundamental dynamics of capitalism, which constantly, through technological innovation, changes its means of production and its products. Urban creative destruction is a similar process, but applied to urban development. Thus, new buildings and even whole neighbourhoods and districts replace old ones over the course of time. New buildings or restored buildings take over, in part or in total,

manufacturing districts and neighbourhoods in many industrial cities. The gentrification process is not really an urban creative destruction for it tends to keep the old buildings but restores them for new dwellers or functions. For instance, lofts used to be manufacturing buildings but have been restored for other purposes, such as a shop or artists' workshop.

urban sociology A specialized field of sociology dedicated to the study of cities, social segregation, and urban culture. It was initiated by Robert Park in the 1920s working at Chicago University.

urban studies An interdisciplinary field of research dedicated to the study of all aspects of cities and urban phenomena.

urbanism Until the 1980s, referred to the meaning given by Louis Wirth in his essay: "the way of life" of city dwellers. Even though this meaning remains valid, it now also includes the specific form taken by urban design within a historical context.

urbanity Designates the way of life and the capacity of inhabitants to take advantage of it.

zoning A planning and municipal instrument to distribute urban activities in space. One objective of zoning is to exclude some activities from urban neighbourhoods. For instance, industrial activities are normally separated from residential neighbourhoods.

Notes

Chapter 1

1. The notion of use value refers to the definition given by Karl Marx in his seminal work *Das Kapital*, where he explains that the "use" category is directly related to the utility of something. If we refer to a use value to describe the relationship someone has with a particular commodity, we underline that this commodity is "something useful" for him or her. Therefore, the same commodity can also have another meaning when inscribed within an exchange market, and it is no longer its direct usefulness but its appreciation through an abstract equivalent, in money usually, that counts. The use value can easily be converted to an exchange value when traded like a commodity in commercial exchange. Even if linked, use value and exchange value are fundamentally opposed categories. There is an artificial aspect as well as an abstract side in the exchange value by comparison to use value. Lived space, as referred to here, is fundamentally a use value if we think of it as a living place where daily life is occurring. It is not defined as an abstract milieu, although urban developers sometimes define it that way, but as an essential place for social expression and solidarity.

Chapter 2

1. The interest raised by the theoretical statements made by Castells has been contagious. Castells attracted the attention of researchers examining the transformation of contemporary cities and the economic, political, and cultural processes at work. He certainly gave a second wind to urban sociology.
2. Use and exchange values refer here to their Marxist meaning (see also Chapter 1, note 1). For Marx an exchange value is defined in relation to the abstract character and value of a commodity when traded in a market for another commodity. By contrast, the use value is defined by the utility some commodity has for someone in his or her daily life, no matter the price this commodity can bring to its owner on any particular market.

Chapter 3

1. The *phalanstère* ("phalanstery" in English) is a form of social and economic organization conceived of by Charles Fourier. It is organized around a building or a set of buildings where a small community lives and works. This form of community organization has been criticized for its totalitarian conception. Like may written utopias since Plato's

Republic, life in a phalanstery is well regulated; conflicts, tensions, rivalry—indeed, freedom of choice and of lifestyle—are limited, if not abolished altogether. A *phalanstère* may best be thought of as a form of military organization for production—hence the word origin, *phalanx*, which is a shape given by a body of infantry in Ancient Greece.

Chapter 4

1. According to Kenneth T. Jackson, the growth of suburbs goes back even to the beginning of the nineteenth century: "Whether the attraction was easy access, pleasant surroundings, cheap land, or low taxes, the suburb was growing at a faster rate than the city by 1800, and in almost every decade until the Civil War its population approximately doubled" (1985: 29).

Chapter 5

1. Although *ethnic* and *ethnicity* are still terms widely used in urban studies, they should perhaps be definitively abandoned for expressions less charged and more accurate. In ancient Greek, *ethnos* means a people or a nation. When immigrants arrive in Canada, they leave their country behind and chose another one. They of course keep many of the cultural habits and values they have been socialized in, and they maintain ties with their country of origin, but they expose themselves to new cultural forms and symbols. Moreover, some religious groups were, in the past, defined as ethnic groups while in fact they came from many different places and do not form peoples or nations in the modern sense of the word. Jews and Muslims, who have migrated to Canada and are still doing so, are not drawn from only one nation or people but from many. *Cultural* and *culturality* are thus better terms to use to talk about values, attitudes, habits, languages, and ways of life that are brought in and kept by migrating people.

   Ethnocultural, as is sometimes used, is not much better. As for *race*, one would hope that the term would, due to past abuses, disappear from the modern conception of a common humanity, as its stands in international institutions, such as the United Nations, and in national charters of rights and freedom. If the term *visible minorities* has cropped up in recent Canadian census data, we believe that researchers and official agencies should be colour-blind and use their sociological imagination to provide new concepts to describe people according to some sociologically relevant categories and not the colour of their skin. One wonders what is truly gained in the census by using "visible minorities" in addition to "immigrant status." Statistics Canada formally defines immigrants as "'people who are, or have been, landed immigrants in Canada. A landed immigrant is a person who has been granted the right to live in Canada permanently" (Statistics Canada, Census 1996, Census Metropolitan Areas Profile).

2. See the Metropolis website for more information. The address is given at the end of Chapter 5 under "Related Websites."

3. "This concept is built from the observation that different groups have different outcomes in terms of their acceptance and adaptation to urban life and that all groups, because of circumstance and disadvantage, cannot be treated the same way. Instead of the assimilation that European immigration has taught us to expect, some groups struggle to retain their culture within the urban environment and yet also try to find their place in urban life. Whether a result of personal cultural commitments or of discrimination and prejudice, or both, these groups struggle to make difficult adjustments to city living." (Peters, 2010: 155)

4. These percentages and the underlying data have to be taken with caution for at least three reasons. First, on many occasions when the census was going on a "number of reserves" refused to participate in the consultation process. Second, the different categories of Aboriginal people (Métis, Inuit, First Nations) are not present in cities in the same proportion. For example, Métis are more urbanized than other categories (in their case, 70 per cent live in urban settings). Third, a lot of variations exist between the main Canadian cities. If in Montréal and Toronto the total of Aboriginal residents amount for only 0.5 per cent of the CMA, in Winnipeg that number is 10.0 per cent of the CMA.

5. As John Lorinc explains, this ambivalence is defined around "a mix of opportunity, invisibility, and segregation, accompanied by an internal struggle to carve out an Aboriginal vision of urban living" (2006: 45).

6. As mentioned by Lorinc (2006: 52).

Chapter 6

1. Here we refer to an understanding of governance that goes back to the 1980s. But one should keep in mind that governance has also a more ancient meaning. According to Ali Kazancigil, the dates of its first appearance are diverse: either the thirteenth century, the end of the fourteenth, or the end of the fifthteenth century depending on the sources we are referring to (2010: 18–19).

2. However, it is important to mention that Kazancigil (2010) also recognizes that a tension exists in the literature between governance, defined on one hand as a tool for market and finance and, on the other hand, as an auxiliary of participatory democracy.

3. The position of the new regionalists that emerged at the beginning of the 1990s has to be contrasted with that of the "old regionalists." For

the "old regionalists," urban problems were going to be solved by creating a metropolitan government able to redistribute resources within the municipalities and impose regional concerns and planning. The new regionalists also believe that metropolitan planning is necessary, but for them, this should be achieved through co-operation and governance, instead of through top-down planning.

4. In 2006, the population of the megacity of Toronto was 2,500,281 inhabitants. For the metropolitan region, this figure rises to 5,113,149.

5. In 2006, the population of Montréal Island was 1,854,442 inhabitants. For the metropolitan region, this figure rises to 3,635,571.

6. As in Toronto, the municipal reform in Montréal was also controversial. In the western part of the Island—where much of the anglophone community of Montréal lives—the mayors succeeded in convincing the Liberal party that the reform was unjust to the anglophone community because it did not respect anglophones' culture and identity. When the Liberal party came to power in 2003, it gave amalgamated municipalities the possibility to recover their past status. On the Montréal Island, 15 reconstituted cities existed as of January 1, 2006; 19 boroughs were still remaining. These 34 entities meet at the Montréal Agglomeration Council, which was created in order to discuss shared matters (including public transit, water treatment, social housing, and property assessment) between the reconstituted cities and the city of Montréal.

7. Several tensions exist between Montréal and other regions of the province. Somehow, from a political standpoint, strengthening Montréal might weaken the position of the provincial government given the intergovernmental rivalries characterizing the relations between Québec and the federal government.

Chapter 7

1. We offer these words from Le Corbusier (1994 [1925]: 8): "*Je pense donc bien froidement qu'il faut arriver à cette idée de démolir le centre des grandes villes et de le rebâtir*" ("I coldly believe that one has to come to the idea that the centre of large cities should be demolished and rebuilt").

Chapter 8

1. The following paragraphs are based on ongoing research on urban governance of combined climate change and biodiversity issues. Samuel Couture collected the information while he was a master's degree student at Laval University with Louis Guay. We are very grateful for his diligent and competent documentary research.

References

Abbott, A. 1988. *The System of Professions: An Essay on the Division of Expert Labor*. Chicago: University of Chicago Press.

Abrams, P. 1968. *The Origins of British Sociology, 1834–1914*. Chicago: University of Chicago Press.

Abu-Lughod, J. 1999. *New York, Chicago, Los Angeles: America's Global Cities*. Minneapolis: University of Minnesota Press.

Adger, W.N., S. Hug, M.J. Mace, and J. Paavola (Eds.). 2006. *Fairness in Adaptation to Climate Change*. Cambridge: MIT Press.

Alber, G. and K. Kern. 2008. "Governing Climate Change in Cities: Modes of Urban Governance in Multi-level Systems." Conference presented at the: *Competitive Cities and Climate Change*. 08/10. Milan, pp. 171–96. [Conference proceedings] Online at www1.oecd.org/regional/regional-policy/50594939.pdf.

Alexander D. and R. Tomalty. 2002. "Smart Growth and Sustainable Development: Challenges, Solutions, and Policy Decisions." *Local Environment* 7, 4: 397–409.

Alexander, D. 2000. "The Best So Far: Vancouver's Remarkable Approach to the Southeast False Creek Redevelopment Is a Big Step Towards Sustainable Development Planning for Urban Sites." *Alternatives* 26, 3: 10–14.

Anderson, N. 1923. *The Hobo*. Chicago: University of Chicago Press.

Andrew, C. 2010. "Récit d'une recherche-action: la participation et le passage de frontières de femmes immigrantes à la ville d'Ottawa." *Sociologie et sociétés* XL11, 1: 227–43.

Andrew, C. and B. Milroy (Eds.). 1988. *Life Spaces, Gender, Household, Employment*. Vancouver: University of British Columbia Press.

Andrew, C., J. Biles, M. Siemiatycki and E. Tolley. 2008. "Conclusion." In Andrew, C., J. Biles and M. Siemiatycki (Eds.). *Electing a Diverse Canada: The Representation of Immigrants, Minorities, and Women*. Vancouver: UBC Press, pp. 255–69.

Ansel, C. 2006. "The Sociology of Governance." In Bevir, M. (Ed.), *Encyclopedia of Governance*. London: Sage.

Antier, G. 2005. *Les stratégies des grandes métropoles. Enjeux, pouvoirs et aménagement*. Paris: Armand Colin.

Archer, D. 2009. *The Long Thaw. How Humans Are Changing the Next 100,000 Years of Earth's Climate*. Princeton: Princeton University Press.

Artibise, A.F.J. and G.A. Stelter (Eds.). 1979. *The Usable Past: Planning and Politics in the Modern Canadian City*. Toronto: Macmillan.

Aubin, B. 2010. "People of the Year: The Pushbackers." *The Gazette*, December 16: A23.

Bacqué, M.-H. and J-P. Lévy. 2009. "Ségrégation." In J.-M. Stébé and H. Marchal (Eds.), *Traité sur la ville*. Paris: PUF, pp. 303–52.

Bacqué, M.-H. and Y. Sintomer (Eds.). 2011. *La démocratie participative: Histoire et généalogie*. Paris: La Découverte.

Bacqué, M.-H., H. Rey and Y. Sintomer. (Eds.). 2005. *Gestion de proximité et démocratie participative*. Paris: La Découverte.

Bairoch, P. 1985. *De Jérico à Mexico: Villes et économie dans l'histoire*. Paris: Gallimard.

Bairoch, P. and R. Kozul-Wright. 1996. *Globalization Myths: Some Reflections on Integration, Industrialization and Growth in the World Economy*. Geneva: UNCTAD, Discussion Paper 113.

Balakrishnan, T.R. and G.K. Jarvis. 1991. "Is the Burgess Concentric Zonal Theory of Spatial Differentiation Still Applicable to Urban Canada?" *Canadian Review of Sociology and Anthropology/ Revue canadienne de sociologie et d'anthropologie* 28, 4: 526–39.

Ball, N.R. (Ed.). 1988. *Building Canada*. Toronto: The University of Toronto Press. In French: *Bâtir un pays: Histoire des travaux publics au Canada*. Montréal: Boréal.

Bash, H.H. 1995. *Social Problems & Social Movements: An Exploration into the Sociological Construction of Alternative Realities*. New Jersey: Humanity Press.

Bauman, Z. 2000. *Liquid Modernity*. London: Polity Press.

Bauman, Z. 2001. *The Individualized Society*. Cambridge: Polity Press.

Beauregard, R.A. 1993. *Voices of Decline. The Postwar Fate of US Cities*. Cambridge: Basil Blackwell.

Beck, U. 1997. *The Reinvention of Politics: Rethinking Modernity in the Global Social Order*. Cambridge: Polity Press.

Beck, U. 2009. *World at Risk*. Cambridge: Polity.

Beck, U. and E. Beck-Gernsheim. 2001. *Individualization*. London: Sage.

Bell, D. 1973. *The Coming of Post-Industrial Society: A Venture in Social Forecasting*. New York: Basic Books.

Benevolo, L. 1967. *The Origins of Modern Town Planning*. London: Routledge & Kegan Paul.

Benevolo, L. 1993. *The European City*. Oxford: Blackwell.

Berger, B.M. 1961. "The Myth of Suburbia." *Journal of Social Issues* 17, 1: 38–49.

Bherer, L. and P. Hamel. 2012. "Overcoming Adversity, or Public Action in the Face of New Urban Problems: The Example of Montréal." In Horak, M. and R. Young (Eds.), *Sites of Governance: Multilevel Governance and Policy Making in Canada's Big Cities*. Montréal: McGill-Queen's University Press, p. 104–35.

Bicknell, J., D. Dodman and D. Satterthwaite (Eds.). 2009. *Adapting Cities to Climate Change: Understanding and Addressing the Development Challenges*. London: Earthscan.

Biello, D. 2011. "How Green Is My City: Retrofitting Is the Best Way to Clean Up Urban Living." *Scientific American* September: 66–69.

Bijker, W. 1997. *Of Bicycles, Bakelites, and Bulbs: Toward a Theory of Sociotechnical Change*. Cambridge: MIT Press.

Bird, K. 2008. "Many Faces, Few Places: The Political Under-Representation of Ethnic Minorities and Women in the City of Hamilton." In Andrew, C., J. Biles and M. Siemiatycki (Eds.), *Electing a Diverse Canada: The Representation of Immigrants, Minorities and Women*. Vancouver: UBC Press, pp. 136–55.

Blanc, M. 2009. "Gouvernance." In Stébé, J.-M. and H. Marchal (Eds.), *Traité sur la ville*. Paris: PUF, pp. 207–57.

Bocking, S. 2011. *Building Postwar Toronto: When Planning and Politics Collide*. Toronto Public Library. Online at http//spacingtoronto.ca/2011/11/11 [Accessed 3 July, 2012].

Boddy, T. 2004. "New Urbanism: The Vancouver Model." *Places* 16, 2: 14–20.

Boddy, T. 2005. *INSIGHT: Vancouverism vs Lower Manhattanism: Shaping the High Density City*. ArchNewsNow. Online at www.archnewsnow.com/features/Feature177.htm [Accessed 1 March, 2012].

Body-Gendrot, S., M. Garcia and E. Mingione. 2012. "Comparative Social Transformations in Urban Regimes." In Sales, A. (Ed.), *Sociology Today: Social Transformations in a Globalizing World*. Los Angeles: Sage, pp. 359–80.

Bogdanowicz, J. 2006. "Vancouverism." *Canadian Architect*, August 1. Online at www.canadianarchitect.com/news/vancouverism/1000205807/.

Bohman, J. 2007. *Democracy across Borders: From Dêmos to Dêmoi*. Cambridge: MIT Press.

Boli, J. and G.M. Thomas (Eds.). 1999. *Constructing World Culture: International Nongovernmental Organizations Since 1875*. Stanford: Stanford University Press.

Boone, C.G. and A. Modarres. 2006. *City and Environment*. Philadelphia: Temple University Press.

Boudreau, J.-A., P. Hamel, B. Jouve and R. Keil. 2006. "Comparing Metropolitan Governance: The Cases of Montréal and Toronto." *Progress in Planning* 66, 2: 1–54.

Boudreau, J.-A., P. Hamel, B. Jouve and R. Keil. 2007. "New State Spaces in Canada: Metropolitanization in Montréal and Toronto Compared." *Urban Geography* 28, 1: 30–53.

Boudreau, J.-A., R. Keil and D. Young. 2009. *Changing Toronto: Governing Urban Neoliberalism*. Toronto: Toronto University Press.

Bourdieu, P. and J.-C. Passeron. 1970. *La reproduction: Éléments d''une théorie du système d'enseignement*. Paris: Les Éditions de Minuit.

Bourne, L.S. 1996. "Reinventing the Suburbs: Old Myths and New Realities." *Progress in Planning* 46, 3: 163–84.

Bourne, L.S. and J.W. Simmons. 2003. "New Fault Lines? Recent Trends in the Canadian Urban System and Their Implications for Planning and

Public Policy." *Canadian Journal of Urban Research* 12, Joint Issue Supplement: 22–47.

Bourne, L.S., J.N.H. Britton and D. Leslie. 2011. "The Greater Toronto Region: The Challenges of Economic Restructuring, Social Diversity, and Globalization." In Bourne, L.S., T. Hutton, R.G. Shearmur and J. Simmons (Eds.), *Canadian Urban Regions: Trajectories of Growth and Change.* Toronto: Oxford University Press, pp. 236–68.

Bourne, L.S., T. Hutton, R.G. Shearmur and J. Simmons (Eds.). 2011. *Canadian Urban Regions: Trajectories of Growth and Change.* Toronto: Oxford University Press.

Bowen, W.M., R.A. Dunn and D.O. Kasdan. 2010. "What Is 'Urban Studies'? Context, Internal Structure, and Content." *Journal of Urban Affairs* 32, 2: 199–227.

Bradford, N. 2004. "Place Matters and Multilevel Governance: Perspectives on a New Urban Policy Paradigm." *Policy Options* 25, 2: 39–44.

Braudel, F. 1979. *Civilisation matérielle, économie et capitalisme (XVe–XVIIIe siècle): Les structures du quotidien.* Paris: Armand Colin.

Brenner, N. 2000. "The Urban Question as a Scale Question: Reflections on Henri Lefebvre, Urban Theory and the Politics of Scale." *International Journal of Urban and Regional Research* 24, 2: 361–78.

Brenner, N. 2004. *New State Spaces: Urban Governance and the Rescaling of Statehood.* London: Oxford University Press.

Brugmann, J. 2009. *Welcome to the Urban Revolution: How Cities Are Changing the World.* New York: Bloomsbury Press.

Bugliarello, G. 2006. "Urban Sustainability: Dilemmas, Challenges and Paradigms." *Technology in Society* 28, 1–2: 19–26.

Bulkeley, H. and K. Kern. 2006. "Local Governance and the Governing of Climate Change in Germany and the UK." *Urban Studies* 43, 12: 2237–59.

Bulkeley, H. and M. M. Betsill. 2003. *Cities and Climate Change.* London: Routledge.

Bulmer, M. 1984. *The Chicago School of Sociology: Institutionalization, Diversity, and the Rise of Sociological Research.* Chicago: University of Chicago Press.

Burgess, E.W. 1925. "The Growth of the City." In Park, R.E, E.W. Burgess and R. McKenzie (Eds.), *The City.* Chicago: University of Chicago Press.

Buttel, F.H. 2000. "Ecological Modernization as a Social Theory." *Geoforum* 30, 1: 57–65.

Canada. 2008. *Federal Sustainable Development Act.*

Castells, M. 1972. *La question urbaine.* Paris: Maspéro.

Castells, M. 1983. *The City and the Grassroots: A Cross-cultural Theory of Urban Social Movements.* London: Arnold.

Castells, M. 1996. *The Rise of the Network Society: The Information Age: Economy, Society and Culture, Vol. I.* Malden: Blackwell.

Castells, M. 2009. "The Networked City: Réseaux, espace, société." EspacesTemps.net. Online at http://espacestemps.net/document7443.html. [Accessed 11 November, 2011].

Castells, M. and M. Ince. 2003. *Conversations with Manuel Castells.* Cambridge: Polity Press.

Castonguay, S. and M. Dagenais (Eds.). 2011. *Metropolitan Natures: Environmental History of Montréal.* Pittsburgh: University of Pittsburgh Press.

Caulfield, J. and L. Peake (Eds.). 1996. *City Lives & City Forms: Critical Research & Canadian Urbanism.* Toronto: University of Toronto Press.

Chapoulie, J.-M. 2001. *La tradition sociologique de Chicago, 1892–1961.* Paris: Éditions du Seuil.

Charbonneau J. and A. Germain 2002. "Les banlieues de l'immigration." *Recherches sociographiques* 43, 2: 311–28.

Charbonneau, H. and R. Cole Harris. 1987. "Le repeuplement de la vallée du Saint-Laurent." In Coles, R.C., G.J. Matthews, L. Deschênes and M. Paré (Eds.), *Atlas Historique du Canada I: Des origines à 1800.* Montréal: Presses de l'Université de Montréal, planche 46.

Charles, C.Z. 2003. "The Dynamics of Racial Residential Segregation." *Annual Review of Sociology* 29: 167–207.

Chen, W.H., J. Myles and G. Picot. 2011. *Why Have Poorer Neighbourhoods Stagnated Economically, While the Richer have Flourished? Neighbourhood Income Inequality in Canadian Cities.* Canadian Market and Skills Researcher Network. Working Paper 82.

Childe, V. Gordon. 2000 [1950]. "The Urban Revolution." In LeGates, R.T. and F. Stout (Eds.), *The City Reader* (2nd ed.). London: Routledge, pp. 22–30.

Chinitz, B. 1964. "City and Suburb." In Chinitz, B. (Ed.), *City and Suburb: The Economies of Metropolitan Growth*. Englewood Cliffs: Prentice-Hall, pp. 3–50.

Choay, F. 1965. *L'urbanisme, utopies et réalités: Une anthologie*. Paris: Seuil.

Choko, M. 1988. *Une cité-jardin à Montréal: La Cité-jardin du tricentenaire, 1940–1947*. Montréal: Méridiens.

Clark, W.A.V. 1986. "Residential Segregation in American Cities: A Review and Interpretation." *Population Research and Policy Review* 5, 2: 95–127.

Clark, W.A.V. and S.A. Blue. 2004. "Race, Class, and Segregation Patterns in U.S. Immigrant Gateway Cities." *Urban Affairs Review* 39, 6: 667–88.

Clark, W.C. 2007. "Sustainability Science: A Room of its Own." *Proceedings of the National Academy of Sciences of the United States of America* 104, 6: 1737–8.

Clarke, S.E. 1995. "Institutional Logics and Local Economic Development: A Comparative Analysis of Eight American Cities." *International Journal of Urban and Regional Research* 19, 4: 513–33.

Clarke, S.E. and G.L. Gaile. 1998. *The Work of the Cities*. Minneapolis: University of Minnesota Press.

Collin, J.-P. 2002. "La réforme de l'organisation du secteur municipal au Québec: La fin ou le début d'un cycle?" *Revue Organisations et territoires* 11, 3: 5–13.

Collin, J.-P., É. Champagne, P.J. Hamel and C. Poitras. 1998. "La Rive-Sud de Montréal: Dynamique intermunicipale et intégration métropolitaine." Montréal: *INRS-Urbanisation* XX: 274.

Conference Board of Canada. 2011. *Canadian Income Inequality*. Online at www.conferenceboard.ca/hcp/hot-topics/caninequalty.asx [Accessed 18 May, 2012].

Coutard, O. and J-P. Lévy (Eds.). 2010. *Écologies urbaines*. Paris: Economica-Anthropos.

Cressey, P.G. 1932. *The Taxi-Dance Hall*. Chicago: University of Chicago Press.

Cronon, W. 1991. *Nature's Metropolis: Chicago and the Great West*. New York: Norton.

Cuin, C.-H. 2004. "Division du travail, inégalités sociales et ordre social: Note sur les tergiversations de l'analyse durkheimienne." *Revue européenne des sciences sociales* XLII, 129: 95–103.

Curran, D. and R. Tomalty. 2003. "Living It up." *Alternatives* 29, 3: 10–18.

Dagenais, M. 2000. *Des pouvoirs et des hommes*. Montréal: Institut d'administration publique du Canada.

Davies, J.S. 2011. *Challenging Governance Theory: From Networks to Hegemony*. Bristol: Policy Press.

Davis, K. 1996. "The Urbanization of the Human Population." In LeGates, R.T. and F. Stout (Eds.), *The City Reader* (2nd ed.). London: Routledge, pp. 3–13.

Davis, M. 2006 [1992]. *City of Quartz: Excavating the Future in Los Angeles* (2nd ed.). London: Verso. [New York: Vintage Books].

Davis. M. 2000. *Magical Urbanism: Latinos Reinvent the U.S. Big City*. London/New York: Verso.

Dear, M. (Ed.). 2002a. *From Chicago to LA: Making Sense of Urban Theory*. Thousand Oaks/London: Sage.

Dear, M. 2002b. "Preface." In Dear, M. (Ed.), *From Chicago to L.A.: Making Sense of Urban Theory*. Thousand Oaks/London: Sage, pp. vii–xi.

Dear, M. 2003. "The Los Angles School of Urbanism: An Intellectual History." *Urban Geography* 24: 493–509.

Dear, M. and M. Dahmann. 2008. "Urban Politics and the Los Angeles School of Urbanism." *Urban Affairs Review* 4, 2: 266–79.

Dear, M. and S. Flusty. 2002. "The Resistible Rise of the L.A. School." In Dear, M.J. (Ed.), *From Chicago to L.A.: Making Sense of Urban Theory*. Thousand Oaks/London: Sage, pp. 5–19.

Dear, M., A. Burridge, P. Marolt, J. Peters and M. Seymor. 2008. "Critical Responses to the Los Angeles School of Urbanism." *Urban Geography* 29, 2: 101–12.

Dennis, R. 2008. *Cities in Modernity: Representations and Productions of Metropolitan Space, 1840–1930*. Cambridge: Cambridge University Press.

Desfor, G. and R. Keil. 2004. *Nature and the City: Making Environmental Policy in Toronto and Los Angeles*. Tucson: University of Arizona Press.

Deslauriers, M., C. Durand and G. Duhaime. 2011. "Que se cache-t-il derrière les portraits statistiques nationaux? Le cas des Amérindiens au Québec." *Sociologie et sociétés* LIII, 2: 143–74.

Dewey, J. 1915. *The Public and its Problems.* Carbondale: University Press Drive.

Divay, G. and M. Gaudreau. 1984. *La formation des espaces résidentiels.* Sillery: Presses de l'Université du Québec.

Dogsé, P. 2004. "Toward Urban Biosphere Reserves." *Annals of the New York Academy of Sciences* 1023, 1: 10–48.

Dreier, P., J. Mollenkopf and T. Swanstrom. 2001. *Place Matters: Metropolitics for the Twenty-First Century.* Lawrence: University Press of Kansas.

Driedger, L. 1999. "Immigrant/Ethnic/ Racial Segregation: Canadian Big Three and Prairies Metropolitan Comparison." *Canadian Journal of Sociology/Cahiers canadiens de sociologie* 24, 4: 485–509.

Drori, G., J. Meyer, F. Ramirez and E. Schoferet. 2003. *Science and the Modern World Polity: Institutionalization and Globalization.* Stanford: Stanford University Press.

Drouilly, P. 1996. *L'espace social de Montréal, 1951–1991.* Montréal: Septentrion.

Dubet, F. 2000. *Les inégalités multipliées.* La Tour d'Aigues: Éditions de l'Aube.

Dubet, F. 2009. *Le travail des sociétés.* Paris: Seuil.

Dufour, P., D. Masson and D. Caouette (Eds.). 2010. *Transnationalizing Women's Movements: Solidarities beyond Borders.* Vancouver: UBC Press.

Dumesnil, F. and C. Ouellet. 2003. "La réhabilitation des friches industrielles: Un pas vers la ville viable?" *Vertigo* 3, 2. Online at http://vertigo.revues.org/3812.

Durkheim, É. 1997 [1893]. *The Division of Labor in Society.* New York: Free Press.

Eisenstadt, S. (Ed.). 1986. *The Origin and Diversity of Axial Age Civilizations.* Albany: State University Press of New York.

Ekers, M., P. Hamel and R. Keil 2012. "Governing Suburbia: Modalities and Mechanisms of Suburban Governance." *Regional Studies* 46, 3: 405–22.

Ellin, N. 1996. *Postmodern Urbanism.* Cambridge: Blackwell.

Erickson, E.G. 1980. *The Territorial Experience: Human Ecology as Symbolic Interaction.* Austin: University of Texas Press.

Erie, S.P. 2004. *Globalizing L.A. Trade, Infrastructure, and Regional Development.* Stanford: Stanford University Press.

European Conference on Sustainable Cities & Towns. 1994. *Charter of European Cities & Towns Towards Sustainability.* Online at http://ec.europa.eu/environment/urban/pdf/aalborg_charter.pdf.

Fainstein, S.S. 2010. *The Just City.* Ithaca, NY: Cornell University Press.

Faure, A. 2010. "Banlieue (pl. banlieues)." In C. Topalov, L. Coudroy de Lille, J.C. Depaule and B. Marin (Eds.), *L'aventure des mots de la ville à travers le temps, les langues, les sociétiés.* Paris: Robert Laffont, pp. 72–7.

Federation of Canadian Municipalities/ Fédération canadienne des municipalités. (2005). *Sustainable Communities Knowledge Network.* Centre for Sustainable Community Development. Online at www.fcm.ca

Filion, P. 2000. "Balancing Concentration and Dispersion? Public Policy and Urban Structure in Toronto." *Environment and Planning C: Government and Policy* 18, 2: 163–89.

Filion, P. 2003. "Towards Smart Growth? The Difficult Implementation of Alternatives to Urban Dispersion." *Canadian Journal of Urban Research/ Revue canadienne de recherche urbaine* 12, Joint Issue Supplement: 48–70.

Firey, W. 1945. "Sentiment and Symbolism as Ecological Variables." *American Sociological Review* 10, 2: 140–48.

Fischer, C.S. 1984. *The Urban Experience* (2nd ed.). San Diego/Toronto: Harcourt Brace Jovanovich.

Fischler, R. 2007. "Development Controls in Toronto in the Nineteenth Century." *Urban History Review/Revue d'histoire urbaine* 36, 1: 16–30.

Fisette, J. and M. Raffinot. 2010. *Gouvernance et Appropriation Locale du Développement: Au-delà des modèles importés.* Ottawa: Presses de l'Université d'Ottawa.

Fishman, R. 1987. *Bourgeois Utopias: The Rise and Fall of Suburbia.* New York: Basic Books.

Flanagan, W.G. 1995. *Urban Sociology: Images and Structure.* Boston: Allyn and Bacon.

Florida, R. 2002. *The Rise of the Creative Class.* New York: Basic Books.

Florida, R. 2003. "Cities and the Creative Class." *Cities & Communities* 2, 1: 3–19.

Fong E. 2011. "Immigration and Race in the City." In Hiller, H.H. (Ed.), *Urban Canada* (2nd ed.). Toronto: Oxford University Press, pp. 132–54.

Fong, E. and E. Chan. 2010. "The Effect of Economic Standing, Individual Preferences, and Co-ethnic Resources on Immigrant Residential Clustering." *International Migration Review* 44, 1: 111–41.

Fong, E. and F. Hou. 2009. "Residential Patterns across Generations of New Immigrant Groups." *Sociological Perspectives* 52, 3: 409–28.

Fong, E. and R. Wilkes. 2003. "Racial and Ethnic Residential Patterns in Canada." *Sociological Forum* 189, 4: 577–602.

Fong, E. and S. Shibuya. 2005. "Multiethnic Cities in North America." *Annual Review of Sociology* 31: 285–304.

Fontan, J.-M., P. Hamel, R. Morin and E. Shragge. 2008. "Le développement local dans un contexte métropolitain: La démocratie en quête d"un nouveau modèle?" *Politique et Sociétés* 25, 1: 99–127.

Forester, J. 1988. *Planning in the Face of Power.* Berkeley/Los Angeles: University of California Press.

Forester, J. 1999. *The Deliberative Practitioner.* Cambridge: MIT Press.

Fortier, R. (Ed.). 1996. *Les villes industrielles planifiées.* Montréal: Boréal.

Fortin, A. and M. Bédard. 2003. "Citadins et banlieusards: Représentations, pratiques et identités." *Canadian Journal of Urban Research/Revue canadienne de recherche urbaine* 12, 1: 58–76.

Fortin, A., C. Després and G. Vachon (Eds.). 2002. *La banlieue revisitée.* Québec: Nota Bene.

Fougères, D. 2004. *L'approvisionnement en eau à Montréal: Du privé au public, 1796–1865.* Québec: Septentrion.

Fourcaut, A. 2000. "Pour en finir avec la banlieue." *Géocarrefour* 75, 2: 101–105.

Fraser, N. 1996. *Social Justice in the Age of Identity Politics: Redistribution, Recognition and Participation.* The Tanner Lectures on Human Values. 04/30–05/02. Stanford University. Online at http://tannerlectures.utah.edu/lectures/documents/Fraser98.pdf.

Freidson, E. 1986. *Professional Powers: A Study of the Institutionalization of Formal Knowledge.* Chicago: University of Chicago Press.

Friedan, B. 1963. *The Feminine Mystique.* New York: W.W. Norton & Company.

Friedman, J. and C. Weaver. 1979. *Territory and Function: The Evolution of Regional Planning.* Berkeley/Los Angeles: University of California.

Friedmann, J. 1981. *Retracking America.* New York: Anchor Press.

Friedmann, J. 1986. "The World City Hypothesis." *Development and Change* 17, 1: 69–83.

Friedmann, J. 1987. *Planning and the Public Domain: From Knowledge to Action.* Princeton: Princeton University Press.

Friedmann, J. 2005. *China's Urban Transition.* Minneapolis: University of Minnesota Press.

Friedmann, J. and G. Wolf. 1982. "World City Formation: An Agenda for Research and Action." *International Journal of Regional and Urban Research* 6, 3: 309–44.

Frisken, F. 2001. "The Toronto Story: Sober Reflections on Fifty Years of Experiments with Regional Governance." *Journal of Urban Affairs* 23, 5: 513.41.

Frisken, F. 2007. *The Public Metropolis.* Toronto: University of Toronto Press.

Gagnon, R. 2006. *Questions d'égouts: Santé publique, infrastructures et urbanisation à Montréal au XIXe siècle.* Montréal: Boréal.

Gagnon, R. and N. Zwarich. 2008. "Les inégnieurs sanitaires à Montréal, 1870–1945: Lieux de formation et exercice de profession." *Urban History Review/Revue d'histoire urbaine* 37, 1: 3–20.

Gans, H.J. 1967. *The Levittowners: Ways of Life and Politics in a New Suburban Community.* New York: Random House.

Gans, H.J. 1968. *People and Plans.* Harmonsworth: Penguin Books.

Garde, A.M. 2004. "New Urbanism as Sustainable Growth? A Supply Side Story and Its Implications for Public Policy." *Journal of Planning Education and Research* 24, 2: 154–70.

Garreau, J. 1991. *Edge City: Life on the New Frontier.* New York: Doubleday.

Geddes, P. 1904. *Civics: As Applied Sociology.* Dodo Press.

Geddes, P. 1949 [1915]. *Cities in Evolution.* London: Williams & Norgate.

Genestier, P. 1998. "Le vocable ville: Métonymie, antiphrase, euphémisme." In Haumont, N. (Ed.), *L'urbain dans tous ses états.* Paris: L'Harmattan, p. 289–306.

Germain, A. 1984. *Les mouvements de réforme urbaine à Montréal au tournant du siècle.* Montréal: Université de Montréal.

Germain, A. and D. Rose. 2000. *Montréal: The Quest for a Metropolis*. New York: Wiley.

Ghorra-Gobin, C. 2009. "À L'heure de la deuxième mondialisation, une ville mondiale est-elle une ville globale?" *Confins* 5.

Giddens, A. 1990. *The Consequences of Modernity*. Cambridge: Polity.

Giddens, A. 1991. *Modernity and Self-Identity: Self and Society in the Late Modern Age*. Stanford: Stanford University Press.

Giddens, A. 2009. *The Politics of Climate Change*. Cambridge: Polity.

Gilliland, J. 2002. "The Creative Destruction of Montréal: Street Widening and the Urban (re)Development in the Nineteenth Century." *Urban History Review* 31, 1: 37–51.

Glaeser, E. 2011. *The Triumph of the City*. London: Macmillan.

Glaeser, E.L., M. Resseger and K. Tobio. 2008. *Urban Inequality*. Cambridge: Harvard Kennedy School, Taubman Center for State and Local Government. Working paper.

Gobster, P.H. 2001. "Vision of Nature: Conflicts and Compatibility in Urban Park Restoration." *Landscape and Urban Planning*, 56: 35–51.

Godard, F. 2001. *La ville en mouvement*. Paris: Gallimard.

Goldberg, M. and J. Mercer. 1986. *The Myth of North American City: Continentalism Challenged*. Vancouver: UBC Press.

Goldsmith, M. 2001. "Urban Governance." In Paddison, R. (Ed.), *Handbook of Urban Studies*. London: Sage, pp. 325–35.

Goonewardena, K., S. Kipfer, R. Milgrom and C. Schmid (Eds.). 2008. *Space, Difference, Everyday Life. Reading Henri Lefebvre*. New York: Routledge.

Gordon, D.M. 1978. "Capitalist Development and the History of American Cities." In W. Tabb and L. Sawers. (Eds.), *Marxism and the Metropolis*. New York: Oxford University Press, pp. 21–53.

Gottdiener, M. and R. Hutchison. 2011. *The New Urban Sociology* (4th ed.). Boulder: Westview Press.

Gottman, J. 1961. *Megalopolis: The Urbanization of the Northeast Seaboard of the United States*. New York: Twentieth Century Fund.

Gouvernement du Québec. 2000. *Projet de loi no 134 instituant la Communauté métropolitaine de Montréal*. Québec: Éditeur officiel du Québec.

Grafmeyer, J. and I. Joseph. 1979. *L'École de Chicago: Naissance de l'écologie urbaine*. Paris: Éditions du Champ Urbain.

Grant, J. 2006. "The Ironies of New Urbanism." *Canadian Journal of Urban Research/Revue canadienne de recherche urbaine* 15, 2: 158–74.

Grant, J. 2008. "The History of Canadian Planning." In Grant, J. (Ed.), *A Reader in Canadian Planning: Linking Theory and Practice*. Toronto: Nelson, pp. 21–6.

Grant, J. (Ed.). 2008. *A Reader in Canadian Planning: Linking Theory and Practice*. Toronto: Nelson.

Gross, M. 2009. "Collaborative Experiments: Jane Addams, Hull-House, and Experimental Social Work." *Social Sciences Information* 48, 1: 81–95.

Gross, M. 2010. *Ignorance and Surprise: Science, Society, and Ecological Design*. Cambridge: MIT Press.

Guay, L. 1978. "Les dimensions de l'espace social urbain: Montréal 1951, 1961, 1971." *Recherches sociographiques* 19, 3: 307–48.

Guay, L. 1981. "Différenciation et ségrégation urbaines: Québec 1951, 1961 et 1971." *Recherches sociographiques*, 22: 237–55.

Guay, L. 2004. "Introduction: Le concept de développement durable en contexte historique et cognitif." In Bouthillier L., G. Debailleul, L. Doucet and L. Guay (Eds.), *Les enjeux et les défis du développement durable: Connaître, décider, agir*. Québec: Les Presses de L'Université Laval, pp. 1–31.

Guay, L. 2005. "Controverses socio-techniques, participation et decisions publiques." In Guay L., P. Hamel, D. Masson and J-G. Vaillancourt (Eds.), *Mouvements sociaux et changements institutionnels*. Sainte-Foy: Presses de L'Université du Québec, pp. 377–420.

Guay, L. and N. Émond. 2010. "Infrastructures urbaines et développement durable." In *Institut du nouveau monde. L'état du Québec 2010*. Montréal: Boréal, pp. 109–15.

Guay, L. and P. Hamel. 2010. "Urban Change and Policy Response in Québec." In Hiller, H.H. (Ed.), *Urban Canada* (2nd ed.). Toronto: Oxford University Press, pp. 297–322.

Gutmann, A. and D. Thompson. 2004. *Why Deliberative Democracy?* Princeton/ Oxford: Princeton University Press.

Haas, P.M. 2004. "When Does Power Listen to Truth? A Constructivist Approach to the Policy Process." *Journal of European Public Policy* 11, 4: 569–92.

Hajer M.E. (Ed.). 2009. *Authoritative Governance: Policy-making in the Age of Modernization.* Oxford: Oxford University Press.

Hajer, M.A. and H. Wagenaar. 2003. "Introduction." In Hajer, M.A. and H. Wagenaar (Eds.), *Deliberative Policy Analysis: Understanding Governance in the Network Society (Theories of Institutional Design).* New York: Cambridge University Press, pp. 1–32.

Hall, P. 1966. *The World Cities.* London: Heineman.

Hall, P. 1980a. *Urban and Regional Planning.* Harmondsworth: Penguin.

Hall, P. 1980b. *Great Planning Disasters.* London: Weidenfeld and Nicolson.

Hall, P. 1988. *Cities of Tomorrow: An Intellectual History of Urban Planning and Design in the Twentieth Century.* Oxford: Blackwell.

Hall, P. 1998. *Cities in Civilization.* London: Weidenfeld & Nicolson.

Hall, P. 2006. "The Metropilitan Explosion." In Brenner, N. and R. Keil (Eds.), *The Global City Reader.* London and New York: Routledge, pp. 23–24.

Hamel, P. 2001. "Enjeux métropolitains: Les nouveaux défis." *International Journal of Canadian Studies/Revue Internationale d'Études Canadiennes* 24, Fall: 105–27.

Hamel, P. 2005. "Municipal Reform in Québec: The Trade-off between Centralization and Decentralization." In Garcea, J. and E.C. LeSage Jr. (Eds.), *Municipal Reform in Canada: Reconfiguration, Re-Empowerment, and Rebalancing.* Don Mills: Oxford University Press, pp. 149–73.

Hamel, P. 2008. *Ville et débat public: Agir en démocratie.* Québec: Presses de L'Université Laval.

Hamel, P. and B. Jouve. 2006. *Un modèle québécois? Gouvernance et participation dans la gestion publique.* Montréal: Presses de L'Université de Montréal.

Hamlin, C. 1990. *A Science of Impurity: Water Analysis in the Nineteenth Century Britain.* Berkeley/Los Angeles: University of California Press.

Hampton, K.N. 2010. "Social Ties and Community in Urban Places." In Hiller, H.H. (Ed.), *Urban Canada* (2nd ed.). Toronto: Oxford University Press, pp. 86–107.

Hannigan, J. 2010. "Analysing and Interpreting the City: Theory and Method." In Hiller, H.H. (Ed.), *Urban Canada* (2nd ed.). Toronto: Oxford University Press, pp. 41–60.

Harris, R. 2004. *Creeping Conformity: How Canada Became Suburban, 1900–1960.* Toronto: University of Toronto Press.

Harvey, D. 1973. *Social Justice and the City.* Oxford: Blackwell.

Harvey, D. 1985a. *The Urban Experience.* Baltimore: Johns Hopkins University Press.

Harvey, D. 1985b. *The Urbanization of Capital: Studies in the History and Theory of Capitalist Urbanization.* Baltimore: Johns Hopkins University Press.

Harvey, D. 1989. *The Condition of Postmodernity.* Oxford: Basil Blackwell.

Harvey, D. 1996. *Justice, Nature & the Geography of Difference.* Oxford: Blackwell.

Hatvany, M. 2001. "L'expansion urbaine du XXe siècle." In Courville, S. and R. Garon (Eds.), *Québec, ville et capitale.* Sainte-Foy: Presses de l'Université Laval, pp. 256–79.

Haus, M. and J.E. Klausen. 2010. "Urban Leadership and Community Involvement: Ingredients for Good Governance?" *Urban Affairs Review* 47, 2: 256–79.

Hawley, A.E. 1986. *Human Ecology: A Theoretical Essay.* Chicago: University of Chicago Press.

Healey, P. 1997. *Collaborative Planning: Shaping Places in Fragmented Societies.* Vancouver: UBC Press.

Heisz, A. and L. McLeod. 2004. "Public Transit Use Among Immigrants." *Canadian Journal of Urban Research* 13, 1: 170–991.

Held, D. and A. McGrew. 2002. *Globalization/ Anti-Globalization.* Cambridge: Polity.

Held, D., A. McGrew, D. Goldblatt and J. Perraton. 1999. *Global Transformations: Politics, Economics and Culture.* Stanford: Stanford University Press.

Hérault, B. 2008. "La participation des citoyens et l'action publique." In *La participation des citoyens et l'action publique, Rapports et Documents.* Paris: La Documentation.

Hiller, H.H. 2010a. "Canadian
Urbanization in Historical and Global
Perspective." In Hiller, H.H. (Ed.),
Urban Canada (2nd ed.). Toronto:
Oxford University Press, pp. 2–30.

Hiller, H.H. 2010b. "The Dynamics of
Canadian Urbanization." In Hiller, H.H.,
(Ed.), *Urban Canada* (2nd ed.). Toronto:
Oxford University Press, pp. 19–39.

Hirst, P. 2000. "Democracy and
Governance." In Pierre, J. (Ed.),
*Debating Governance: Authority, Steering
and Democracy.* Oxford: Oxford
University Press, pp. 13–35.

Hodge, G. 1985. "The Roots of Canadian
Planning." *Journal of the American
Planning Association* 51, 1: 8–22.

Hodge, G. and I.M. Robinson. 2001.
Planning Canadian Regions. Vancouver:
UBC Press.

Hohenberg, P.M. and L.H. Lees. 1985. *The
Making of Urban Europe: 1000–1950.*
Cambridge: Harvard University Press.

Hommels, A. 2005a. "Studying Obduracy
in the City: Toward a Productive Fusion
Between Technology Studies and Urban
Studies." *Science, Technology & Human
Values* 30, 3: 323–51.

Hommels, A. 2005b . *Unbuilding Cities:
Obduracy in Urban Socio-Technical
Change.* Cambridge: MIT Press.

Hou, F. 1996. "Spatial Assimilation
of Racial Minorities in Canada's
Immigrant Gateway Cities." *Urban
Studies* 43, 7: 1189–1213.

Hou, F. and T.R. Balakrishnan. 1996.
"The Integration of Visible Minorities
in Contemporary Canadian Society."
*Canadian Journal of Sociology/Cahiers
canadiens de sociologie* 21, 3: 307–26.

Hough, M. 1995. *Cities and Natural
Processes.* London and New York:
Routledge.

Howard, E.1965 [1902]. *Garden Cities of
Tomorrow.* Cambridge: MIT Press.

Huber, J. 2008. "Pioneer Countries and
the Global Diffusion of Environmental
Innovations: Theses from the Viewpoint
of Ecological Modernization Theory."
Global Environmental Change 18, 3:
360–67.

Huff, T.E. 2011. *Intellectual Curiosity and
the Scientific Revolution.* Cambridge:
Cambridge University Press.

Hughes, E.C. 1958. *Men and Their Work.*
Glencoe: The Free Press.

Hughes, T.P. 1983. *Networks of Power:
Electrification in Western Society,
1880–1930.* Baltimore: Johns Hopkins
University Press.

Hugill, P.J. 1999. *Global Communications
since 1844: Geopolitics and Technology.*
Baltimore: Johns Hopkins Press.

Hulbert, F. 1994. *Essai de géopolitique urbaine
et régionale: La comédie urbaine de Québec*
(2nd ed.). Québec: Méridien.

Hulchanski, J.D. 2007. *The Three Cities
Within Toronto:. Income Polarization
Among Toronto's Neighbourhoods, 1970–
2005.* Toronto: Cities Centre Press,
University of Toronto.

Hutton, T. 2004. "The New Economy of the
Inner City." *Cities* 21, 2: 89–108.

Innis. H. 1995. *Staples, Markets, and
Cultural Change.* Montréal/Kingston:
McGill/Queen's.

IPCC (Intergovernmental Panel on Climate
Change) 2007. *Climate Change 2007:
The Physical Science Basis.* Cambridge:
Cambridge University Press.

Jackson, K.T. 1985. *Crabgrass Frontier: The
Suburbanization of the United States.*
Oxford: Oxford University Press.

Jacobs, J. 1961. *The Death and Life of Great
American Cities: The Failure of Town
Planning.* New York: Random House.

Jacobs, J. 1984. "Why TVA Failed." *New
York Review of Books* 31, 8.

Jansen, M.A., K. Börner, W. Ke and
M.L. Schoon. 2006. "Scholarly
Networks on Resilience, Vulnerability
and Adaptation within the Human
Dimensions of Global Environmental
Change." *Global Environmental Change*
16, 3: 240–52.

Jayal, N.G. 2007. "Review Essay: On
Governance." *Current Sociology* 55, 1:
126–35.

Jessop, B. 1979. "Corporatism,
Parliamentarism and Social Democracy."
In Schmitter, P.C. and G. Lembruch
(Eds.), *Trends Towards Corporatist
Intermediation.* London: Sage, pp. 185–212.

Jorgensen, A. and P.H. Gobster (2010).
"Shades of Green: Measuring the
Ecology of Urban Green Space in the
Context of Human Health and Well-
Being." *Nature and Culture,* 5: 338-63.

Jouve, B. 2003. *La gouvernance urbaine en
questions.* Paris: Elsevier.

Jouve, B. 2005. "La démocratie en métropoles: Gouvernance, participation et

citoyenneté." *Revue française de science politique* 55, 2: 317–37.

Judd, D.R. 2011. "Theorizing the City." In Judd, D.R. and D.W. Simpson (Eds.), *The City, Revisited: Urban Theory from Chicago, Los Angeles, New York.* Minneapolis: University of Minnesota Press, pp. 3–20.

Judd, D.R. and D.W. Simpson. 2011. *The City, Revisited: Urban Theory from Chicago, Los Angeles, and New York.* Minneapolis: University of Minnesota Press.

Kazancigil, A. 2010. *La gouvernance: Pour ou contre le politique?* Paris: Armand Colin.

Keil, R. 1998. *Los Angeles: Globalization, Urbanization and Social Struggles.* New York: Wiley.

Keil, R. 2002. " Common-Sense Neoliberalism: Progressive Conservative Urbanism in Toronto, Canada." *Antipode* 34, 3: 578–601.

Keney, M.R. 1998. "Remember, Stonewall Was a Riot: Understanding Gay and Lesbian Experience in the City." In Sandercock, L. (Ed.), *Making the Invisible Visible.* Berkeley: University of California Press, pp. 120–32.

Kipfer, S. 2008. "How Lefebvre Urbanized Gramsci: Hegemony, Everdyday Life, and Difference." In Goonewardena, K., S. Kipfer, R. Milgrom and C. Schmid (Eds.), *Space, Difference, Everyday Life: Reading Henri Lefebvre.* New York/London: Routledge, pp. 193–211.

Kline, R. and T. Pinch. 1996. "Taking the Black Box off the Wheels: The Social Construction of the Automobile in Rural America." *Technology and Culture* 37: 776–95.

Knox, P.L. 2008. *Metroburbia, USA.* New Brunswick: Rutgers University Press.

Korneski, K. 2008. "Reform and Empire: The Case of Winnipeg, Manitoba, 1870–1910." *Urban History Review/Revue d'histoire urbaine* 37, 1: 48–62.

Kousky, C. and S.H. Schneider. 2003. "Global Climate Policy: Will Cities Lead the Way?" *Climate Policy* 3, 4: 359–72.

Kuznets, S. 1966. *Modern Economic Growth: Rate, Structure and Spread.* New Haven/London: Yale University Press.

Lacour, R. and S. Puissant (Eds.). (1999). *La Métropolisation. Croissance, Diversité, Fractures.* Paris: Anthropos.

Lafaye, C. 2006. "Gouvernance et démocratie: Quelles reconfigurations?" In Andrew, C. and L. Cardinal (Eds.),

Gouvernance et démocratie. Ottawa: Presses de L'Université d'Ottawa, pp. 57–87.

Lafrance, M. and A. Charbonneau. 1987. "Les villes." In Coles, R.C., G.J. Matthews, L. Deschênes and M. Paré, *Atlas Historique du Canada I: Des origines à 1800.* Montréal: Presses de L'Université de Montréal, planche 49.

Laliberté, P. 2002. "Un développement urbain pour réduire concrètement la dépendance à l'automobile." *Vertigo* 3, 2. Online at http://vertigo.revues.org/3815.

Lamonde, P. and Y. Martineau. 1992. *Désindustrialisation et restructuration économique: Montréal et les autres grandes métropoles nord-américaines, 1971–1991.* Montréal: Institut National de la Recherche Scientifique (INRS-Urbanisation).

Landes, D.S. 1969. *The Unbound Prometheus: Technological Change and Industrial Development in the Western Europe from 1750 to the Present.* Cambridge: Cambridge University Press.

Lascoumes, P. and P. Le Galès. 2007. *Sociologie de l'action publique.* Paris: Armand Colin.

Latour, B. 2005. *Re-assembling the Social:. An Introduction to Actor-Network Theory.* Oxford: Oxford University Press.

Lavedan, H. 1970. *Histoire de l'urbanisme: Époque contemporaine.* Paris: H. Laurens.

Le Corbusier. 1957. *La Charte D'Athènes.* Paris: Éditions de Minuit/Points.

Le Corbusier. 1994 [1925]. *Urbanisme.* Paris: Champs Flammarion.

Le Galès, P. 1995. "Du gouvernement des villes à la gouvernance urbaine." *Revue française de science politique* 45, 1: 57–95.

Le Galès, P. 2002. *European Cities: Social Conflicts and Governance.* Oxford: Oxford University Press.

Le Goix, R. 2005. *Villes et mondialisation: Le défi majeur du XXIe siècle.* Paris: Ellipses.

Léautier, F. (Ed). 2006. *Cities in a Globalizing World: Governance, Performance & Sustainability.* Washington: World Bank.

Lees, A. 1985. *Cities Perceived: Urban Society in European and American Thought, 1820–1940.* Manchester: Manchester University Press.

Lefebvre, H. 1968. *Le droit à la ville.* Paris: Anthropos.

Lefebvre, H. 1970. *La révolution urbaine.* Paris: Gallimard.

Lefebvre, H. 1996. *Writings on Cities.* Cambridge: Blackwell Publishers.

Lefebvre, H. 2003. *The Urban Revolution.* Minneapolis: The University of Minnesota Press.

Lefèvre, C. 1998. "Metropolitan Government and Governance in Western Countries: A Critical Review." *International Journal of Urban and Regional Research* 22, 1: 9–25.

Lefèvre, C. 2009. *Gouverner les métropoles.* Paris: Lextenso Éditions.

LeGates, R. and F. Stout. 2000. *The City Reader* (2nd ed.). New York: Routledge.

LeSage, E.C. and L. Stefanick. 2004. *New Regionalist Metropolitan Action: The Case of the Alberta Capital Regional Alliance.* [Paper presented at] The Canadian Political Science Association meetings, Winnipeg, 3 June.

Levi-Faur, D. 2012. "From 'Big Government' to 'Big Governance'?" In Levi-Faur, D. (Ed.), *The Oxford Handbook of Governance.* Oxford: Oxford University Press, pp. 3–18.

Ley, D. 1999. "Myths and Meanings of Immigration and the Metropolis." *The Canadian Geographer/Le géographe canadien* 43, 1: 2–19.

Ley, D. 2007. "Countervailing International and Domestic Migration in Gateway Cities: Australian and Canadian Variations on an American Theme." *Economic Geography* 83, 3: 231–54.

Lightbody, J. 2006. *City Politics, Canada.* Orchard Park: Broadview Press.

Linteau, P.-A. 1981. *Maisonneuve ou comment des promoteurs fabriquent une ville.* Montréal: Boréal.

Linteau, P.-A. 1988. "Le transport en commun dans les villes." In Ball, N.R. (Ed.), *Bâtir un pays: Histoire des travaux publics au Canada.* Montréal: Boréal, pp. 73–100.

Logan, J.R. and H.L. Molotch. 1987. *Urban Fortunes: The Political Economy of Place.* Berkeley: University of California Press.

Logan, J.R., B.J. Stults and R. Farley. 2004. "Segregation of Minorities in Metropolis: Two Decades of Change." *Demography* 41, 1: 1–22.

Lorinc, J. 2006. *The New City: How the Crisis in Canada's Urban Centre is Reshaping the Nation.* Toronto: Penguin Canada.

Lortie, A. (Ed.). 2004. *Les années 60: Montréal voit grand.* Montréal: Le Centre canadien d'architecture.

Lyotard, J.-F. 1979. *La condition postmoderne: Rapport sur le savoir.* Paris: Éditions de Minuit.

Macdonald, S. and R. Keil. 2012. "The Ontario Greenbelt: Shifting the Scales of the Sustainability Fix?" *The Professional Geographer* 64, 1: 125–14.

Macionis, J.J. and V.N. Parrillo. 2010. *Cities and Urban Life.* Boston/Montréal: Prentice Hall.

Mancebo, F. 2006. *Le développement durable.* Paris: Armand Colin.

Mannheim, K. 1936. "Ideology and Utopia." In Mannheim, K. (Ed.), *Ideology and Utopia: An Introduction to the Sociology of Knowledge.* New York: Harvest Book, pp. 55–108.

Manuel, F.E. and F.P. Manuel. 1979. *Utopian Thought in the Western World.* Oxford: Basil Blackwell.

Marlow, I. 2012. "Urban Shift Threatens to Swallow Little India." *The Globe and Mail*, December 2012, A 22.

Martell. L. 2010. *The Sociology of Globalization.* Cambridge: Polity.

Massey, D.S. and Mullan, B.P. 1984. "Processus of Hispanic and Black Spatial Assimilation." *American Journal of Sociology* 89, 4: 836–73.

Massey, D.S. and N.A. Denton. 1985. *American Apartheid: Segregation and the Making of the Underclass.* Bloomington: Indiana University Press.

Massey, D.S. and N.A. Denton. 1988. "The Dimensions of Residential Segregation." *Social Forces* 67, 2: 281–315.

Mauss, M. 1978. *Sociologie et anthropologie.* Paris: Presses Universitaires de France.

May, T. and B. Perry. 2005. "The Future of Urban Sociology." *Sociology* 39, 2: 343–70.

McCormick, J. 1989. *Reclaiming Paradise: The Global Environmental Movement.* Bloomington and Indianapolis: Indiana University Press.

McCue, H. 2012. "Aboriginal Reserves." *The Canadian Encyclopedia.* Online at www.thecanadianencyclopedia.com/ articles/indian-reserve.

McGahan, P. 1986. *Urban Sociology in Canada* (2nd ed.). Toronto: Butterworth & Co.

McGee, T. (Ed.). 2007. *China's Urban Space.* London and New York: Routledge.

McGranahan, G. and D. Satterthwaite. 2003. "Urban Centers: An Assessment of Sutainability." *Annual Review of Environment and Resources* 28: 243–74.

McHarg, I. 1969. *Design with Nature.* Garden City: Natural History Press.

McNeill J.R. 2000. *Something New Under the Sun: An Environmental History of the*

Twentieth-Century World. New York: Norton.

Meller, H. 1990. *Patrick Geddes: Social Evolutionist and City Planner*. London: Routledge.

Melosi, M.V. 2000. *The Sanitary City: Urban Infrastructure in America from Colonial Times to the Present*. Baltimore: Johns Hopkins University Press.

Mendez, P. 2009. "Immigrant Residential Geographies and the Spatial Assimilation Debate in Canada, 1997–2007." *International Migration & Integration* 10, 1: 89–108.

Mercier, G. 2002. "Essai de schématisation des modèles urbains de revitalisation du quartier Saint-Roch à Québec." In Sénéchal, G., J. Malézieux and C. Mazagol (Eds.), *Grands projets urbains et requalification*. Montréal: Presses de L'Université du Québec/Paris: Publications de la Sorbonne, pp. 101–15.

Merlin, P. 1972. *Les villes nouvelles: Urbanisme et aménagement*. Paris: Presses Universitaires de France.

Merlin, P. 1982. *L'aménagement de la région parisienne et les villes nouvelles*. Paris: Documentation française.

Methot, M. 2003. "Herbert Brown James: Political Reformer and Enforcer." *Urban History Review/Revue d'"histoire urbaine* 31, 2.

Metropolis. 2004–2011. *Our Diverse Cities*. Ottawa: Citizenship and Immigration Canada.

Millennium Ecosystem Assessment. 2003. *Ecosystems and Human Well-being: A Framework for Assessment*. Washington: Island Press.

Miller, D.L. 1997. *City of the Century: The Epic of Chicago and the Making of America*. New York: Touchstone.

Ministry of Infrastructure of Ontario. 2006. *Growth Plan of the Greater Golden Horseshoe*.

Ministry of Municipal Affairs and Housing of Ontario. 2005. *Greenbelt Act*.

Modarres, A. and A. Kirby 2010. "The Suburban Question: Notes for a Research Program." *Cities* 27, 2: 114–21.

Monkkonen, E.H. 1988. *America Becomes Urban: The Development of U.S. Cities & Towns, 1780–1980*. Berkeley: University of California Press.

Morisset, L. 2001. *La mémoire du paysage: Histoire de la forme urbaine d'un centre-ville: Saint-Roch, Québec*. Sainte-Foy: Presses de L'Université Laval.

Müller, N., P. Werner and J.G. Kelcey (Eds.). 2010. *Urban Biodiversity and Design*. New York and Oxford: Wiley-Blackwell.

Mumford, L. 1938. *The Culture of Cities*. New York: Harcourt Brace Jovanovich.

Mumford, L. 1961. *The City in History: Its Origins, its Transformations, and its Prospects*. New York: Harcourt, Brace & World.

Murphy, R. and M. Murphy. 2012. "The Tragedy of the Atmospheric Commons: Discounting Costs and Risks in Pursuit of Immediate Fossil-Fuel Benefits." *Canadian Review of Sociology/Revue canadienne de sociologie* 49, 3: 247–70.

Myers, D. 2002. "Demographic Dynamism in Los Angeles, Chicago, New York, and Washington, DC." In Dear, M.J. (Ed.), *From Chicago to L.A.: Making Sense of Urban Theory*. Thousand Oaks/London: Sage, pp. 55–84.

Myles, J. and F. Hou. 2004. "Changing Colours: Spatial Assimilation and the New Racial Minority Immigration." *Canadian Journal of Sociology/Cahiers canadiens de sociologie* 29, 1: 29–58.

Myllyla, S., and K. Kuvaja. 2005. "Societal Premises for Sustainable Development on Large Southern Cities." *Global Environmental Change* 15, 3: 224–37.

National Round Table on the Environment and the Economy (NRTEE). 2008. *Getting to 2050: Canada's Transition to a Low-Emission Future*. Ottawa.

Naylor, R.T. 2006. *Canada in the European Age, 1453–1919*. Montréal: McGill/Queen's University Press.

Newman P. and A. Thornley. 2004. *Planning World Cities: Globalization and Urban Politics*. Basingstoke: Palgrave Macmillan.

Newman, P. and A. Thornley. 1996. *Urban Planning in Europe: International Competition, National Systems and Planning Projects*. London/New York: Routledge.

Newman, P. and Kenworthy, J. 1999. *Sustainability and Cities*. Washington Island Press.

Nicolaides, B.M. and A. Wiese. (Eds.). 2006. *The Suburb Reader*. London: Routledge.

Nisbet R.A. 1993. *The Sociological Tradition*. New Brunswick: Transaction.

Notteridge, H.E. 2007. *The Sociology of Urban Living*. London: Routledge.

OECD. 2011. *Divided We Stand: Why Inequality Keeps Rising*. Online at www.oecd.library.org/ [Accessed 18 May, 2012].

Offe, C. 2008. *The Decline and Rise of Public Spaces*. Berlin: Hertie School of Governance. Working paper 39. Online at www.hertie-school.org/binaries/addon/1056_publicspaces.pdf.

Offe, C. 2009. "Governance: An 'Empty Signifier.'" *Constellation* 16, 4: 550–62.

Orfield, M. 2002. *American Metropolitics: The New Suburban Reality*. Washington: Brookings Institution Press.

Ouellet, M. 2006. "Le 'smart growth' et le nouvel urbanisme: Synthèse de la littérature récente et regard sur la situation canadienne." *Cahiers de géographie du Québec* 50, 140: 175–93.

Palen. J. John. 1975. *The Urban World*. New York: McGraw-Hill.

Papadopoulos, Y. 2002. "Is 'Governance' a Form of Deliberative Democracy? " Paper presented at the ECPR Joint Sessions of Workshops, The Politics of Metropolitan Governance. Turin, 3 Feb.

Papadopoulos, Y. 2012. "The Democratic Quality of Collaborative Governance." In Levi-Faur, D. (Ed.). *The Oxford Handbook of Governance*. Oxford: Oxford University Press, pp. 512–26.

Park, R.E., W. Burgess and R. McKenzie (Eds.). 1925. *The City*. Chicago: University of Chicago Press.

Peach, C. 1996. "Good Segregation, Bad Segregation." *Planning Perspectives* 11, 4: 379–98.

Purcell, M. 2002. "Excavating Lefebvre: The Right to the City and Its Urban Politics of the Inhabitant." *GeoJournal*, 58: 99–108.

Perkin. H. 1969. *The Rise of Professional Society: England Since 1880*. London: Routledge.

Perkin, H. 1996. *The Third Revolution: Professional Elites in the Modern World*. London: Routledge.

Perry, B. and A. Harding. 2002. "The Future of Urban Sociology: Report of Joint Sessions of the British and American Sociological Associations." *International Journal of Urban and Regional Research* 26, 4: 844–53.

Peters, B.G. and J. Pierre. 2001. "Developments in Intergovernmental Relations: Towards Multilevel Governance." *Policy and Politics* 29, 2: 131–35.

Peters, E.J. 2010. "Aboriginal Peoples in Urban Areas." In Hiller, H.H. (Ed.), *Urban Canada* (2nd ed.).

Toronto: Oxford University Press, pp. 156–74.

Piattoni, S. 2010. *The Theory of Multi-level Governance: Conceptual, Empirical and Normative Challenges*. New York: Oxford University Press.

Pickett, S.T.A., M.L. Cadenasso, J.M. Grove, C.H. Nilon, R.V. Pouyat, W.C. Zipperer and R. Costanza. 2001. "Urban Ecological Systems: Linking Terrestrial Ecological, Physical, and Socioeconomic Components of Metropolitan Areas." *Annual Review of Ecology and Systematics* 32: 127–57.

Pierre, J. 2000. "Conclusions: Governance Beyond State Strength." In Levi-Faur, D. (Ed.), *The Oxford Handbook of Governance*. Oxford: Oxford University Press, pp. 241–46.

Pincetl, S. 2010. "From the Sanitary City to the Sustainable City: Challenges to Institutionalizing Biogenic (Nature's Services) Infrastructure." *Local Environment: The International Journal of Justice and Sustainability* 15, 1: 43–58.

Pinçon, M. and M. Pinçon-Charlot. 1989. *Dans les beaux quartiers*. Paris: Seuil.

Pinçon, M. and M. Pinçon-Charlot. 2004. *Sociologie de Paris*. Paris: La Découverte.

Pinçon, M. and M. Pinçon-Charlot. 2007. *Les Ghettos du Gotha*. Paris: Seuil.

Pineo, P.C. 1988. "Socioeconomic Status and the Concentric Zonal Structure of Canadian Cities." *Canadian Review of Sociology and Anthropology/Revue canadienne de sociologie et d'anthropologie* 25, 3: 421–38.

Platt, R.H. 2004. "Regreening the Metropolis: Pathway to More Ecological Cities." *Annals of the New York Academy of Sciences* 1023: 49–61.

Poitras, C. 2000. *La cité au bout du fil: Le téléphone à Montréal de 1879 à 1930*. Montréal: Presses de L'Université de Montréal.

Porter, R. 1997. *The Greatest Benefit to Mankind: A Medical History of Humanity*. New York: Norton.

Portes, A. and E. Vickstrom. 2011. "Diversity, Social Capital and Cohesion." *Annual Review of Sociology* 37: 461–79.

Poulantzas, N. 1968. *Pouvoir politique et classes sociales*. Paris: François Maspéro.

Préteceille, E. 1973. *La production des grands ensembles*. Paris: Mouton.

Punter, J. 2003. *The Vancouver Achievement: Urban Planning and Design.* Vancouver: UBC Press.

Putman, R.D. 2000. *Bowling Alone: The Collapse and Revival of American Community.* New York: Simon & Schuster.

Québec. 2008. *Plan d'action. Le Québec et les changements climatiques: Un défi pour L'avenir.*

Québec (City of). 2010. *Plan de mobilité durable.* Document de consultation.

Ramadier, T. and C. Després 2004. "Les territoires de mobilité et les représentations d'une banlieue vieillissante de Québec." *Recherches sociographiques* 45, 3: 521–48.

Rast, J. 2006. "Environmental Justice and the New Regionalism." *Journal of Planning Education and Research* 25, 3: 249–63.

Richards, J. 2010. *Reducing Lone-Parent Poverty: A Canadian Success Story.* C.D. Howe Institute Commentary. Social Policy No 305. Toronto: C.D. Howe Institute.

Robertson, R. 1992. *Globalization.* Thousands Oaks: Sage.

Robinson, P.J. and C.D. Dore. 2005. "Barriers to Canadian Municipal Response to Climate Change." *Canadian Journal of Urban Research/ Revue canadienne de recherche urbaine* 14, 1: 102–20.

Rome, A. 2001. *The Bulldozer in the Countryside: Surbuban Sprawl and the Rise of American Environmentalism.* Cambridge: Cambridge University Press.

Rui, S. 2004. *La démocratie en débat: Les citoyens face à l'action publique.* Paris: Armand Colin.

Rusk, D. 1993. *Cities without Suburbs.* Baltimore: Johns Hopkins University Press.

Rutherford, P. 1984. "Tomorrow's Metropolis: The Urban Reform Movement in Canada, 1880–1920." In Stelter, G.A. and A.F.J. Artibise (Eds.), *The Canadian City. Essays in Urban History.* Toronto: Macmillan, pp. 368–92.

Ryan, J. 1994. "Women, Modernity and the City." *Theory, Culture & Society* 11, 1: 35–63.

Rydin, Y. 2010. *Governing for Sustainable Urban Development.* London: Earthscan.

Sancton, A. 2000. *Merger Mania: The Assault on Local Government.* Montréal: McGill-Queen's University Press.

Sancton, A. 2005. "The Governance of Metropolitan Areas in Canada." *Public Administration and Development* 25, 4: 317–27.

Sandercock, L. 1995. "Voices from the Borderlands: A Meditation on a Metaphor." *Journal of Planning Education and Research* 14, 2: 77–88.

Sandercock, L. 1998. *Towards Cosmopolis.* Chischester: John Wiley & Sons.

Sandercock, L. 2004. "Towards a Planning Imagination for the 21st Century." *Journal of the American Planning Association* 70, 2: 133–41.

Sassen, S. 1991. *The Global City: New York, London, Tokyo.* Princeton: Princeton University Press.

Sassen, S. 1994. *Cities in a World Economy.* Thousands Oaks: Pine Forge.

Sassen, S. 2000. "New Frontiers Facing Urban Sociology at the Millennium." *British Journal of Sociology* 51, 1: 143–59.

Sassen, S. 2004. "Local Actors in Global Politics." *Current Sociology* 52, 4: 649–70.

Sassen, S. 2005. "Cities as Strategic Sites." *Sociology* 39, 2: 352–57.

Sassen, S. 2007. *A Sociology of Globalization.* New York/London: Norton.

Sassen, S. 2008. "Re-assembling the Urban." *Urban Geography* 29, 2: 113–26.

Sassen, S. 2009. "Cities in Today's Global Age." *SAIS Review XXIX*, 1 Winter/ Spring: 3–32.

Satzewich, V. and N. Liodakis. 2007. *"Race" and Ethnicity in Canada: A Critical Introduction.* Toronto: Oxford University Press.

Saunders, P. 1981. *Social Theory and the Urban Question.* London: Hutchinson & Co.

Savage, M. 2005. "Urban Sociology in the Third Generation." *Sociology* 39, 2: 357–61.

Savage, M. and A. Ward. 1993. *Urban Sociology, Capitalism and Modernity.* Houndmills: Macmillan.

Savitch, H.V. 1989. *Post-industrial Cities: Politics and Planning in New York, Paris, and London.* Princeton: Princeton University Press.

Savitch, H.V. and P. Kantor. 2002. *Cities in the International Marketplace.* Princeton/ Oxford: Princeton University Press.

Savitch, H.V. and R.K. Vogel. 2000. "Paths to New Regionalism." *State and Local Government Review* 32, 3: 158–68.

Savitch, H.V. 2007. "Globalisation et changement d'échelle dans le gouvernement urbain." *Métropoles* 2: 133–66.

Scott, A.J. (Ed.). 2001. *Global City-Regions: Trends, Theory, Policy.* Oxford/New York: Oxford University Press.

Schwartz Cowan, R. 1997. *A Social History of American Technology*. Oxford: Oxford University Press.

Schwirian, K.P. 2006. "The Political Ecology of Plague in the Global Network of Cities: The Sars Epidemic of 2002–2003." In McCright A.M. and T.N. Clark (Eds.), *Community and Ecology (Research in Urban Policy, Volume 10)*. Emerald Group Publishing Limited, pp. 241–68.

Scott, A.J. 2006. "Creative Cities: Conceptual Issues and Policy Questions." *Journal of Urban Affairs* 28, 1: 1–17.

Scott, M. 1969. *American City Planning Since 1890*. Berkeley and Los Angeles: University of California Press.

Séguin, A-M. and P. Villeneuve. 1997. "Du rapport hommes-femmes au centre de la haute-ville de Québec." *Cahiers de Géographie du Québec* 31, 83: 189–204.

Selin, H. and S.D. VanDeVeer. 2009. *Changing Climates in North American Politics: Institutions, Policymaking, and Multilevel Governance*. Cambridge: MIT Press.

Sen, A.K. 1993. "Capability and Well-being." In Nussbaum, M.C. and A.K. Sen (Eds.), *The Quality of Life*. Oxford: Clarendon Press, p. 30–53.

Sénécal, G. 2007. "Métaphores et modèles en géographie urbaine: Le continuum de L'École de Chicago à celle de Los Angeles." *Annales de Géographie* 657, 5: 513–32.

Sénécal, G., J. Malézieux and C. Manzagol (Eds.). 2002. *Grands Projets Urbains et Requalification*. Québec: Presses de l'Université du Québec.

Shearmur R. and N. Rantisi. 2011. "Montréal: Rising Again from the Same Ashes. In Bourne L., T. Hutton, R. Shearmur and J. Simmons (Eds.), *Canadian Urban Regions: Trajectories of Growth and Change*. Toronto: Oxford University Press, pp. 173–201.

Shearmur, R. and J. Simmons (Eds.). *Canadian Urban Regions: Trajectories of Growth and Change*. Toronto: Oxford University Press, pp. 236–68.

Shevsky, E. and W. Bell. 1955. *Social Area Analysis*. Stanford: Stanford University Press.

Shils, E. 1982. *The Constitution of Society*. Chicago: University of Chicago Press.

Shorter, E. 1987. *The Health Century*. New York: Doubleday.

Simmel, G. 1950 [1903]. "The Metropolis and Mental Life." In Wolff, K.H. (Ed.), *The Sociology of Georg Simmel*. Glencoe: The Free Press.

Simpson, D. and T.M. Kelly. 2008. "The New Chicago School of Urbanism and the New Daley Machine." *Urban Affairs Review* 44, 2: 218–38.

Sinclair, B., N.R. Ball and J.O. Petersen (Eds.). 1974. *Let Us Be Honest and Modest: Technology and Society in Canadian History*. Toronto: Oxford University Press.

Sitte, C. 1996 [1889]. *L'art de bâtir les villes: L'urbanisme selon ses fondements artistiques*. Paris: Seuil.

Sjoberg, G. 1960. *The Preindustrial City: Past and Present*. New York: The Free Press.

Sklair, L. 1991. *Sociology of the Global System*. Baltimore: Johns Hopkins University Press.

Sklair, L. 2001. *The Transantional Capitalist Class*. Oxford/New York: Blackwell.

Smart Growth Canada Network/Réseau canadien de développement intelligent. July 2013. Online at www.smartgrowth.ca

Smil, V. 2005. *Creating the Twentieth Century: Technical Innovations of 1867–1914 and Their Lasting Impact*. Oxford: Oxford University Press.

Smith, H. and D. Ley. 2008. "Even in Canada: The Multiscalar Construction and Experience of Concentrated Immigrant Poverty in Gateway Cities." *Annals of the Association of American Geographers* 98, 3: 686–713.

Soja, E.W. 2000. *Postmetropolis: Critical Studies of Cities and Regions*. Oxford: Blackwell.

Soja, E.W. 2010. *Seeking Spatial Justice*. Minneapolis: University of Minnesota Press.

Soroka, L. 1999. "Male-Female Urban Income Distributions in Canada: The Service Sector in a Dependency Model." *Urban Studies* 36, 3: 563–74.

Spivak, A.L., L.E. Bass and C. St. John. 2011. "Reconsidering Race, Class, and Residential Segregation in American Cities." *Urban Geography* 32, 4: 531–67.

Star, S.L. and J.R. Greisemer. 1989. "Institutional Ecology, 'Translations' and Boundary Objects: Amateurs and Professionals in Berkeley's Museum of Vertebrate Zoology, 1907–39." *Social Studies of Science* 19, 3: 387–420.

Starr, P. 1982. *The Social Transformation of American Medicine*. New York: Basic Books.

Statistics Canada. 1996. Census 1996, Census Metropolitan Areas Profile.

Statistics Canada. 2011. *Census of Population, 1851 to 2006. Population, Urban and Rural, by Province and Territory*. Online

at www.statcan.gc.ca/tables-tableaux/
sum-som/l01/cst01/demo62a-eng.htm
[Accessed 20 Feb., 2012].

Steger, M.B. 2003. *Globalization: A Very
Short Introduction.* Oxford: Oxford
University Press.

Stelter, G.A. and A.F.J. Artibise (Eds.).
1979. *The Canadian City:. Essays in
Urban History.* Toronto: Macmillan.

Stelter, G.A. and A.F.J. Artibise (Eds.).
1986. *Power and Place: Canadian Urban
Development in the North American
Context.* Vancouver: UBC Press.

Stern, N. 2009. *The Global Deal: Climate
Change and the Creation of a New Era of
Progress and Prosperity.* New York: Public
Affairs.

Sutcliffe, A. 1981. *Towards the Planned City:
Germany, Britain, the United States, and
France, 1790–1914.* Oxford: Blackwell.

Taeuber, K.E. and A.F. Taeuber. 1965.
Negroes in Cities. New York: Aldine
Press.

Tarr, J. and G. Dupuy (Eds.). 1988.
*Technology and the Rise of the Networked
City in Europe and America.* Philadelphia:
Temple University Press.

Tastsoglou, E. and B. Miedema. 2003.
"Immigrant Women and Community
Development in the Canadian
Maritimes: Outsiders Within?"
*Canadian Journal of Sociology/Cahiers
canadiens de sociologie* 28, 2: 203–34.

Taylor, P.J. 2004. *World City Network:. A
Global Urban Analysis.* London/New
York: Routledge.

Tellier, L.-N. 2009. *Urban World History: An
Economic and Geographical Perspective.*
Québec: Presses de l'Université du
Québec.

Tencer, D. 2011. "Canada Income
Inequality: Which Canadian Cities Are
Seeing the Fastest Ghettoization?" *The
Huffington Post Canada*, 12 May.

The Economist. 2008. "Urban Idylls:
Vancouver Remains the Most Liveable
City; Harare Is Still Intolerable." 28 Apr.

Tilly, C. 2007. *Democracy.* Cambridge:
Cambridge University Press.

Toner, G. and J. Meadowcroft. 2009.
"Spinning Wheels and Loosing
Traction: The Struggle of the Canadian
Government to Move from Rhetoric
to Action on the Institutionalization
of Sustainable Development." In
VanNijnatten, D. and R. Boardman
(Eds.), *Canadian Environmental Policy:*

Context and Cases (3rd ed.). Don Mills/
New York: Oxford University Press.

Topalov, C. 2008. "Sociologie d'un étiqu-
etage scientifique: Urban Sociology,
Chicago 1925." *L'Année sociologique* 58,
1: 203–34.

Toronto Environment Office. (2008). *Ahead
of the Storm: Preparing Toronto for Climate
Change.* Toronto.

Toulmin, S. 1990. *Cosmopolis. The Hidden
Agenda of Modernity.* New York: Free Press.

Toulmin, S. 2001. *Return to Reason.*
Cambridge: Harvard University Press.

Touraine, A. 1965. *Sociologie de L'action.*
Paris: Éditions du Seuil.

Touraine, A. 1969. *La société post-industrielle:
Naissance d'une société.* Paris: Denoël.

Turcotte, M. 2001. "L'opposition rural/
urbain a-t-elle fait son temps? Le cas
du moralisme traditionnel." *Canadian
Journal of Sociology/Cahiers canadiens de
sociologie* 26: 1–29.

Turcotte, M. 2007. "L'opposition ville/ban-
lieue: Comment la mesurer." *Tendances
sociales*, Hiver: 2–13.

Turmel, A. and L. Guay. 2008. "Une
sociologie historique des problèmes
urbains: la montée de l'état aménagiste."
In Fyson, D. and Y. Rousseau (Eds.),
*L'État au Québec: Perspectives d'analyse
et expériences historiques.* Québec: Giéc,
pp. 33–8.

UK Sustainable Development Commission.
2009. *Prosperity without Growth?
Transition to a Sustainable Economy.*
Online at www.sd-commission.org.uk.

UN-Habitat 2008/2009. *State of the World's
Cities.* London: Earthscan.

UN-Habitat 2010/2011. *State of the World's
Cities.* London: Earthscan.

United Nations. 1992. United Nations
Framework Convention on Climate
Change (UNFCCC).

Urry, J. 2007. *Mobilities.* Cambridge: Polity.

Van Nus, W. 1979. "The Fate of City
Beautiful Thought in Canada,
1893–1930." In Stelter, G.A. and
A.F.J. Artibise (Eds.), *The Canadian
City: Essays in Urban History.* Toronto:
Macmillan, pp. 162–85.

Velt, P. 1996. *Mondialisation, villes et territoires: L'économie d''archipel.* Paris: PUF.

Vieillard-Baron, H. 2001. *Les Banlieues: Des
singularités françaises aux réalités mondia-
les.* Paris: Hachette.

Wagner, P. 2008. *Modernity as Experience
and Interpretation.* London: Polity Press.

Wagner, P. 2012. *Modernity: Understanding the Present*. Cambridge: Polity Press.

Wallerstein, I. 1974. *The Modern World-System. Volume 1*. New York: Academic Press.

Wallerstein, I. 2004. *World-System Analysis: An Introduction*. Durham: Duke University Press.

Waltner-Toews, D., J.J. Kay and N-M. Lister (Eds.). 2008. *The Ecosystem Approach: Complexity, Uncertainty, and Managing for Sustainability*. New York: Columbia University Press.

Ward, S.V. 1990. "The Garden City Tradition Re-examined." *Planning Perspectives* 5, 3: 249–56.

Ward, S.V. 1999. "The International Diffusion of Planning: A Review and a Canadian Case." *International Planning Studies* 4, 1: 53–77.

Ward, S.V. 2002. *Planning the Twentieth-Century City: The Advanced Capitalist World*. Chichester: Wiley.

Waters, M. 1995. *Globalization*. London/New York: Routledge.

Weaver, J.C. 1984. "Tomorrow's Metropolis Revisited: A Critical Assessment of Urban Reform in Canada, 1880–1920." In Stelter, G.A. and A.F.J. Artibise (Eds.), *The Canadian City: Essays in Urban History*. Toronto: Macmillan, pp. 393–418.

Weber, M. 1958. *The City*. New York: Collier Books.

Welter, V.M. and J. Lawson. 2000. *The City after Patrick Geddes*. Oxford/New York: Peter Lang.

Werkele, G.R. 2010. "Gender and the Neo-Liberal City: Urban Restructuring, Social Exclusion, and Democratic Participation." In Hiller, H.H. (Ed.), *Urban Canada* (2nd ed.). Toronto: Oxford University Press, pp. 211–33.

White, N. 2004. "Creating Community: Industrial Paternalism and Town Planning in Corner Brook, Newfoundland, 1923–1955." *Urban History Review/Revue d'histoire urbaine* 32, 2: 45–58.

Whyte, W.F. 1942. *Street Corner Society*. Chicago: University of Chicago Press.

Whyte, W.H. 1956. *The Organization Man*. New York: Simon & Schuster.

Wilson, E. 1992. *The Sphinx in the City: Urban Life, the Control of Disorder, and Women*. Berkeley: University of California Press.

Wilson, W.H. 1989. *The City Beautiful Movement*. Baltimore: Johns Hopkins University Press.

Wirth, L. 1928. *The Ghetto*. Chicago: University of Chicago Press.

Wirth, L. 1938. "Urbanism as a Way of Life." *American Journal of Sociology* 44, 1: 1–24.

Wolfe, J. M. 1984. "Our Common Past: An Interpretation of Canadian Planning History/Retour sur le passé. Un survol historique de L'urbanisme canadien." *Plan Canada* July: 12–34.

Wolfe, J.M. 2003. "A National Urban Policy for Canada? Prospects and Challenges." *Canadian Journal of Urban Research/ Revue canadienne de recherche urbaine* 12, Joint Issue Supplement: 1–21.

World Commission on Environment and Development (WCED). 1987. *Our Common Future*. Oxford: Oxford University Press.

Wright, F.L. 1958. *The Living City*. New York: Mentor Book.

Wright, G. 2007. *Women in Modernism: Making Places in Architecture*. New York: Beverly Willis Architecture Foundation & The Museum of Modern Art Colloquium, 25 Oct.

Wu, W. and P. Gaubatz. 2013. *The Chinese City*. London: Routledge.

Wynn, G. and D. McNabb. 1987. "La Nouvelle-Écosse avant les Loyalistes." In Coles, R. C., G.J. Matthews, L. Deschênes and M. Paré (Eds.), *Atlas Historique du Canada I: Des origines à 1800*. Montréal: Presses de L'Université de Montréal, planche 31.

Xu, J. and A. Ye (Eds.). 2011. *Governance and Planning of Mega-City Regions: An International Comparative Perspective*. Routledge: Abingdon (UK).

Young, M. and P. Willmott. 1957. *Family and Kinship in East London*. London: Routledge & Kegan Paul.

Zorbaurg, H. 1929. *The Gold Coast and the Slum*. Chicago: University of Chicago Press.

Zuberi, D. 2010. "Urban Inequality and Urban Social Movements." In Hiller, H.H. (Ed.), *Urban Canada* (2nd ed.). Toronto: Oxford University Press, pp. 109–30.

Zukin, S. 2009. "Changing Landscapes of Power: Opulence and the Surge for Authenticity." *International Journal of Urban and Regional Research* 33, 2: 545–46.

Index

history and, 58; garden city experiment in, 142; GHG reductions, 170; immigrants in, 98, 100; Maisonneuve City, 61; map of, *128*; Mount Royal Park, 64; planning and, 64, 146–8, 152; Plateau district, 84; population density, 71; population of, 215n5; smart growth and, 160; sustainable development in, 154; telephones and, 57

Montréal Metropolitan Community (MMC), 128

Montréal Urban Community (MUC), 127

morphology: urban, 14, 23, 32, social, 202

Morris, William, 63

mosaic, urban social, 101

multiculturalism, 39

multinational corporations (firms), 17

Mumford, Lewis, 5, 137, 138, 139, 140, 142, 153

municipal governments: authority of, 125; climate change and, 165; planning decisions and, 168; public health and, 54

Municipality of Metropolitan Toronto, 126, 129; map of, *126*

natural areas (social areas), 97

nature, cities and, xvi–xvii, 15, 157–9, 174

neighbourhoods: ethnic status and, 102; inner-city, 123–4

neo-corporatism, 118–19

Neolithic revolution, 5

networks, technological, 7

New France, 46–7

new regionalism, 123–24, 209; vs. old regionalism, 214–15n3

new urbanism, 81, 85, 142, 151, 157, 159, 161–4, 174, 175, 203; basic elements of, 162–3; criticisms of, 163–4; origins of, 162; vs. smart growth, 164

New York, 47, 55, 70, 186, 191

New York-Newark, 182

New Zealand, urbanization of, 179

Nisbet, 1993, 45

Nixon, Richard, 123

North America: Industrial Revolution and, 6–7; planning and, 161–2; public action on housing, 55; sociology in, 24; suburbia in, 79, 80–1; urbanization of, 179

nuclear power, 166

obduracy, 135, 173

Offe, Claus, 112, 116–17

Olmstead, Frederick, 64

Ontario: governance in, 72; settlement of, 47; use of fossil fuels, 166

Oregon, smart growth and, 164

Organisation for Economic Co-operation and Development (OECD), 90

Organization Man, The (Whyte), 77

Ottawa-Gatineau, 69, 90; climate change and, 171; immigrants in, 98, 100; smart growth and, 161

"Our Diverse Cities" (Metropolis), 98

outsiders, 27

Owen, Robert, 60

Paris, 80, 191; planning and, 64, 82; planning in, 61; *Plan Viosin* for, 143

Park, Robert E., xii, 11, 14, 25, 27, 29, 83, 198, 202; development of urban sociology and, 11

Park, R.E., E.W. Burgess, E.W., and R. McKenzie, *The City*, 25, 40

parks, urban, 55–6, 64, 205

participation, public, 72–3, 112, 121–3, 130–1, 167–8, 204, 206; mechanisms, 121–2; in metropolitan areas, 72–3

Perry, Clarence, 162

phalanstère, 63, 212–13n2

Philadelphia, 47

place stratification model, 104

planning, urban, 12, 45, 58–9, 203, 204, 209; development of profession, 58–62; diversity and, 108; ecological, 173; economic and social interests and, 61–2; emergence of profession, 60; in Europe, 161; governance and, xiv; green space and urban parks and, 56; high-density, 150, 154, 208; metropolitan, 82; movement for, 60–1; multiple actors and, 201; new, 164; in North America, 161–2; professional arrogance and confidence in, 143–4; public vs. private interests in, 162; regional, 139; social tensions and, 153; spatial justice and, 108; state and, 59; suburbia and, 76–7, 81, 85; sustainable, 161; training and, 61; urban problems and, 51, 58–62; urban technologies and, 57; urban vs. suburban, 81; world cities and, 188–9

Plan Voisin, 143

Plato, *Republic*, 201

Poitras, Claire, 57

Polanyi, Karl, 191

Polis, 88

political and administrative movement, 53

political economy, 24, 31–6

politics, local, 7–8, 72, 121, 167–8; public participation in, 121–2; rise of urbanization and, 7–8

population: aging, 156; Canadian urban, 48; in CMAS, 69, 70; global and urban growth, 164, 183; shift from rural to urban, 6–7; suburbanization and, 79; urban, 50, 178, 179

population density, in metropolitan areas, 71